THE BOW IN THE CLOUD

THE

BOW IN THE CLOUD

*Springs of Comfort
in Times of Deep Affliction*

EDITED BY

WILLIAM BACON STEVENS

CONTRIBUTIONS BY

JAMES W. ALEXANDER
JAMES BUCHANAN
ROBERT S. CANDLISH
PHILIP DODDRIDGE
JOHN EAST
ARCHBISHOP LEIGHTON
JOHN NEWTON
EDWARD PAYSON
OCTAVIUS WINSLOW

SOLID GROUND CHRISTIAN BOOKS
BIRMINGHAM, ALABAMA USA

Solid Ground Christian Books
PO Box 660132
Vestavia Hills AL 35266
205-443-0311
sgcb@charter.net
www.solid-ground-books.com

THE BOW IN THE CLOUD
Springs of Comfort in Times of Deep Affliction

William Bacon Stevens (1815-1887), Editor

Taken from 1871 edition by Hubbard Bros., Philadelphia

Solid Ground Christian Books Reprint in October 2007

Cover design by Borgo Design of Tuscaloosa, Alabama
Contact them at borgogirl@bellsouth.net

ISBN: 1-59925-103-5

PREFACE.

WE live in a world of sin, and hence in a world of sorrow, for "Man is born unto trouble, as the sparks fly upward."

The Apostle Paul tells us that "we must, through much tribulation, enter into the kingdom of God;" and the Apostle John shows us, in one of the visions of the Revelations, that those who "were arrayed in white robes," who were led by the Lamb "into living fountains of water," and from whose eyes "God shall wipe away all tears," "are they which come out of great tribulation, and have washed their robes and made them white in the blood of the Lamb." Thus it is true that "The path of sorrow, and that path alone, leads to the land where sorrow is unknown." This being so, it becomes us to learn how to transmute tribulations into blessings; how to turn God's chastening rod into a supporting staff; how to discern the bow in the cloud, while we are still wet with its raindrops of sorrow.

It is the design of this volume to aid in doing this comforting work. It seeks to ameliorate sorrow, not by a kind of moral anæsthetic, deadening the sensibility to grief, and making the heart less susceptible of woe, but rather by showing to the afflicted that chastenings are the sure evidences of God's fatherly love. Afflictions, the means whereby, when rightly used, "we become partakers of the divine nature;" and the furnace of trial but the purifying agent to purge away our dross that the Great Refiner may see his own image reflected in our purified souls.

The present work, therefore, has a distinct character of its own in the originality of its design; in the arrangement of its several parts; and in gathering from choice and diverse authors, English and American, the strongest and most scriptural consolation which can be offered to the stricken-hearted.

Believing, as the Editor does, that all our springs of comfort are in Jesus Christ, that they are applied to the soul by the Holy Ghost, that they are to be sought for by the prayer of faith, and that they result from the overflowing grace of our Heavenly Father, he has aimed to keep these points prominently before the reader, being unwilling to lead him to any of the "broken cisterns" of earth for consolation, when the well-spring of Divine comfort, which can alone staunch his bleeding heart, is pouring forth its free and life-giving waters. It is the lot of all to be visited with sorrow. There is "a time to mourn" marked out in every man's life; and when that time comes, and the fainting spirit turns away from the "miserable comforters" of earth, may all who consult these pages find in God a refuge from every storm, and "a very present help" in every time of trouble; and may they be enabled so to look at their sorrows, with the clear-sighted eye of faith, that they shall discern "*a bow*" in every cloud of affliction, and "*covenant mercy*" in every shower of grief.

CONTENTS.

(5)

ILLUSTRATIONS.

Drawn expressly for this Work, by C. Schuessele,

AND ENGRAVED IN THE FIRST STYLE OF ART.

Affliction.

AFFLICTION.

I.

The Chastening Rod in the Father's Hand.

" This is my comfort in mine affliction:"—Ps. cxix. 50.
" He doth not afflict willingly, nor grieve the children of men."—Lam. iii. 33.

ONE of the most solemnly interesting inquiries to which the thoughts of a reflecting mind can be directed is,—To what cause are we to attribute the prevalence and the unequal distribution of affliction in the present state? And the solution of this question will lead to another of equal importance and interest, viz., How far these afflictions should affect our confidence in God, or our future hopes under his government?

In reference to the first of these questions, viz., To what cause we are to attribute the prevalence and the unequal distribution of affliction in the present state, —both reason and Scripture concur in ascribing every affliction with which men are visited, to the *purpose* and *providence* of God. Suffering does not arise fortuitously in his dominions, but is the product of his deliberate

counsel, and the result of laws which he has established
for the government of his subjects.   It is neither a necessary adjunct, nor a casual accident of our nature;
not necessary, for omniscient wisdom and almighty
power might constitute even a created being without
suffering,—such are now the angels in heaven, and such
was man before the Fall; nor accidental, for that were
to exempt the happiness of his creatures from God's
control, and virtually to set aside his overruling providence.   It is true, that suffering sometimes proceeds
so immediately and so manifestly from the conduct of
individual men, that to their follies or vices it may be
ascribed as its proximate cause,—the horrors of disease
being the natural fruit of profligate manners, and the
hardships of poverty resulting naturally from habits of
indolent indulgence, or improvident thoughtlessness.
But even in such cases, these afflictive results are determined by a law which God has established,—a law which
attaches health and comfort to frugal and temperate
habits, and entails disease and penury on the opposite
vices; and God being the author of that constitution
of things under which we live, to his sovereign will we
must look as the ultimate cause of such a connexion
betwixt sin and its appropriate misery.   And, in other
cases, as in the dread visitation of famine, or pestilence,
or the more ordinary occurrence of family bereavement,
we see his hand, as it were, visibly stretched forth : " Is
there evil in a city," saith the sacred writer, " and the
Lord hath not done it ?"   " I form the light and create

darkness, I make peace and create evil; I the Lord do all these things." It was the Lord who rained fire and brimstone out of heaven on the cities of the plain; it was the Lord who sent the deluge on the earth, until all men and every living thing died; it was the Lord who glorified himself in the destruction of the Egyptian host; and he still guards us against the foolish notion that the sufferings of life are fortuitous or accidental, lest we should thereby be led to overlook his hand in them, and so "to despise the chastening of the Lord."

Every affliction, then, with which any of us is visited, is the result of God's deliberate purpose, and no evil befalls us without his permission or appointment. Nor are our afflictions to be regarded as the results of the careless or capricious exercise of almighty power; but, on the contrary, they are to be ascribed to the most comprehensive wisdom, acting according to principles which are fixed and determined as laws of the divine government. God is not a careless or inattentive spectator of what passes amongst his subjects; he does not send evil amongst them at random, nor without cause, nor without a well-defined end in view: such capricious exercise of almighty power is incompatible with the possession of omniscient wisdom; and as his attributes forbid, so no exigency in his government can ever require it. He cannot be taken by surprise, neither can he act from the impulse of momentary feeling: every attribute of his nature, and every principle of his government, are alike stable and excellent; and from

3

these, not from caprice or passion, does affliction spring. Far less can affliction be ascribed to the deliberate exercise of cruelty, or the sudden gust of revenge. If the comprehensive wisdom, the almighty power, and the perfect independence of God, forbid us to imagine that he can, in any case, permit evil to arise through negligence or caprice, surely the infinite benevolence which prompted him to communicate being to his creatures, and to open up for them so many sources of enjoyment, may well forbid the thought that he is capable of cherishing one vindictive feeling, or of taking delight in the infliction of suffering. Infinitely great, and glorious, and happy in himself, what possible motive can exist in the divine mind for the exercise of these cruel and vengeful passions, which he has forbidden his own creatures to cherish, and by which, where they are indulged, his creatures are debased? Shall we attribute to the most glorious Being in the universe those passions by which only the basest of mankind are animated, and which, wherever they exist, render the character hateful, and the bosom which contains them wretched as well as guilty? God forbid: all nature bears witness to the benevolence of its author; and that benevolence assures us, that whatever evils may exist under his government, they are not inflicted in the exercise of cruelty, or for the gratification of passion,—that to whatever other cause they may be ascribed, they cannot be referred to any disposition on the part of God, that would lead him unnecessarily to make his creatures unhappy, or to take

pleasure in their suffering. And, in addition to the
testimony of nature, God does most solemnly disclaim
every such feeling, and assures us, "that he afflicts not
willingly, nor grieves the children of men."

In these words, it is not denied that affliction proceeds
from the hand of God; on the contrary, it is admitted
that *he does* afflict and grieve the children of men: but
then, in regard to the disposition and feelings with
which he does so, it is affirmed that he "afflicteth *not
willingly.*" This cannot be understood to signify that
affliction comes without the will, or contrary to the purpose of God, or that he does not approve of the painful
discipline to which his people are subjected. On the
contrary, every suffering which he inflicts is the fruit
of his deliberate wisdom, and the object of his holy
approbation. But when it is said that he "*afflicteth
not willingly,*" we are given to understand that he has
no pleasure in the misery of his creatures, considered
in itself, and apart from its causes and ends; that he
does not lift the rod merely to render them unhappy,
and far less to gratify his own passion; that, but for
moral considerations, physical happiness is with him a
far more pleasing thing than physical suffering; and
that, while he has no pleasure in making his subjects
wretched, he does delight in their comfort and well-being.
This view, indeed, of the feelings with which God contemplates the sufferings of his creatures, necessarily
arises out of the simplest idea which we can form of his
character, as a perfectly wise and good Being; and to

what cause, then, it may be asked, are we to ascribe
the sufferings which do actually prevail under his administration? The Bible enables us fully to answer
this question, by the views which it presents of God's
character, as the Governor of the world; and of the
present state, as one of respite and trial.

God is revealed, not only as a being of infinite moral
perfection and blessedness, but as the righteous *moral
governor* of his intelligent creatures; and the course of
his providence is represented as not only comprehending
the means by which he preserves them in existence, but
also as constituting the discipline by which the ends of
his moral government are fulfilled. To the idea of a
moral government a law of some kind is absolutely
essential, and a law of any kind being given, it was
necessary that it should be accompanied with such sanctions of reward and punishment, as might put a difference betwixt the obedient and disobedient subjects of
it. Hence, if by any means sin should appear, God
determined that suffering should arise along with it; and
in the very structure of our own being, he has instituted
physical checks as well as moral restraints to disobedience, and has connected therewith not only the pangs
of an accusing conscience, but also a numerous train of
diseases, and the sentence of death. These arrangements, by which suffering is inseparably connected with
sin, are far from being arbitrary; they flow necessarily
from the perfections of the divine nature. Could we,
indeed, entertain, for one instant, the monstrous idea,

that God, although possessed of infinite power, and
wisdom, and benevolence, was nevertheless, in moral
respects, a being of a neutral character,—that he had no
holiness, no rectitude, no justice,—that he had no pre-
dilection for one style of moral character in his subjects,
more than another,—that ingratitude, and sensuality,
and deceit, were not more offensive to him than the
opposite virtues,—then, and then only, could we conceive
of him lavishing the wealth of almighty power and unbounded beneficence on all his creatures alike, and making no difference betwixt seraphic virtue and satanic
guilt; but, being holy and just, as well as good, he
must necessarily approve of what is congenial to his
own character, and conformable to that law which is
but the transcript of his character, and the expression
of his unchangeable will. Although, therefore, from
the benevolence of his nature, he must delight in the
diffusion of happiness, yet, from the holiness and rectitude of his character, the principle, that sin should be
connected with suffering, must be the object of his
moral approbation.

Farther, men are not only represented in Scripture as
the subjects of a moral government, but as subjects
placed in a very peculiar and interesting state, a state
of acknowledged guilt, yet of delayed punishment, in
order to their *probation and trial* for an everlasting
destiny hereafter. Their present state is not one of
"retribution, but of respite,"*—sentence has been

*Dr Gordon

passed against them as guilty, but the effect of that sentence has been for a time suspended, in order to the application of means, on the part of God, for their redemption; and being neither like the angels, perfectly holy and happy, nor like devils, absolutely lost, they occupy a middle state, which may be either the scene of their education for heaven, or of their preparation for hell. To one or other of these departments of the invisible world, all will ere long be transferred; but, meanwhile, they are dealt with as creatures that have incurred condemnation, but who, through the mercy of God, are capable of rising to glory.

These two views, the one of God's character, as a moral governor and judge, and the other of mankind, as sinners in a state of respite and trial, satisfactorily account both for the sufferings which men endure, and for the unequal distribution of them. Were there no sin, there would be no suffering; or were this the place of strict retribution, suffering would be awarded according to the amount of guilt; but it being a middle state, enjoyment and sorrow are so intermingled as to prove, at once, the benevolence and the rectitude of God. To the great moral ends of this economy, the discipline of affliction is, in many respects, needful; and hence the varied evils with which God has seen meet to visit us. Of these afflictions, viewed as parts of his own procedure, and a means of salutary discipline, God must be supposed to entertain a holy moral approbation; and yet, in none of his dispensations, however dark and distressing, does he take pleasure in inflicting unnecessary suffering, or in making his creatures unhappy; for it is expressly declared, that "he has no pleasure in the death of the sinner," and that "he does not afflict willingly, nor grieve the children of men."

These views throw an interesting light, both on the character of God, and on the nature and design of affliction under his government. As God is to be regarded both as an affectionate father and a righteous judge, so affliction is presented in two lights in Scripture, in each of which, it is compatible with the most perfect benevolence in the divine mind. It is there represented as being partly *corrective* and partly *penal ;* at one time, the chastisement of an affectionate father; at another, the award of a righteous judge; while, in both, it is declared to be the result of sin. In neither case is it the spontaneous infliction of one who delights in suffering for its own sake, but the result of principles from which no wise father or judge will ever depart in the management of his children or subjects.

The meaning of the declaration, that "God does not afflict willingly, nor grieve the children of men," may, perhaps, be best illustrated, if, conceiving of him as the father and governor of his rational creatures, we take as an illustration, the parallel case of an affectionate father, or a benevolent judge, among ourselves.

Take the case of an earthly parent: suppose him to be endowed with all the tenderest sensibilities of nature,

—conceive of him as delighting in the health and welfare of his children, and, in the exercise of every benevolent affection, lavishing on them all the riches of a
father's kindness and a father's care. You say, on
looking at his benignant countenance and his smiling
family, this is an affectionate father. But a secret can-
ker of ingratitude seizes one or more of his children,—
they shun his presence, or dislike his society, and at
length venture on acts of positive disobedience; he warns
them, he expostulates with them, but in vain, they re-
volt more and more; and at length, in the exercise of
deliberate thought, he lifts the rod and chastens them;
and he who once was the author of all their happiness,
has become also their calm but firm reprover. And who
that knows the tenderness of a father's heart, will not
acknowledge, that severe as may be the suffering inflicted, such a man doth not afflict willingly, nor grieve the
children of his love?

Again, conceive of a man of benevolent feelings
invested with the office of magistrate or judge,—conceive of Howard, the unwearied friend of his race, who
visited the prisons of Europe to alleviate the miseries
of the worst and most destitute of men,—conceive of
such a man sitting in judgment over the life or liberty
of another; and can you not suppose that, while every
feeling within him inclined him to the side of mercy,
and his every sensibility would be gratified, were it
possible to make the felon virtuous and happy, he might,
notwithstanding, have such a deep moral persuasion of

the importance of virtue and order to the well-being of the state, that he could consign the prisoner to a dungeon or the gallows, and that, too, with the perfect conviction that it was right and good to do so ; while, still, every sentiment of the heart within him, if it could be disclosed, would bear witness that he afflicted not willingly, and that he had no pleasure in the death of the criminal ?

Such a father and such a judge is God; and the sufferings which he inflicts, whether they be viewed as corrective or penal, are compatible with the loftiest benevolence in the divine mind. And unquestionably, the fact, that " God doth not afflict willingly, nor grieve the children of men," may, in one light, be regarded as a *ground of consolation,* inasmuch as it assures us that the Almighty Being, in whose hands our destinies are placed, has no pleasure in the mere infliction of suffering,—that, in his holy mind, not one passion exists which can be gratified by it,—and that, even "as a father pitieth his children, so the Lord pitieth them that fear him."

We confine our present meditation to the mere *negative view* of affliction, that it is not the result of a capricious or cruel delight in suffering on the part of God: hereafter we shall see abundant reason to believe that it is, under a system of grace, the result of pure and comprehensive benevolence, and the means of much *positive good.* In the mean while, let us not allow even the darkest aspects of God's providence to shake our

4 .

faith in the benevolence of his character; and when, through the sharp inflictions of his rod, we are tempted to entertain hard thoughts of Him, let us remember the precious truth, that " God afflicteth not willingly, nor grieveth the children of men."

But while these views are, in some respects, highly consolatory, inasmuch as they assure us of the benevolence of God, yet, to every reflecting mind, another question will suggest itself, to which, without such a revelation as is contained in the Gospel, no satisfactory answer can, in our opinion, be returned.   The benevolence of God being admitted, the question arises, How far the afflictions which do prevail, notwithstanding, should affect our hopes of future happiness under His government?   To those who rest their hopes of exemption from future punishment on the mere general benevolence of God, this should be a very serious and solemn inquiry; for God is, at this moment, a Being of infinite benevolence, and yet, suffering to a great extent prevails in his empire; and the question may well be entertained, whether, being afflicted now under his administration, we may not, *for the same reasons*, be equally or still more afflicted *hereafter?*   And this inquiry becomes the more serious, when we connect affliction with the causes to which it is ascribed.   What are these causes? why, they are the sins with which we are chargeable on the one hand, and the holiness and justice of God's character on the other.   But an effect can only be prevented by the removal of its cause; and is it not

a very solemn reflection, that the holiness and justice
of God are unchangeable attributes of his nature ; and
that, if we continue to be chargeable with sin, they
must, for aught we know, perpetuate our sufferings ?
So far from allaying our apprehensions from this cause,
the fact that God " afflicteth not willingly, nor grieveth
the children of men," gives a very awful sanction to the
moral principles of his government, when, notwithstanding his benevolence, he does visit his creatures with
severe calamity.   The benevolence of God being admitted, the whole course of his providence may be
regarded as a very solemn exhibition of the holiness
and justice of the divine government.   And unless, in
these circumstances, we can discover some way of escaping from guilt, or can entertain the delusive hope, that
God's holy and righteous government is to be radically
changed, we cannot fail to have many dark thoughts,
and many anxious fears, respecting our future prospects.
We see that God is wise, and righteous, and benevolent,
and yet notwithstanding, or rather for that very reason,
we feel that God is pouring many a bitter ingredient
into our cup,—that he is visiting us with trials of a very
severe and confounding nature ; and can we help inquir-
ing whether it will be so for ever ? whether this life is
to be the pattern of our immortal existence? or whether,
in the eternity which awaits us, we have reason to expect either the unmingled good, or the unmingled evil
which are combined, at present, in the chequered scene
of life ?   We want some assurance, on this point, to

remove our doubts, and misgivings, and fears; and, without such assurance, we feel that our eternal prospects are dark and uncertain indeed.

These misgivings are not without a foundation in reason; for manifold as are the proofs which our own experience supplies of the benevolent character of God, and explicit as is the sanction which Scripture gives to the indications of nature, there are many things, notwithstanding, both in nature and in Scripture, which are fitted to awaken alarm respecting the relation in which we stand to that august Being, and the mode in which he may yet deal with us here and hereafter. God may be perfectly wise, and just, and good; yet, conceiving of him as the moral Governor and Judge of mankind, we cannot fail to understand that he must put a difference betwixt the righteous and the wicked,— that his administration may require the sanction of punishment, and that the very perfection of his character may thus become the strongest reason for the infliction of suffering, where his law has been dishonoured, and his authority contemned. The infinite power, and rectitude, and wisdom of God, which, to innocent beings, must be a source of the highest and purest delight, may thus become, to fallen creatures, the occasion of alarm, and suspicion, and jealousy; and a secret distrust of *their* interest in his favour will prey upon their minds, even in the midst of all the riches of his benevolence which nature displays.

Accordingly, may I not appeal to every human being,

whether he has not felt in his own bosom many a secret misgiving respecting his personal interest in the favour of his Judge, and many a dark foreboding in respect to his future prospects, and that, too, while he could not shut his eyes to the evidence, nor bring himself to deny the reality of God's wisdom, and rectitude, and love? The reason is, that every man knows and feels that he is guilty; that he has violated the law, and forsaken the service of God; and that God, being a righteous governor, may, notwithstanding his benevolence, be disposed to punish transgressors. Conscience makes this suggestion, and the course of God's providence confirms it; else, why so much suffering, if a benevolent God entertains no hatred against sin? The feelings of our own minds must convince us, that the present course of God's providence is utterly irreconcilable with the idea, either of his wisdom or benevolence, unless, in our own conduct, he finds a holy reason for his method of dealing with us; and no conscience can be so blinded as not to perceive much in the state and conduct of every man, that may warrant a Holy God in inflicting suffering and death.

The Bible does unquestionably, in the first instance, confirm the testimony of nature and conscience in respect to the present state of trial. It acknowledges the existence of sorrow and suffering, under the government of a most wise and benevolent God; it declares that, notwithstanding the moral faculties which God hath given to us, and the moral indications which the

course of providence affords, good and evil are not here
dealt out according to the strict measure of desert;
and the reason which it assigns for the sufferings that
prevail in the world, is the prevalence of sin, while it
attributes the regular distribution of good and evil, to
the nature of the present state, as one of respite and
trial for an eternal state after death.   Had its commu-
nications stopped at this point, it would have *confirmed
our worst fears*, and deepened our most distressing
thoughts; for, when revealing, as it does, the benevolence of God, it declares notwithstanding, that even
under his government, sin must be connected with suffering; and when it points to an eternal state, where
the principles of his holy and righteous administration
shall have their ultimate issue, and be more fully un-
folded, how could we avoid the apprehension that we
are obnoxious to the displeasure of our Almighty Judge,
and in danger of an eternal state of retribution from
his righteous hand?   So far from allaying these apprehensions, in the first instance, or declaring them to be
unreasonable in themselves, or inconsistent with our
just deserts, it is one leading object of the Bible to confirm their certainty, to impress their truth on the heart,
and to assure us that judgments, infinitely more awful
than those which prevail in the present world, await the
transgressors of the Divine law, in a future state of
strict judicial retribution.   The Bible sanctions all the
judgments which conscience has ever pronounced against
us ; it delineates our characters in the darkest shades

of guilt; and it affirms that, notwithstanding the benevolence of God, sin cannot escape punishment, without
inferring a violation of those eternal principles on which
the government of the universe is conducted, and on
the maintenance of which, the glory of God, and the
happiness of his obedient creatures depend.

Are any who now meditate on this serious subject
along with me ready to exclaim, How, then, can the
Bible be our comfort in affliction—the Bible, which presents a more humiliating view of our character, and a
more distressing view of our state, and a more alarming
view of our everlasting prospects, than what is contained
in any other book, or what has been suggested from
any other quarter, or what, fearful and desponding as
we are, we have ever been willing to entertain? Ah!
brethren, you see how true it is, that the Bible does
not seek to comfort you by denying the evils of your
condition, or by withdrawing your attention from them,
or by soothing you with partial views of their extent,
or by delusive expectations of their removal. It probes
your case to the very bottom. It unfolds all the evil
that is within, or around, or before you. And this it
does, not only from a regard to truth, which, however
dark and distressing, cannot be compromised in any
communication from God to his creatures, but also,
and especially, with a view to shatter your confidence
in every spring of spurious comfort, and every false
ground of hope, and to lead you in simplicity to a
ground of consolation, which alone can cheer your

hearts amidst your present sorrows, and support your spirits in the prospect of what is yet before you; and which, bearing as it does the impress of God's hand, shall endure, when all other confidences are shattered, and all other hopes destroyed.

BUCHANAN.

SCRIPTURAL SELECTIONS.

FURTHERMORE, we have had fathers of our flesh which corrected us, and we gave them reverence: shall we not much rather be in subjection unto the Father of spirits, and live?—*Heb.* xii. 9.

And all the inhabitants of the earth are reputed as nothing: and he doeth according to his will in the army of heaven, and among the inhabitants of the earth: and none can stay his hand, or say unto him, What doest thou?—*Dan.* iv. 35.

All the paths of the Lord are mercy and truth unto such as keep his covenants and his testimonies.—*Ps.* xxv. 10.

For the rod of the wicked shall not rest upon the lot of the righteous; lest the righteous put forth their hands unto iniquity.—*Ps.* cxv. 3.

As many as I love, I rebuke and chasten: be zealous, therefore, and repent.—*Rev.* iii. 19.

That be far from thee to do after this manner, to slay the righteous with the wicked; and that the righteous should be as the wicked, that be far from thee: Shall not the Judge of all the earth do right?—*Gen.* xviii. 25.

I know, O Lord, that thy judgments are right, and that thou in faithfulness hast afflicted me.—*Ps.* cxix. 75.

And I will cause you to pass under the rod, and I will bring you into the bond of the covenant.—*Ez.* xx. 37.

SANCTIFIED AFFLICTION.

LORD, unafflicted, undismayed,
In pleasure's path how long I strayed:
But thou hast made me feel thy rod,
And turned my soul to thee, my God.

What though it pierced my fainting heart.
I bless thy hand that caused the smart;
It taught my tears awhile to flow,
But saved me from eternal woe.

O, hadst thou left me unchastised,
Thy precepts I had still despised,
And still the snare in secret laid
Had my unwary feet betrayed.

I love thy chastenings, O my God,
They fix my hopes on thy abode;
Where, in thy presence fully blest,
Thy stricken saints for ever rest.

Uses of Chastisement.

E VERY man," says the excellent Bishop Hall, "hath his turn of sorrow, whereby (some more, some less) all men are in their times miserable. I never yet could meet with the man that complained not of somewhat. Before sorrow come, I will prepare for it. When it is come, I will welcome it. When it goes, I will take but half a farewell of it, as still expecting its return."

There is then no one who can take up these humble pages without finding in them something applicable to his own case. And, therefore, I am encouraged to proceed with the following address to sufferers, of whatever kind.

It is only in the Word of God that we learn to consider affliction as a blessing. The utmost which the most refined philosophy can effect, is to remove from our sorrows that which is imaginary, to divert the attention from the cause of distress, or to produce a sullen and stoical resignation, more like despair than hope. The religion of the gospel grapples with the evil itself, overcomes it, and transforms it into a blessing. It is by no means included in the promises made to true

Christians that they shall be exempt from suffering.
On the contrary, chastisement forms a necessary part
of that paternal discipline, by which our heavenly
Father fits his children for their eternal rest and glory.
The Psalmist asserts the blessedness of the man who is
chastened by the Lord, with this qualification as necessary to constitute it a blessing, that he is also instructed
in divine truth. *Psalm* xciv. 12. By this we understand that the influence of chastisement is not physical;
that mere suffering has no inherent efficacy; but that
the afflictions of this life are, in the hand of God, in-
strumental in impressing divine truth upon the heart,
awakening the attention of the believer to the consideration of his own character and situation, the promises of
the gospel, and the rewards of heaven. The child of
God is assured that all things work together for his
good: in this is plainly included the pledge, that chastisements and afflictions shall eventually prove a blessing; and this is verified by the experience of the whole
church.

The subject can scarcely ever be inappropriate. We
are all familiar with suffering, in our own persons, or
the persons of those whom we love: we are either now
enduring, or shall at some future time endure severe
afflictions. Among our readers, it is natural to suppose
that some are at this very moment labouring under
burdens of grief. Some, it may be, are experiencing
the infirmities and pains of a diseased body, others are
mourning over the loss of friends and relatives, and

others still are living in the dread of trials yet to come. There are few of us therefore to whom the inquiry may not be interesting, How is affliction a blessing?

1. Chastisement is useful, because it tends to convince the believer of his misery, and shows him that without Christ he cannot be happy.   And in order to bring this subject more directly before the mind, let me for a moment consider my readers as suffering under the pangs of some great affliction.   You will at once agree with me in the position, that if you had more faith, you would have less trouble of mind; or rather, that if you had faith sufficient, you would be altogether clear from the deep impressions which afflict you.   Because we very well know from our own experience, that there are cases in which the most severe bodily pains, or mental distresses, have, so to speak, been neutralized by considerations of a spiritual kind.   This is exemplified in the history of the whole Christian Church, and of every individual believer, and most remarkably in the sufferings and death of the Martyrs.   There is then a certain point of elevation in divine trust, confidence in God, reliance on the providence, grace, and promise of God; that is, a certain degree of faith, which would entirely free you from these trials of mind.   I take it for granted that you heartily concur in this, and that you feel at this very moment of suffering that no gift of God would so effectually bless you, as this gift of faith.   Your trials and afflictions, therefore, produce in your soul a deep feeling of want.   You are now sen-

sible that you need more of the presence of Christ : that your piety is not in sufficient exercise to make you happy under your chastisements. In the moments when forebodings and fears become most oppressive, you are most strongly impressed with the truth, that you still lack a great deal; and your desires are quickened for that measure of faith which shall enable you, with filial confidence, to leave all in the hands of God.

If these are your feelings, you are now ready to acknowledge, that chastisement has already produced in you one part of its intended effect. You are brought to feel that you are totally dependent on God for your comfort ; that nothing but high measures of piety can render you independent of these clouds of trial, and that the attainments which you have made are insufficient to this end. You are brought to desire of God that grace which shall be sufficient for you, and to say, with the disciples : " Lord, increase our faith !" This is one great end of chastisement, to humble man from his self-sufficiency, and make him feel, in the most profound manner, that in God he lives, and moves, and has his being. Afflicted brethren, you never felt in your hours of ease (we venture to affirm) so fully dependent upon God's will, as you do at this present time. Perhaps, if entire prosperity had continued, you would never have felt this persuasion ; thus a most important point is gained in your spiritual progress. It is so in this respect, it prepares you for receiving the blessing. It is not God's method, in the ordinary economy of His grace, to give favours of a spiritual kind, until the soul feels its need of them. He "will be inquired of for these things," even when he purposes to vouchsafe them. It is in answer to earnest longings, pantings, hungering and thirstings of the spirit, that the Lord manifests himself in the most remarkable manner. You have been brought by chastisement to the very point, where you ought to desire to be brought; and where perhaps nothing but this affliction would have brought you, the total renunciation of your own strength, and the casting of yourself upon the strength of God. Now you begin more deeply to feel your need of Christ. Now you are convinced that something more is necessary than that vague and intermitted trust which you commonly indulge; that Christ must be embraced by your faith, and not visited merely by occasional devotions; in a word, that you must constantly be "looking to Jesus."

If these things are so; if you are persuaded that nothing except strong faith can heal your wounded spirit; if you are conscious that you still lack such faith; if you earnestly and constantly desire it; the question becomes exceedingly interesting to you: "Can I attain it?" And if this could be at once answered in the affirmative, to your full satisfaction, it would go far towards an entire banishment from your soul of these poignant distresses. Now in proportion as your soul is engaged in seeking this inestimable blessing, in just that proportion will your acts of faith be increased. As Christ becomes more and more present to your mind,

you will, with more and more confidence, lean upon him
with son-like assurance.   And, therefore, without endeavouring to resolve the question, when, how, or in
what precise manner, God will give you the grace which
you need, it is sufficient for our present purpose to know,
that one great end of your affliction is answered, when
you are led to commence and persevere in a faithful and
earnest application to Christ, as the great Physician.

Ah! how little do Christians ponder on the truth,
that by their lives of carelessness they are rendering
afflictions necessary !   While they are at ease in Zion,
forsaking their first love, and declining from the path
of strict piety, the cloud is gathering darker and darker
over their heads ; that cloud of judgment and of mercy
which is to drive them up from their unlawful resting-
places, and alarm them into a renewal of their pilgrimage.   Afflicted brethren ! ye thought not, while ye were
at ease, that these trials were in reserve for you, though
often forewarned by the preachers of the gospel, and
the experience of your brethren.   The trial has now
come ; you have now to retrace your steps ; you now
feel that none but Christ can bring you back to happiness ; and you are humbly asking for the blessings of
his hand.   Thus it is that chastisement convinces the
believer of his misery, and shows him that afar from the
Saviour he can never be at peace.

2. Chastisement is useful, as it leads the believer to
see and feel his exceeding sinfulness.   It is one of the
strongest proofs that our sanctification is imperfect, and

our self-love inordinate, that we are wrought upon so
much more readily by stripes than by favours.   Though
the Lord's goodness ought to lead us to repentance, yet
we generally observe that the heart grows hard under
the smiles of Providence, and thus loudly calls for the
necessary strokes of God's correcting hand.   It is a
favourable indication of reigning grace, when any soul,
in the sunshine of great worldly prosperity, is consider-
ate, humble, and constant in walking with God.   In
too many cases, it is far otherwise.   And when sudden
affliction breaks in a storm upon the head of one who
has been relapsing into carnal security, the surprise
and consternation are great and almost insupportable.
After the first tumult of the soul, it is natural to look
around for some solace or support ; and in the case of
a true Christian, the resort will at once be to the consolations of religion.   Like the little child which strays
from its watchful and tender parent, during the hours
of play, but hastens back at the approach of alarm, so
the believer, overtaken by calamity, awakes from his
dream, and endeavours to retrace his steps to the neg-
lected mercy-seat.   But ah ! in how many cases does
he here learn his lamentable distance from God ; and
how mournfully is he made to cry, "O that I knew
where I might find him !"   He who is habitually walking with God does not suffer this, for the whole armour
of God protects him from the most unexpected assaults :
"he is not afraid of evil tidings, his heart is fixed, trusting in the Lord ;" but the slumbering and lukewarm

G

professor sinks disheartened. In vain does he apply himself to earthly solaces for alleviation of his grief. With shame and pain of conscience, does he endeavour to ask deliverance of his offended Father. Every petition that he utters, is accompanied with a sense of weakness. The blessedness which once he spake of is gone; the habit of devout waiting upon God is suspended; the way to the throne of grace is obstructed. How confidently would he offer his petitions, if he were persuaded of his own acceptance: how gladly would he plead the promises, if he felt his title to them secured in Christ! But alas! it is not with him as in days that are past, when the candle of the Lord shone on him.

Now his repentings are kindled: now he knows how evil and bitter a thing it is to forsake the Lord, and to depart from his fear; and when he considers how long God has borne with him, how many favours he has received, and how brutish has been his ingratitude, his heart is broken, his tears flow, he seeks the lowest place in the dust of abasement, wonders that affliction has not long since overtaken him for his carelessness and neglect, and bows before the Lord without a murmur. At such a time the language of the afflicted soul will be : " Wherefore doth a living man complain, a man for the punishment of his sins? Let us search and try our ways, and turn again to the Lord: let us lift up our heart with our hands unto God in the heavens : we have transgressed and have rebelled, thou hast not pardoned, thou hast covered thyself with a cloud that our prayer should not pass through : mine eye trickleth down and ceaseth not, without any intermission, till the Lord look down and behold from heaven."

When chastisement has its proper operation, the believer will seek not to be comforted merely, but to be taught of God. "Blessed is the man whom thou chastenest, O Lord, and teachest him out of thy law." He seeks to know why God contends with him, and lies very low in contrition, when the still small voice of the Lord says to him, "The Lord hath a controversy with his people, and he will plead with Israel : O my people, what have I done unto thee, and wherein have I wearied thee, testify against me." And this exercise leads to godly sorrow which is not to be repented of. It is under deep affliction that we feel most deeply the connexion between sin and misery, and acknowledge that the connexion is just and holy. Smarting under the rod, we know that the Lord hath not dealt with us after our sins, nor rewarded us according to our iniquities ; and that it is of his mercies that we are not consumed.

Times of affliction afford some natural facilities for cultivating repentance. Occasions of sin are then removed ; the world is excluded. The man confined to the silence of the sick-room, or the house of mourning, cannot, by idle pursuits, divert his mind. He is forced to think ; and to think of his sins. He considers his ways bewails his transgression, and renews his covenant. He learns to confess, "Surely it is meet to be said unto God, I have borne chastisement, I will not offend any more; that which I see not teach thou me, and if I have done iniquity, I will do so no more."— *Job*, xxxiv. 31.

Now, in these experiences of the afflicted, there is a real consolation. Such tears are sweet, and it will probably be the unanimous testimony of all true penitents, that they have enjoyed a tender and refined delight in those moments of grief, in which they came to God as a forgiving God, and heard him say to their souls, in accents at once of gentle rebuke and comfort: " Behold, I have refined thee, but not with silver; I have chosen thee in the furnace of affliction," " for mine own sake will I defer mine anger." " For a small moment have I forsaken thee, but with great mercies will I gather thee: In a little wrath I hid my face from thee for a moment, but with everlasting kindness will I have mercy on thee, saith the Lord thy Redeemer."

3. Chastisement is useful as a trial of faith.

To use another expression of Bishop Hall, " untried faith is uncertain faith." There often is in professors of religion enough of the semblance of piety to lull their consciences while they are prosperous, but not enough of the reality to support them in the time of trial. Adversity makes the exercise of faith needful, and puts the strength of that faith to the test. It is compared to the fire, the furnace, the fining-pot or crucible, because it not only purifies, but tries; it not only consumes the dross, but ascertains the gold.

There is no true believer who does not desire this

trial. The very supposition of being found wanting, at the day of judgment, fills him with horror. His daily supplication is: "Search me, O God, and know my heart; try me, and know my thoughts; and see if there be any wicked way in me, and lead me in the way everlasting." Christian reader, give a moment's thought to this question, "Is your faith sufficient to support you in the hour of death, if that hour (as is very possible) should soon and suddenly arrive?" Are you not ready to sink under ordinary afflictions? How then will you bear this greatest of trials? To adopt the language of Jeremiah (xii. 5), "If thou hast run with the footmen, and they have wearied thee, then how canst thou contend with horses? And if, in the land of peace, wherein thou trustest, they wearied thee, then how wilt thou do in the swellings of Jordan?"

This trial of your faith is plainly important, and it is the office of chastisement to constrain you to such a trial. If your standing in the covenant is so firm, through humble trust in God, that you can say, "But he knoweth the way that I take, when he hath tried me I shall come forth as gold," you are happy indeed. But this conviction is not likely to be strong in those who have not passed through the furnace. The apostle Peter, in comforting the dispersed saints, explains to them this end of their chastisement, "If need be, ye are in heaviness through manifold temptations, that the trial of your faith being much more precious than of gold that perisheth, though it be tried with fire, might

be found unto praise, and honour, and glory, at the appearing of Jesus Christ."

We have already seen, in the course of our medita
tions, some of the ways in which faith is tried by affliction. If any be afflicted, he will pray. But there can
be no comfort in prayer, where there is not a belief
that prayer is heard, and will be answered. The supplication of one who pours out strong crying and tears,
in a great fight of afflictions, is a very different thing
from the formal addresses of one at ease. The sufferer
cannot be consoled until he finds that God is his friend;
he cannot find this without faith: and in this manner,
most directly, chastisement convinces the soul, that it
is still unprovided with the shield of faith, or awakens
the exercise of this grace, with great and unspeakable
satisfaction. And thus the tribulations which have succeeded one another through life, give us stronger and
stronger reliance on God, for the approaching hour of
death.

4. Chastisement is useful, as it strengthens faith, by
leading the believer to the promises, and especially to
the Lord Jesus Christ.

There is no expression in the Word of God better
suited to reconcile the Christian to trials than that of
the Apostle Paul: "He [that is God] chastens us for
our profit, that we may be partakers of His holiness"—
partakers of His holiness! What words are these!
This is the very summit of your desires. This you
have been toiling for, and longing after. This you

have earnestly implored, and are you now ready to
shrink from the very means by which your Father in
heaven is about to promote your sanctification ?   By no
means will you be led to relinquish this appointment of
God for your good.   Now it is by these very trials that
your graces are to be invigorated.

We have seen that such trials disclose the reality and
degree of our faith.   We may go further, and observe,
that faith is greatly increased and strengthened by the
same process.   Faith is strengthened by exercise.   As
the touch, or any natural faculty, becomes obtuse, and
often useless, by want of exercise, or the removal of its
proper objects, so faith languishes and seems ready to
perish, when those truths which are to be believed are
long kept out of the mind.   The most valuable truths
of the Christian are, "the exceeding great and precious
promises."   He does not feel his need of these promises
while he is indulging in that self-pleasing which usually
accompanies prosperity.   In penning these lines, it is
said advisedly, no man can fully value health who has
not been sick, nor appreciate the services of the kind
and skilful physician, until he has been healed by him.
And thus also, no man can fully prize, or fully understand the promises of the Scriptures, until they are made
necessary to his support in adversity.   Many of the
most precious portions of revelation are altogether a
dead letter to such as have never been exercised by the
trials to which they relate.

The believer who is in sufferings or straits of any

kind, comes to God by prayer; and in attempting to
pray, seeks some promise suitable to his precise wants.
Blessed be God! he needs not to search long—so rich
are the treasures of the Word. These promises he takes
as the very truth of God. He pleads them at the throne
of grace; he believes them, relies on them, rejoices in
them. This is faith; these exercises are vital exercises
of the renewed soul. So long as the Christian is oppressed with affliction, these exercises must be continual; and in proportion as the trial is great, must the
faith be great also, so that he often finds every earthly
support cut away, and is taught with implicit trust, to
hang on the simple word of Divine faithfulness. This
is emphatically the life of piety; and it is encouraged,
developed, and maintained in time of trial.

Affliction is sanctified when we are made to feel that
nothing can satisfy us but God, and when we actually
wait upon God, and rely on him as our only hope. It
is then that the believer finds the promises confirmed
to him; "Whom the Lord loveth he chasteneth, and
scourgeth every son whom he receiveth." "No chastening for the present is joyous, but grievous," &c. Then
he rolls his burden on the Lord, commits his way to
Him, leans upon Him, trusts in Him with all his heart,
so that with a meaning altogether new, he can sing with
the church: "God is our refuge and strength, a very
present help in trouble, therefore will we not fear,
though the earth be removed, and though the mountains
be carried into the midst of the sea."

Some appear to entertain the mistaken opinion that the only relief which is afforded to the Christian in suffering, must arise from some hope of speedy deliverance or escape. This is so far from being true, that perhaps the greatest solace under afflictions is derived from direct acts of faith upon the Lord Jesus Christ, and communion with Him; in which the soul is so much absorbed that the present suffering is forgotten, and the mind wholly occupied in its exercises of piety. And herein the chastisement is profitable. In pain, and despondency, and grief, we go to Jesus as to a friend that sticketh closer than a brother : we pour our sorrows into his friendly ear, and ask his aid, and then, when he reveals to us his love, and speaks his promises, and unveils his face, even though he give no assurance that we shall be set free, he does more,—he gives us *Himself*, and faith is refreshed and nourished by receiving him. And shall we not regard as a mercy, that sickness, or that bereavement, or that alarm, which so embitters the world's cup, as to lead us to Christ, that we may see his beauty, and be filled with his love ?

Prosperity leaves us to wander, and offers temptations to wandering. Afflictions alarm us, and drive us back to the right path. Prosperity casts a glittering but delusive veil over divine realities, and encourages unbelief. Afflictions rend and destroy this covering, and show us the truths of another world. Prosperity seldom leads to increase of faith. Affliction, by God's

7

blessing, is, in many cases, made the instrument of sanctification to such as are truly pious.

Dear brethren, that God who "doth not afflict willingly, nor grieve the children of men," offers you in your trials these "peaceable fruits of righteousness." Taste of the sweetness of his promises, and each of you shall say with David : "It is good for me that I have been afflicted."

5. Chastisement is useful, because it leads the believer to exercise entire submission to the Divine will.

It is an undeniable truth, and one of which the child of God is very deeply convinced, that "the Lord reigneth;" that it is infinitely right and fit that he should reign ; and that the first duty of every intelligent being, is to submit promptly, cheerfully, and unreservedly to every ordinance and dispensation of God. It is not very difficult to keep the soul in correspondence with this truth, so long as our self-love is not interfered with, nor our present happiness invaded ; but when the sovereignty of God is manifested in despoiling us of our most precious possessions and delights, our souls are often ready to falter, and our weakness betrays itself when, with hesitating lips, we endeavour to say, "Shall not the Judge of all the earth do right?" It is common to hear those who are ignorant of the Scriptures cavilling at the representation of Job as a man of eminent patience ; but where, except in his biography, shall we look for the instance of a man, suffering in one day the total loss of immense wealth, and of ten beloved children, and still saying, "The Lord gave, and the Lord hath taken away, blessed be the name of the Lord."

Without exercise, Christian graces do not grow, and severe afflictions are probably intended to cultivate this important grace of entire submission.   Nothing is more common than for persons, under chastisement, to indulge in such thoughts as these, "I could endure almost any affliction better than this; it is that which I have most dreaded, for which I was least prepared, and now it has overtaken me! It is so strange, new, and unexampled, that I am unmanned, and my soul sinks within me." These are the symptoms of a rebellious and unsubdued will; the murmurings of a proud and stubborn heart, which must be humbled in the dust. This is just the trial by which, perhaps, God graciously intends to bring down the imaginations and high thoughts of your soul into captivity to the obedience of Christ. And patience will not have had its perfect work in any case, until the afflicted soul is prepared to make no reservation, to claim no direction, but to give up all into the hands of the most wise, most righteous, and most merciful Creator. If the suffering were less, it would not have this humbling efficacy, and he mistakes the nature of the covenant, who supposes that such peculiar trials are excluded. It was, no doubt, a visitation sudden and alarming as a stroke of lightning, when Aaron beheld his sons consumed by fire from the Lord. It was an awful sanction to that rule, "I will be sanctified in them that come nigh me, and before all the people I will be glorified." Yet, on seeing and hearing these things, the bereaved father "held his peace." *Lev.* x. 3. It is a bitter medicine, but the soul which is convinced of God's justice and goodness, lays down every thought of rebellion and discontent.

This is the temper which sanctified affliction always begets, so that the prostrate soul dares no longer to impose terms on Jehovah, but yields itself to his sovereign discretion. There is peace in such a surrender, a peace which is altogether independent of any expected mitigation of the stroke.

Wave after wave often goes over the child of God, before he is brought to this state of self-renunciation. Murmuring may for a time prevail, yet the Great Physician, who applies the painful remedy, cannot be baffled, and triumphs to his own glory, and the unspeakable benefit of the believer's soul.

"Humble yourselves, therefore, under the mighty hand of God, that he may exalt you in due time," yet, if his rod should long abide upon you, if you are ready, like Job, to cry, from repeated and continued strokes, "He hath set me up for his mark. He breaketh me with breach upon breach. He hath fenced up my way so that I cannot pass, and he hath set darkness in my paths," yet even then, "remember the patience of Job, and the end of the Lord," and say, "Though he slay me, yet will I trust in him."

Some may be disposed to think, in the time when all

God's waves and billows go over them, that they could acquiesce and be comforted, if they perceived any way of escape, if they could reasonably expect deliverance; and this is the whole of what is sometimes called Christian resignation. Yet, the comfort in this case is merely worldly. The grace of God can do more than this; it can make you willing still to endure, and in enduring, still to praise.

Say not, "I could be content if I were sure of deliverance." God has not promised absolutely to remove the chastisement. Perhaps it is his holy will not to deliver. Perhaps it is this very thing in your afflictions which is to insure you the blessing from the Lord. The apostle Paul earnestly desired, and thrice besought the Lord to deliver him from that trial which he calls the thorn in his flesh, the messenger of Satan to buffet him. Yet, as far as we are informed, it was continued to the end of his life. But mark the glorious indemnification: "My grace is sufficient for thee, for my strength is made perfect in weakness." Upon this declaration, the apostle calmly, nay joyfully, goes forward under his burden, singing as he pursues his pilgrimage: "Most gladly, therefore, will I rather glory in my infirmities, that the power of Christ may rest upon me; therefore I take pleasure in infirmities, in reproaches, in necessities, in persecutions, in distresses, for Christ's sake, for when I am weak, then am I strong." The sweet support under every possible calamity is, that God can turn it into a blessing, and that if we have faith he will do so. With respect, therefore, to the use of afflictions, "all things are possible to him that believeth."

6. Finally. Chastisement is useful, because it leads the believer to look for complete happiness in heaven only.

And at this stage of our reflections, let us rejoice, dear brethren, that the consolation offered is liable to no exception or abatement: it is adapted to every case; perfect and entire. If the comfort which you need depended upon the hopes of deliverance in this world, there would be many cases which we should be forced to leave as hopeless: for there are many in which no expectation of exemption in this life can be indulged. But let the worst, most lingering, and most aggravated instance of suffering be presented, and the hope of heaven is still sufficient to mitigate its ills. You may have been reduced to hopeless poverty; you may have suffered from the treachery and ingratitude of supposed friends; from cruel mockings and persevering calumny; you may labour under incurable disease, or follow to the grave beloved objects of your affections, who can never be replaced in this world. Still there is a country, and you are rapidly approaching it, "where the wicked cease from troubling, and the weary are at rest." It is well if you have learned to look beyond all secondary, earthly, imperfect comforts, to God, the source of good, and to that world where all tears are wiped away. It is well if the trial of your faith has enabled you to say, "I know in whom I have believed, and that he is able to keep that which I have committed to him against that day."

This is a benefit of affliction, which is striking and great in proportion to the failure of earthly consolation. For it may be doubted whether any man fully yields himself up to the view and prelibation of heaven, until he is disentangled and rent away from all hope of blessedness on this side of the grave. It is natural to seek resting-places by the way; and trials, losses, sufferings, bereavements, are thrice blessed when they engrave upon our hearts that we have here no continuing city, but must seek one above. So long as we can flatter ourselves with any refuge in this world, we are prone to lean on an arm of flesh, and to look upwards only for the supply of what is deficient here. But let all expectation of worldly peace and satisfaction be cut off, and the released soul, which is truly sanctified and full of faith, rises, like a bird from the snare, and rejoices to say, "My soul, wait thou only upon God, for my expectation is from him. Then shall I be satisfied when I awake in thy likeness!" Think not, however, to enjoy this fruit of chastisement, while you cast long and lingering looks on that country whence you came out. Nothing but the hope of a glorious resurrection upheld the apostle Paul, when troubled on every side, perplexed, persecuted, cast down, and (as to the outward man) perishing. Hear the method of his escape out of sorrow, "Our light affliction, which is but for a mo-

ment, worketh for us a far more exceeding and eternal
weight of glory."

He is the happy man who dwells most on the thoughts
of heaven.   Like Enoch, he walks with God.   Like Job,
he can say, " I know that my Redeemer liveth," &c.
Like David, he glories, " Thou wilt show me thy salvation."   Like Paul, he triumphs, " for I am now ready
to be offered," &c.

This happiness we sometimes witness; but where
have we found it ?   In the house of prosperity, where
death has never invaded the family circle; where all
have more than heart could wish; where health, and
opulence, and honour unite to expel all care ?   No! but
in the hovel of the poor, where one affliction hath followed another, till earthly hope is almost extinct.   In
the darkened chamber of mourning, whence all that was
most loved and cherished has taken its last flight.   In
the bed of lingering, incurable disease, and in the very
gasp of death !   Here religion hath set up her trophies ;
here is happiness, here, where things hoped for are sub-
stantiated to the believing soul, where things unseen
are evidenced to faith by divine influence.

In every case of suffering it is the prime wisdom of
the Christian to fix his eyes upon the heavenly crown.
In every other hope you may be disappointed, in this
you cannot.   Try, as you may, all other fountains for
your solace, there is a time coming when you must be
driven to this.   Become familiar with the meditation of
heavenly glory !   Daily contemplate that joyful deliver-

ance from evil, that indissoluble and ecstatic union with the Lord Jesus Christ! Then, when death lays upon you his cold hand, you can say, " I am prepared for this hour. I have longed for this deliverance to meet my Lord in his temple. I have lived in communion with the blessed Lord of heaven." " Lo, this is my God, I have waited for him, and he will save me, this is the Lord, I have waited for him; I will rejoice and be glad in his salvation."

ALEXANDER.

SCRIPTURAL SELECTIONS.

FOR he doth not afflict willingly, nor grieve the children of men. Wherefore doth a living man complain, a man for the punishment of his sins?—*Lam.* iii. 33, 39.

Surely it is meet to be said unto God, I have borne chastisement, I will not offend any more:—

That which I see not, teach thou me: if I have done iniquity, I will do no more.—*Job*, xxxiv. 31, 32.

Howbeit, thou art just in all that is brought upon us; for thou hast done right, but we have done wickedly.—*Neh.* ix. 33.

Before I was afflicted I went astray: but now have I kept thy word.

It is good for me that I have been afflicted; that I might learn thy statutes.—*Ps.* cxix. 67, 71.

By this therefore shall the iniquity of Jacob be purged.—*Is.* xxvii. 9.

And I will turn my hand upon thee, and purely purge away thy dross, and take away all thy tin.—*Is.* i. 25.

Christ the Purifier.

" He shall sit as a refiner, and purifier of silver."—Mal. iii. 3.

He that from dross would win the precious ore,
　Bends o'er the crucible an earnest eye,
The subtle searching process to explore,
　Lest the one brilliant moment should pass by,
When in the molten silver's virgin mass
He meets his pictured face as in a glass.

Thus in God's furnace are his people tried;
　Thrice happy they who to the end endure:
But who the fiery trial may abide?
　Who from the crucible come forth so pure?
That He whose eyes of flame look through the whole,
May see his image perfect in the soul?

Nor with an evanescent glimpse alone,
　As in that mirror the refiner's face;
But, stampt with heaven's broad signet, there be shown
　Immanuel's features full of truth and grace.
And round that seal of love this motto be,
"Not for a moment, but—eternity!"

III.

THE STONES OF THE HEAVENLY TEMPLE
PREPARED ON EARTH.

And the house, when it was in building, was built of stone made ready before it was brought thither: so that there was neither hammer, nor axe, nor any tool of iron, heard in the house while it was in building."—1 KINGS, VI. 7.

THE Temple of Solomon was the noblest structure ever built by human hands.

In the Architect who devised it, in the materials employed, in the labour bestowed, in the costliness of the work, and in the grandeur of its whole design, it surpassed the proudest edifices of the world. From its first erection in the wilderness until the time of Solomon, over four centuries, the "Tabernacle," containing the ark of the covenant and its sacred treasures, was but a movable tent pitched where peace or convenience would permit. When David selected Jerusalem to be his royal city, and "the Lord had given him rest round about from all his enemies," he said to the prophet Nathan, "Lo, I dwell in an house of cedars, but the ark of the covenant of the Lord remaineth under curtains," thus expressing his uneasiness that he should be more sumptuously lodged than the ark of God, and inti-

C. Schuessele.

J. C. McRae.

"And the house, when it was in building, was built
of stone made ready before it was brought thither: so
that there was neither hammer, nor axe, nor any tool
of iron heard in the house while it was in building."

1 Kings VI. 7.

mating his desire to build an house of the Lord. This very proper desire the Lord would not suffer him to execute, because he had been a warrior, and his hand had been stained with human blood; but He announced to him through the prophet that his son should build an house to Him, and thus accomplish what he had so piously designed. Though divinely hindered from building the house, he yet busied himself in collecting materials for it of the most ample and costly character, and four years after his decease, Solomon, who reigned in his stead, began the work of erecting the Temple which his father David had planned in all its parts by the Spirit of God. Seven years were consumed by an immense army of labourers in this gigantic work, ere the Temple crowned the summit of Mount Moriah, and was dedicated to the worship of the one living and true God. There it stood for many years, the pride of Israel and the glory of the world. Grand in the massiveness of its structure—magnificent in the arrangement of its courts and porches, and gates, and holy, most holy places— splendid in the glittering radiance which its walls of dazzling whiteness flashed upon the beholder as the morning or evening sun was reflected from it, "glistering stones," glorious as a Temple erected for the worship of Almighty God, but pre-eminently honoured as the place where the Most High condescended to dwell between the Cherubim in the Holy of Holies by a visible emblem, and where he communed with his anointed servant from off the mercy seat of the ark of the cove-

nant   In every aspect, human and divine, it was the
most remarkable building ever erected on earth—remarkable in its human aspects—in its foundations—
its materials—its structure—its costliness—its splendour ; and in its divine, as the only house of wood and
stone in which Jehovah resided by the symbol of
His presence.   Leaving, however, the many interesting points suggested by this stupendous work, let us
bend our thoughts upon the remarkable fact spoken of
by the sacred historian in the 1st Book of Kings, 6th
chapter and 14th verse : " And the house, when it was
in building, was built of stone made ready before it was
brought thither : so that there was neither hammer, nor
axe, nor any tool of iron, heard in the house while it was
in building."   It is difficult to understand how a work so
vast and so complicated could be erected in such a silent
manner.   And this fact will appear the more remarkable
if we consider the nature and dimensions of materials
used.   The heavy work was all of stone or marble, and
some of the great and costly stones spoken of in the Book
of Kings were blocks eighty feet long, ten high, and
twelve wide, and many of its pillars were socketed in
solid masonry.   Its massive rafters were tenoned and
mortised into corresponding beams ; yet these ponderous
masses were hewn, squared, carved and fitted to their
places before they were brought to Mount Moriah, with
such nicety and skill, that Josephus says that " the
smallest interstices were not perceptible between the
stones," and yet no hammer, axe, or any tool of iron

was needed to adjust them to their several places, and frame them together in grand yet harmonious proportions. How all this could be accomplished in so unusual a manner can only be accounted for by supposing that God presided over his own Temple, and gave the builders this unusual art and skill.

This gorgeous Temple was destroyed by Nebuchadnezzar nearly twenty-five hundred years ago. Another and another temple has risen on the same spot and met the same fate; the Lord of the Temple himself has come into his earthly court, not by the emblematic Shekinah, but in bodily form, and has gone back to his original glory; the nation which worshipped in those sanctuaries has been scattered to the four winds of heaven; yet the deep instruction furnished by this passage remains: and let us, through God's assistance, attempt to search out and apply the lesson.

In the New Testament the Church is termed " God's building"—" the temple of God"—" the temple of the Holy Ghost"—" the temple of the living God"—" an holy temple of the Lord"—" an habitation of God in the Spirit"—" the house of Christ." These terms denote that as God by the bright symbol of his glory manifested his presence in the movable tabernacle erected by Moses, and the stately temple built by Solomon, so does he by his spirit dwell in the hearts of Christians as individuals and in the church collectively. In looking then at this Christian temple, let us observe, first, the stones of which it is composed; secondly, the preparation of them; and thirdly, their destination. St. Peter says of Christians, that as lively stones they are built up a spiritual house. A stone is a shapeless mass of rock. It is inert—lifeless—could never split itself from its native quarry—could never fashion itself into classic shape and beauty, and could never set itself up as a lintel or column in any edifice of man. And such by nature is the spiritual state of all men—having no power to move—hear—see—feel—believe, because of the moral inertia which makes them as passive, hard, insensible as the stones of the earth. Hence, when God would express the hardened condition of a person or people, he speaks of such as having "hearts of stone."

But believers having been hewn out from the quarry of humanity by the electing grace of God, are termed living stones; not inert masses of rock, not senseless blocks of marble, but full of life, feeling, action; and they are thus designated because Christ, as the tried corner stone, the sure foundation, is called a living stone, and diffuses his own life through all parts of the spiritual temple which rests on him. So that every stone in it, from the foundation of the apostles and prophets to the topmost coping, is made a precious, a glistering, a living stone, through the preciousness and glory and life of Jesus, the prince of life. So long then as the soul of the believer rests on Jesus Christ alone for salvation, and on nothing else, it has spiritual life—build it upon any other foundation and it is a senseless stone still—only as laid by the Holy Ghost upon the foundation of the prophets and apostles, Jesus Christ being the chief corner stone, can it receive in itself the life of Christ, and become through the impartation of his own vitality a living stone.

The way in which these living stones are prepared for the temple, furnishes a subject of interesting and profitable thought. The wood and stone used in Solomon's Temple were carefully prepared at a distance from the place where the edifice was to be built. The sacred house was planned out in minutest detail by David, under the direction of the Spirit of God. Each stone, column, lintel, architrave, capital, beam, rafter, had its special and appointed place, but as yet the wood was waving its branches in the forests of Lebanon, and the stone was unquarried in the mountains of Judea. Under the direction of appointed overseers, the Hebrew workman went up to the sides of Lebanon and cut down the designated tree, and there, before carrying it to Jerusalem, he trimmed and fashioned it by much hewing and carving for its destined place. The Phœnician stonecutter went to the mountain and split out masses of rock from the quarry, and there, by many ponderous blows, he dressed it and shaped it for its appointed position. Many an axe and sharp-edged tool passed over that tree before it became a stately pillar, and many a hammer and instrument of iron was used on that once unsightly block ere as a polished stone it was fitted for the Temple's wall. Most beautifully does all this illustrate the way of God in building up His spiritual and

9

living temple. In the mind of Him who seeth the end
from the beginning, and who has devised all things in the
counsel of his own will, this temple is already planned
in its minutest part—He knows each living stone that
shall compose its walls—He has designated them for
their several places before the foundation of the world,
though as yet many of them are still swaying their
green branches in the forests of worldliness, or lie buried
in the stony ledges of hardened impenitence. But the
Great Architect knows what tree and what rock he
wants, and he lays the axe of converting grace at the
root of this tree, and speaking by his spirit to the in-
sensate stone, his word becomes, in his own expressive
language, as a fire, and like a hammer that breaketh
the rock in pieces. But when the tree is thus felled,
when the stone is thus quarried out, is it immediately
fitted for its destined place in heaven? In most cases
we answer, no. Though at conversion the child of God
is a marked man, though he is justified freely by the
grace that is in Christ Jesus, yet how much spiritual
trimming and dressing, how much hewing and squaring
does he need to fashion him aright for the position which
the Divine Architect intends he shall occupy hereafter!
There are sharp angles of character to be rounded off—
unsightly protuberances of conduct to be chipped away
—many roughnesses of temper to be smoothed down,
many flaws and cracks of mind and heart to be chiselled
out; and then, when the general form of the stone is
prepared, how much severe friction is required to give

it the right polish, and bring out all its beauties, so that
its smooth surface may fling back the rays of the Sun
of Righteousness!

Our earth is the place where this is to be done; for,
as there was no noise of any axe or hammer, or tool of
iron heard on Mount Moriah while the Temple was building, so in the New Jerusalem above there will be heard
no crushing strokes of conviction, no sharp hewings of
an awakened conscience, no sound of preparatory discipline. Heaven is not the place to prepare men for
glory—but to receive them when prepared. Earth,
then, is the preparing place for heaven, and the preparation is effected by the axe, the hammer, and the tools
of iron of God's wise dispensations. All God's dealings
with us have respect to our future existence; and these
are so wisely adapted to the peculiarities of each case
that no two persons pass through the same course, and
no two result in the same development. We are not
arbitrarily classed together like the Linnæan system of
plants under certain genera and species, and then each
group made to experience the same indiscriminate treatment. Far from it: each individual in the whole train-
ing of his moral nature is as much under the eye and
care of God as if there was no other being in the universe; and there is not a peculiarity of mind or heart or
body—not a changing phase of life from the cradle to
the coffin—that is not expressly met by infinite wisdom
in the arrangement of his Providence and Grace. Nor
does he set in motion a course of preparation suited to

your case, and then, leaving it like a piece of machinery to do its allotted work, go off to some other part of his wide domain to superintend some other of his vast designs. No. For as the refiner of silver never removes his eye from the molten mass in the crucible of his furnace until he sees his own image reflected in the purged and shining metal, so God never leaves the individual soul which he has placed in the furnace fires of this world, until he either sees his own image reflected in the purified spirit, or proves it to be but sinful dross.

The greater part of the preparation to which we are subjected as professing Christians, is of a disciplinary character, and hence is fitly represented by the axe, the hammer, and the tool of iron. Prosperity not only is the destruction of fools, but in the great majority of cases hardens the heart of the nominal Christian, so that Christ himself was forced to say "how hardly shall they that have riches enter into the kingdom of heaven," and for many hundreds of years God by the voice of Jeremiah has complained, "I spake unto thee in thy prosperity; but thou saidst I will not hear. This hath been thy manner from thy youth, that thou obeyedst not my voice." Afflictions come more immediately to the heart, and operate with a more searching and purifying influence upon the life. These show one his weakness and sinfulness—lay open the moral anatomy of his nature—subject to severest test his principles of action, and cause him to retire into the chambers of his soul and learn there in the light of the Bible and in the light of conscience, his relations and duties to God and man. Now the axe seems driven into the root of his happiness—now he is broken as a block of granite under the blows of the hammer of God's Word, and now the iron of a sore adversity has entered into his soul, and he feels himself stricken, smitten, and afflicted. In these dispensations, however severe, he is being fitted by the hand of God himself for a place in glory. God knows for what position in that heavenly temple he has designed us, and he knows when we are prepared for that position; nor will he permit us to receive a single blow or cut more than is necessary to accomplish his divine purpose concerning us. Let the Christian, then, who is passing through trials and afflictions fiery and discouraging, remember that God is thus hewing and squaring him here, that as a well prepared and lively stone he may by and by be built up into the living temple not made with hands, eternal in the heavens. The preparing process may be severe; the strokes frequent and heavy; the hewing into shape painful to the flesh; the polishing into beauty rasping to the spirit: yet every blow aids to bring it into form; every tool of iron, though it cuts deep, leaves behind some chiselled beauty; and every grating file of sorrow that rasps the sensitive fibres of the heart, only gives it a higher polish, and makes it reflect a brighter glory. And who will complain of such dealings, when such blissful ends are attained by it? Who will murmur at the roughness of a road that leads to such eternal joys?

who will repine at any chastenings, and not rather esteem them as light afflictions which are but for a moment, when his Heavenly Father assures him that they shall work out for him a far more exceeding and eternal weight of glory? And Oh, let the afflicted saint remember also that as those portions of the earthly Temple which were to be most conspicuous and beautiful, had more cutting and carving and polishing than others, so those whom God designs for eminence in glory, for pillars in his temple, are subjected to heavier blows, deeper chiselings, severer raspings in the process of bringing out in them higher beauties and a more excelling glory.

And this leads us to consider, lastly, the end for which these living stones, thus prepared on earth, are designed. We have seen that the stones quarried out and elaborately hewn by the Sidonians, were taken after due preparation to Jerusalem and set up in the Temple. As the house erected for God by Solomon was the most magnificent of all earthly structures, and was designed to show forth the praise of God, and be his earthly abode; so when he would speak of the glory of Heaven, where he dwells in full and visible presence, where he is worshipped in pure and perfect devotion, where he receives his people into close and holy communion, and where he manifests the unveiled perfections of the Godhead; he speaks of it under the figure of a temple—a house—a building: of a temple, because he is worshipped there; of a house, because he entertains his children there in its many mansions or apartments; of a building, because it has been slowly augmented since the foundation of the world.

The real end, then, for which God hath chosen us in Christ Jesus before the world began, and fitted us on earth by his providential dispensations, is, "that in the dispensation of the fullness of time he might gather together in one, all things in Christ, both which are in heaven and which are on earth, even in Him." And this recapitulation of all things in Christ is to be effected by building all things on Christ as the sure foundation which God himself has laid in Zion; and Christians, as living stones chosen of God and precious, are, in the language of St. Paul, built upon the foundation of the apostles, "In whom all the building fitly framed together, groweth unto an holy temple in the Lord. In whom ye also are builded together for an habitation of God through the Spirit." This structure the same apostle designates in another place as "a building of God, a house not made with hands, eternal in the heavens." And now if we will with the eye of St. John gaze into the opening heaven, we shall with him behold no temple there. Why? because, says this beloved disciple, "the Lord God Almighty and the Lamb are the temple thereof." Ah yes! Christ, in whom all things are gathered together—on whom as a corner stone all living stones are built—in whom dwelleth all the fullness of the Godhead bodily, is the temple of Heaven! and because we are Christ's, and Christ is

God, we also, by being, in the words of St. Paul, "partakers of the divine nature," become a holy temple of
the Lord, having for its walls salvation, and for its gates
praise.

This spiritual temple God is now building up, and
it progresses just as fast as the living stones are prepared to take their places above.   The first living stone
ever built upon this precious corner stone was righteous
Abel, and since then Enoch, and Noah, and Abraham,
and Moses, and David, and Daniel, and multitudes of
others having been hewn and squared here, have been
fitted into their places in this living temple.   But since
Christ came, how gloriously has it increased !   Apostles,
and martyrs, and confessors, and saints ; bishops, and
priests, and deacons, and laity ; the aged, the middle
aged, the young and the infant ; the rich, the learned,
the poor and the ignorant ; kings, and captains, and
statesman, and scholars, have been added layer upon
layer ; sometimes, when persecution has raged, a thousand stones a day ; and sometimes long years have
passed, and scarce a living stone has been transferred to
heaven.   And this building process is going on every
day, in our midst, under our own eyes.   The prattling
infant, the loving child, the youth of promise, the doat-
ing mother, the cherished wife, the fond husband, the
revered parent, the loved sister, the manly brother, all
have been taken from our midst, and while household after household have put on mourning and uttered
piercing cries of anguish as the beloved but stricken one

has been taken away; angels have shouted for joy
that another lively stone has been set up in the heavens,
to abide for ever in glory. And who of those who hope
that we are lively stones, who are now passing through
the trials and afflictions of our needed preparation;
who of us will next be taken—in what family will God
select the next lively stone that shall be borne from
this earthly to that heavenly temple? Or if God
keep you longer on earth, and cause you to suffer trials
and afflictions of mind and body, and home and friends,
and business and fortune, can you, will you repine
when you know why he keeps you here, and what these
tribulations are designed to accomplish in you? Keep
before your souls God's ultimate purpose, and it will
make you always to rejoice in God's present dealings.
Look frequently at the glorious end, and you will murmur less at the sorrows of the way, and remember that
the moment that you are fitted in the eye of the Great
Architect to take your place as a living stone above, he
will place you there, whether with the preliminary call
of sickness or the sudden summons, " Come up hither,"
and when up thither all the preparation and disciplines
of earth are over, and as the Saints look back to the
quarry whence they were hewn, and compare their rough
and unshapen appearance then with their present grace
and beauty, will they not bless God who did not leave
them in the stony ledge of impenitence, or lying as
unseemly blocks at the quarry's mouth; but who
caused to pass over them the axe and the hammer, and
10

the tool of iron of his afflictive dispensation, and thus made them lively stones fitted to abide in eternal beauty in the New Jerusalem above?

But this exceeding glory will be ours only as we become living stones, by being united to Jesus Christ the corner stone by a living faith. Have we this faith? do we cling to Christ alone? have we hid our lives in him by a self-consecration that will never recall its covenant vows? Do we walk by faith, and does this faith purify the heart, enabling us to resist the devil, overcome the world, and rejoice in hope of the glory of God?

Have we evidences that we are now, as the apostle says, "temples of the Holy Ghost?" Are our souls under the constant, controlling, sanctifying, influences of this blessed spirit? For if we are not temples of the Holy Ghost on earth, we can never become "living stones" in the temple of heaven. Does Christ dwell in our hearts by faith, and do we feel the presence and the preciousness of such an indwelling Saviour? If we do, then have we daily evidence that we are of his chosen ones, and that ere long, after a few more strokes from the axe and the hammer, he will raise us to glory; but if not, oh wait not another day, but, while the Spirit of God even now strives with your soul, embrace the offers of his abounding grace, that you also may so look for, and long for his appearing, as to be constrained to say with the enraptured spirit of the banished apostle: "Amen. Even so, come quickly, Lord Jesus!"

STEVENS.

Scriptural Selections.

For whom the Lord loveth he chasteneth, and scourgeth every son whom he receiveth.

If ye endure chastening, God dealeth with you as with sons: for what son is he whom the father chasteneth not?

But if ye be without chastisement, whereof all are partakers, then are ye bastards, and not sons.

Furthermore, we have had fathers of our flesh which corrected us, and we gave them reverence: shall we not much rather be in subjection unto the Father of spirits, and live?

For they verily for a few days chastened us after their own pleasure; but he for our profit, that we might be partakers of his holiness.

Now no chastening for the present seemeth to be joyous, but grievous: nevertheless, afterward it yieldeth the peaceable fruit of righteousness unto them which are exercised thereby.—*Heb.* xii. 6—11.

We are troubled on every side, yet not distressed; we are perplexed, but not in despair;

Persecuted, but not forsaken; cast down, but not destroyed;

Always bearing about in the body the dying of the Lord Jesus, that the life also of Jesus might be made manifest in our body.—2 *Cor.* iv. 8—10.

For which cause we faint not; but though our outward man perish, yet the inward man is renewed day by day.

For our light affliction, which is but for a moment, worketh for us a far more exceeding and eternal weight of glory;

While we look not at the things which are seen, but at the things which are not seen: for the things which are seen are temporal; but the things which are not seen are eternal.—2 *Cor.* iv. 16—18.

The New Jerusalem.

" And I saw the Holy City, new Jerusalem, coming down from God out of heaven, prepared as Bride adorned for her husband."

The Holy Jerusalem
From highest heaven descending,
  And crowned with a diadem
  Of Angel bands attending,
The Living City built on high,
Bright with celestial jewelry!

  She comes, the Bride, from heaven gate,
  In nuptial new Adorning,
    To meet the Immaculate,
    Like coming of the morning.
  Her streets of purest gold are made,
  Her walls a diamond palisade.

  There with pearls the gates are dight
  Upon that Holy Mountain;
    And thither come both day and night,
    Who in the Living Fountain
  Have washed their robes from earthly stain,
  And borne below Christ's lowly chain.

  By the hand of the Unknown
  The Living Stones are moulded
    To a glorious Shrine, ALL ONE,
    Full soon to be unfolded;
  The building wherein God doth dwell,
  The Holy Church Invisible.

IV.

Jesus Veiling his Dealings.

" Jesus answered and said unto him, What I do thou knowest not now; but thou shalt know here after."—John, xiii. 7.

OUR Lord, when he spake these words, had just risen from the lowliest act of his most lowly life. Around that act there was thrown a veil of mystery which partially concealed its purport and its end from the view of his wondering disciple. There was much in this simple but expressive incident of the Saviour's life which filled his mind with perplexing thought. His first feeling was that of resistance, to be succeeded by one of astonishment, still deeper. He had marked each step in the strange proceeding—the loosened sandal, the bathing of the feet, the replacing of the robe; but the deep significance of the whole was to his view wrapped in impenetrable mystery. And how did the Saviour meet his perplexity? Not by denying its mysteriousness, but by a promise of clearer light anon. "Jesus answered and said unto him, What I do thou knowest not now; but thou shalt know hereafter." And this explanation and assurance satisfied the mind of the amazed disciple. "Simon Peter saith unto him, Lord, not my feet only, but also my hands and my head."

Each individual believer has a personal interest in
this subject, especially those to whom these pages are
inscribed,—the Father's chastened ones.   These words
imply a concealment of much of the Lord's procedure
with his people.   It is our wisdom to know that no
pure, unmixed sorrow, ever befalls the Christian sufferer.
Our Lord Jesus flung the curse and the sin to such an
infinite distance from the church, that could his faith
but discern it, the believer would see nothing but love
painting the darkest cloud that ever threw its shadow
upon his spirit.   Akin to the preceding subject is the
one upon which we now propose briefly to address the
suffering reader.   It speaks of a veiling of Christ's dealings, with the promise of an unveiling in a day far
sunnier and happier than this.   "What I do thou
knowest not now; but thou shalt know hereafter."

With regard to our heavenly Father, there can be
nothing mysterious, nothing inscrutable to him.   A
profound and awful mystery himself, yet to his infinite
mind there can be no darkness, no mystery at all.   His
whole plan—if plan it may be called—is before him.
Our phraseology, when speaking of the divine procedure, would sometimes imply the opposite of this.   We
talk of God's foreknowledge, of his foresight, of his
acquaintance with events yet unborn; but there is in
truth no such thing.   There are no tenses with God—
no past—nor present—nor to come.   The idea of God's
Eternity, if perfectly grasped, would annihilate in our
minds all such humanizing of the Divine Being.   He is

one—E TERNAL N OW. All events to the remotest period
of time, were as vivid and as present to the divine mind
from eternity, as when at the moment they assumed a
real existence and a palpable form.

But all the mystery is with us, poor finite creatures
of a day. And why, even to us, is any portion of
the divine conduct thus a mystery ? Not because
it is in itself so, but mainly and simply because
we cannot see *the whole* as God sees it. Could it
pass before our eye, as from eternity it has before his,
a perfect and a complete whole, we should then cease
to wonder, to cavil and repine. The infinite wisdom,
purity, and goodness, that originated and gave a character, a form, and a colouring, to all that God does,
would appear as luminous to our view as to his, and
ceaseless adoration and praise would be the grateful
tribute of our loving hearts.

Throw back a glance upon the past, and see how
little you have ever understood of all the way God has
led you. What a mystery—perhaps, now better ex-
plained—has enveloped his whole proceedings ! When
Joseph, for example, was torn from the homestead of
his father, sold, and borne a slave into Egypt, not a
syllable of that eventful page of his history could he
spell. All was to his mind as strange and unreadable
as the hieroglyphics of the race, whose symbolical
literature and religion now for the first time met his
eye. And yet God's way with this his servant was
perfect. And could Joseph have seen at the moment

that he descended into the pit, whither he was cast by
his envious brethren, all the future of his history as
vividly and as palpably as he beheld it in after years,
while there would have been the conviction that all was
well, we doubt not that faith would have lost much of
its vigour, and God much of his glory. And so with
good old Jacob. The famine,—the parting with Benja-
min,—the menacing conduct of Pharaoh's prime minister, wrung the mournful expression from his lips, "All
these things are against me." All was veiled in deep
and mournful mystery. Thus was it with Job, to whom
God spake from the whirlwind that swept every vestige
of affluence and domestic comfort from his dwelling.
And thus, too, with Naomi, when she exclaimed, "Call
me not Naomi, call me Mara : for the Almighty hath
dealt very bitterly with me. I went out full, and the
Lord hath brought me home again empty." How easy
were it to multiply these examples of veiled and yet
all-wise dispensations !

And is this the way of the Lord with you, my reader ?
Are you bewildered at the mazes through which you are
threading your steps ; at the involved circumstances of
your present history ; the incidents which seem so netted
and interlaced one with the other as to present to your
view an inextricable labyrinth ? Deem yourself not
alone in this. No mystery has lighted upon your path
but what is common to the one family of God : "This
honour have all his saints." The Shepherd is leading
you, as all the flock are led, with a skilful hand and in

a right way. It is yours to stand if he bids you, or to
follow if he leads. "He giveth no account of any of
his matters," assuming that his children have such confidence in his wisdom, and love, and uprightness, as, in
all the wonder-working of his dealings with them, to
"be still and know that he is God." That it is to the
honour of God to conceal, should in our view justify all
his painful and humiliating procedure with us. "It is
the glory of God to conceal a thing," as it will be for
his endless glory by and by fully to reveal it all. But
there is one thing, Christian sufferer, which he cannot
conceal. He cannot conceal the *love* that forms the
spring and foundation of all his conduct with his saints.
Do what he will, conceal as he may ; be his chariot the
thick clouds, and his way in the deep sea ; still his love
betrays itself, disguised though it may be in dark and
impenetrable providence. There are under tones, gentle
and tender, in the roughest accents of our Joseph's voice.
And he who has an ear ever hearkening to the Lord,
and delicately attuned to the gentlest whisper, shall
often exclaim,—"Speak, Lord, how and when and where
thou mayest—it is the voice of my beloved !"

But we have arrived at an interesting and cheering
truth—the full unveiling of all the Lord's dealings in a
holier and a brighter world. "What I do, thou knowest
not now ; *but thou shalt know hereafter*." That there
is a present partial understanding of God's will and
ways concerning us, we readily concede. We may, now
and then, see a *needs be* for his conduct. The veil is

11

just sufficiently lifted to reveal a portion of the "end of the Lord." He will make us acquainted with the evil which he corrects, with the backsliding which he chastens, with the temptation which he checks, and with the dangerous path around which he throws his hedge; so that we cannot escape. We see it, and we bless the hand outstretched to save. He will also cause us to be *fruitful.* We have mourned our leanness, have confessed our barrenness, and lamented the distance of our walk, and the little glory we bring to his dear name,—and lo! the dresser of the vineyard has appeared to prune his sickly branch, "that it may bring forth more fruit." "By this therefore shall the iniquity of Jacob be purged; and this is all the fruit to take away his sin." The deeper teaching, too,—the result of the divine chastenings,—has revealed to some extent the "end of the Lord" in his mysterious conduct. O there is no school like God's school; for "who teacheth like him?" And God's highest school is the school of trial. All his true scholars have graduated from this: "Who are these which are arrayed in white robes? and whence came they? These are they which came out of great tribulation, and have washed their robes, and made them white in the blood of the Lamb." "Blessed is the man, O Lord, whom thou *chasteneth* and *teacheth* him out of thy law." Ask each spiritually, deeply-taught Christian where he attained his knowledge—and he will point you to God's great university—*the school of trial.*

But there is a time coming, a blessed time of " good things to come," when the darkness will all have passed. away, the mystery of God will be finished, and the present conduct of our Saviour will be fully cleared up. " What I do, thou knowest not now; *but thou shalt know hereafter.*" O that " *hereafter*," what a solemn word to the ungodly! *Is* there, then, a *hereafter?* Jesus says there is; and I believe it, because he says it. That *hereafter* will be terrible to the man that dies in his sins. It will be a hereafter, whose history will be ." written in mourning, lamentation, and woe." It had been better for thee, reader, living and dying, impenitent and unbelieving, hadst thou never been born, or. had there been *no* hereafter. But there *is* a *hereafter* of woe to the sinner, as of bliss to the saint. " These shall go away into everlasting punishment: but the righteous into life eternal." (Matt. xxv. 46.)

The position which the Christian shall occupy hereafter, will be most favourable to a full and clear comprehension of all the mysteries of the way. The " clouds and darkness"—emblems in our history of obscurity and distress—which now envelop God's throne, and enshroud his government of the saints, will have passed away; the mist and fog will have vanished, and breathing a purer atmosphere, and canopied by a brighter sky, the glorified saint will see every object, circumstance, incident, and step, with an eye unobscured **by** a vapour, and unmoistened by a tear. "Now we know in part, then shall we know even as we are known." And what shall we know? All the mysteries of *Providence*. Things which had made us greatly grieve, will now be seen to have been causes of the greatest joy. Clouds of threatening, which appeared to us charged with the agent of destruction, will then unveil, and reveal the love which they embosomed and concealed. All the mysteries of *faith* too will be known. " Now we see through a glass, darkly (in a riddle); but then face to face; now I know in part; but then shall I know even as also I am known." The great " mystery of Godliness" will develop and unfold its wonders. His everlasting love to his church—his choice of a people for himself—his sovereign grace in calling them, all, all, will shine forth with unclouded lustre to the eternal praise of his great and holy name. O what a perfect, harmonious, and glorious whole will all his doings in providence and grace appear, from first to last, to the undimmed eye, the ravished gaze of his white-robed, palm-bearing church.

Many and holy are the lessons we may gather from this subject. The first is—the lesson of deep *humility*. There are three steps in the Christian's life. The first is—humility; the second is—humility; the third is—humility. " Thou shalt remember all the way which the Lord thy God led thee these forty years in the wilderness, to *humble* thee, and to *prove* thee, to know what was in thine heart." In veiling his dealings, Jesus would " hide pride" from us. How loftily and self-sufficiently should we walk did we see all our present

and future history plain before us.   We should ascribe
to our own wisdom and skill, prudence and forethought,
the honour which belongs to Christ alone.   Let us,
then, lie low before the Lord, and humble ourselves
under his mysterious hand.   " The meek will he guide
in judgment, and the meek will he teach his way.   All
the paths of the Lord are mercy and truth unto such
as keep his covenant and his testimonies."   Thus
writing the sentence of death upon our wisdom, our
sagacity, and our strength, Jesus—the lowly one—
seeks to keep us from the loftiness of our intellect, and
from the pride of our heart prostrating us low in the
dust at his feet.   Holy posture ! blessed place !   There,
Lord, would I lie ; my trickling tears of penitence and
love, falling upon those dear feet that have never misled,
but have always gone before, leading me by a right
way, the best way, to a city of rest.

> " To cure thee of thy pride—that deepest-seated ill,
>   God humbled his own self—wilt thou thy pride keep still ?"

We should learn from this subject to live by *faith*
amidst the enshrouding dealings of our God.   Therefore are those dealings often so dark.   Could we ever
see all the road, faith would have no play ; this precious,
this Christ-honouring, this God-glorifying grace would
lie dormant in the soul.   But, in " leading the blind by
a way that they know not," he teaches them to confide
in the knowledge, truth, and goodness of their Divine
escort—and that confidence is the calm unquestioning
repose of *faith*.

> "My spirit on thy care,
>   Blest Saviour, I recline;
> Thou wilt not leave me to despair,
>   For thou art love divine.

> "In thee I place my trust,
>   On thee I calmly rest;
> I know thee good, I know thee just,
>   And count thy choice the best.

> "Whate'er events betide,
>   Thy will they all perform:
> Safe in thy breast my head I hide,
>   Nor fear the coming storm.

> "Let good or ill befall.
>   It must be good for me;
> Secure of having thee in all,
>   Of having all in thee."*

Oh, sweet, consoling words of Jesus!—"What I do."
Not what men do—not what angels do—not what thou
doest,--but, "what *I* do." Is the loved one wrenched
from your heart?—"I have done it," says Jesus. Is
the desire of thine eyes smitten down with a stroke?—
"I have done it," says Jesus. Is it the loss of property,
of health, of position, of friends, that overwhelms you
with grief?—"I have done it," says Jesus. "What *I*
do thou knowest not now; but thou shalt know hereafter." How many a mother has this promise soothed,
while with an anguish such as a mother only knows,
she has gazed upon the withered flower on her breast!
How many a father, standing by the couch of death,
grasping the cold clammy hand of the pride of his heart,

* Rev. H. F. Lyte.

has felt the power of these words, more sweet and more soothing than an angel's music—"What I do thou knowest not now; but thou shalt know hereafter." Wait, then, suffering child, the coming glory—yielding yourself to the guidance of your Saviour, and submitting yourself wholly to your Father's will.

WINSLOW

SCRIPTURAL SELECTIONS.

CONFIRMING the souls of the disciples, and exhorting them to continue in the faith, and that we must through much tribulation enter into the kingdom of God.—*Acts,* xiv. 22.

That no man should be moved by these afflictions: for yourselves know that we are appointed thereunto.

For verily, when we were with you, we told you before that we should suffer tribulation; even as it came to pass, and ye know.—1 *Thes.* iii. 3, 4.

For even hereunto were ye called: because Christ also suffered for us, leaving us an example, that ye should follow his steps:

Who did no sin, neither was guile found in his mouth:

Who, when he was reviled, reviled not again; when he suffered, he threatened not; but committed himself to him that judgeth righteously.—1 *Pet.* ii. 21, 23.

Peace in Affliction.

O Lord! how happy should we be,
If we could cast our care on thee,
   If we from self could rest;
And feel at heart that One above,
In perfect wisdom, perfect love,
   Is working for the best.

How far from this our daily life!
Ever disturbed by anxious strife,
   By sudden wild alarms;
O could we but relinquish all
Our earthly props, and simply fall
   On thy Almighty arms!

Could we but kneel, and cast our load.
E'en while we pray, upon our God;
   Then rise with lightened cheer,
Sure that the Father who is nigh
To still the famished raven's cry
   Will hear, in that we fear.

We cannot trust him as we should,
So chafes fallen nature's restless mood
   To cast its peace away;
Yet birds and flow'rets round us preach,
All, all the present evil teach
   Sufficient for the day.

Lord, make these faithless hearts of ours,
Such lessons learn from birds and flowers.
  Make them from self to cease:
Leave all things to a Father's will,
And taste, before him lying still,
    E'en in affliction, peace.

Resignation.

RESIGNATION.

I.

SILENT SUFFERING.

*I was dumb, I opened not my mouth, because thou didst it."—*PSALM XXXIX. 9.

I BELIEVE that there are few of us who have not frequently heard this Psalm read upon funeral occasions; and we must, no doubt, approve the propriety of the choice, as it contains some very weighty reflections on the mortality of human nature, expressed with great solemnity, and intermingled with proper devotional addresses to that great and awful Being who has in righteous judgment passed that sentence on sinful man, by which we and our friends are brought down to the dust: for it is he, as the Psalmist well expresses it (verse 5), who has *made our days as a hand's breadth, and our age as nothing before him;* so that *every man,* in his best state, *is altogether vanity.* When the mind is agitated with strong affections, it is difficult to restrain the tongue from some undue liberty of speech:

at least, there may be an inward language, audible to the ear of God, which may be displeasing to him, if there be not a care to impose silence upon every re-pining thought, as well as to *keep the mouth as with a bridle.* But it is the design of the providence of God, in conjunction with his ordinances, to teach us, what-ever our trials may be, how dear soever the enjoyments which we may lose, and how heavy soever the burthen which we may bear, to be dumb with silence, after the example of the pious Psalmist, and not to open our mouths, because whatever it is that has fallen upon us, has come from the hand of God.

1. Let the Christian reflect that God can do no wrong to him, or to any of his creatures.

Let him not only consider the sovereignty of the Almighty's dominion, which is such that no creature can pretend to contend with him, but also the essential rectitude of his nature, which is such that none can have any right inwardly to censure, or to complain of what he does. "O my soul! he has done it, who holds the reins of universal empire. He, who *does what he pleases in the armies of heaven, and amongst the inha-bitants of earth.* He has done it, *who spake* the crea-ting *word, and it was done;* he who *is the potter, and every creature,* on earth and in heaven, *but as clay* in his hand, to be moulded according to his own will. And *shall the thing formed say to him that formed it, why hast thou made me thus?* Well may it be said in that connexion, 'Nay, O man! who art thou that repliest

against God? Let the potsherds strive with the potsherds of the earth; but woe unto him that strives, with
his Maker!' " This is a silencing thought: nor does
it impose merely such a silence as proceeds from the
dread of superior power, or the despair of being able to
make anything out by resisting it; but with the conviction of such sovereign authority and dominion is necessarily connected that also of infinite perfection. It
cannot be good to the Almighty that he should oppress.
Nothing can tempt Omnipotence in any instance to do
evil. The infinite understanding of God must ever see
what is right; his all perfect mind, seeing it, must approve it; and, approving it, must do it, being infinitely
above all temptation to deviate from it. There is
always reason to say, *Good is the word of the Lord that
he has spoken,* for this very reason, because it is his
word; because it is spoken by him. " O my perverse
heart! what wouldst thou say? Wouldst thou dare to
fly in the face of God himself? Wouldst thou dare to
charge him with tyrannical administration? Wouldst
thou dare to say, Lord, thou art now beginning to act
unworthy of thyself: thou governest other beings wisely
and well; but thou neglectest me, and availest thyself
of thine irresistible power to overbear my rights, and
to oppress me in judgment! God forbid! who would
not rather say, *Let my tongue cleave to the roof of my
mouth,* before I utter such a word; yea, let my mind
lose all its rational faculties rather than harbour such a
thought!"

2. Let the Christian further recollect what God has done for him, as a reason why he should be silent under what God now does to him.

Were he only to consider himself as the creature of God, without attending to what is peculiar to him as being a Christian, he might see enough to silence his complaints. "Has not the blessed God given to me my being? such a being! with such noble powers and endowments as I possess! Has he not set me here at the head of this visible creation? in this spacious and magnificent palace, which he has raised for the human family, and furnished and adorned in this commodious, grand, and beautiful manner? Has he not been the guardian of my infancy, and my childhood? and in riper years my guide and my benefactor in numberless instances? Has he not given to me all that I have; every comfort in life, personal or relative? When I look round about me upon all that I can call my treasure, my possession, does not everything bear his name, as it were, inscribed upon it as the donor? *The gift of God*. May I not be reminded of his bounty by all that I possess; yea, by all that I lose, and all that I suffer? This member, which is the seat of pain or disease, did he not form it? and has he not given to me the easy and comfortable use of it during these many years, though he now lays his hand upon it? This friend, who is now laid in the grave, was she not a creature of his, whom he formed and gave to me; and in whom, perhaps, he blessed me for many years? and is such a friend and benefactor to be quarrelled with, because he sometimes resumes a little of what he has given ?"

But this is not all. I am speaking to you now as Christians : and then consider how the account rises. " Has not God blessed me with the knowledge of his gospel, and of his Son ? Has he not sent to me the tidings of grace and salvation by him ? and has he not by his Holy Spirit made him dear and precious to my heart ; and given to me some cheerful and comfortable hope of an interest in him as my Redeemer and my Saviour ? And can there be matter of complaint against him when I consider this ? Has not *his arm brought salvation* to my view ? A salvation which he himself wrought out in so wonderful a manner ? And ought not that consideration to, reconcile me to everything else which comes from so good a hand ? to all his other doings ?"

3. Let the Christian recollect what God might have done with him, and to him, as a further reason for being silent under the afflicting of the Divine hand.

" The hand of God has now touched me and pained me. True ! but it has not destroyed me. He has not, as Job expresses it, *let loose his hand against me, and cut me off :* and might he not have done that ? He has taken away this and that comfort. True ! but might he not have taken away all ; and have stripped me quite naked and bare ? yea, might he not have taken away my soul ? have destroyed my very existence ?· or, what would have been ten thousand times worse, have sup-

13

ported it only to make it miserable ? God has *chastised me with rods:* but what are those *scorpions* with which he might have scourged me, and have been righteous in doing it ! Hast thou not, O my soul ! by numberless provocations, most righteously exposed thyself to his everlasting vengeance ? What if thou hadst, even now, been in the abodes of the damned, surrounded with eternal darkness and despair ! would he have been unjust in speaking, and unrighteous in judging thus ? Be silent then, O my heart ! before him; and let not God hear the lightest murmur : but rather let me fall down upon my knees, and adore his sovereign goodness that he has yet spared me ; and, much more, that he gives me any hope that he will save me."

4. Let the Christian consider what God is now doing in a wider extent of the prospect than can arise merely from the view of any present affliction.

" Thou, Lord, hast done this. Thou hast afflicted my body ; thou hast disappointed my prospects ; thou hast blasted my hopes ; thou hast slain my friends. But this is not all that thou art now doing : thou still continuest thy goodness to me ; thou *causest thy sun to arise, and thy rain to descend upon me ;* thou feedest and clothest me daily ; thou sparest to me many dear and valuable friends, whom it were base and barbarous ingratitude to slight because some are taken away. Thou art still continuing to me the liberty of access to the throne of grace ; encouraging and inviting me, if I have not this or that remaining comfort in the creature, to come to thee; to tell thee my sorrows and my complaints; to seek in thee what I have lost elsewhere, and more than I have lost. Yea, thou art continuing to me the liberty of thine house, and the privileges of thine ordinances. I am not banished from the solemn assembly by the violence of my enemies, who would gladly long ere this have introduced universal confusion and desolation, and *have burnt up all the synagogues of God in the land.* I am not his prisoner at home, as many of my Christian brethren are, in this land of liberty. Blessed be his name! I can come up to his house, as it is this day. Yea, he *spreads his own table for me.* As if all the blessings of mine were not, as indeed they are not, sufficient, he sets before me the body and blood of his own Son; gives him to me as *the bread of life that comes down from heaven.* It is the blessing of this day and of this hour. And is this a day and hour in which to be complaining of him? as if it were not enough that I am here, unless it were with such and such a fellow creature; possessed of so much silver and gold; arrayed in such or such apparel; with such and such degrees of health and strength and spirits! Oh! surely it may be enough that I am here as a member of Christ, as a child of God! especially when with that is connected this further thought, as an heir of glory." Which leads me to add,

5. Let the Christian further consider what God will further and hereafter do for him, and it must surely silence him under whatever God has now done.

And if you ask, what? Let the Jewish Psalmist answer in these emphatical words, "Thou shalt guide me with thy counsel, and afterwards receive me to glory." "Has God forsaken me, that I should murmur and complain? Is he now doing the last office of kindness and love that he ever intends? No; he will never leave me nor forsake me. This is still his language, 'Fear not, for I am with thee: be not dismayed, for I am thy God.' He will choose my inheritance for me. *He will watch over me for good, and cause all things to work together for* my truest advantage. He will subdue my iniquity; he will strengthen my graces; and, *having begun the good work* in me, *he will carry it on till the day of the Lord.* In a little while, perhaps, a very little, he will do what to an eye of sense indeed looks like a dreadful work, but to faith wears a most cheerful aspect. He will, by his Providence, say to me, as to Moses, *Go up and die.* But that act of his, which consigns this mortal sinful body to the dust and worms, will be the most gracious act that he ever exerted since he regenerated my soul by the power of his Spirit. Then farewell to all my pains and my fears, my disappointments and my sorrows at once. Farewell, for a little while, to all my surviving friends; and welcome more perfect and glorious friends. Welcome the dear deceased Christians, over whom I have so often wept. Welcome, above all, the bosom of my Saviour, in which I also shall rest with them. O abyss of joy and delight! and yet not all that I hope. The resurrection of the body shall complete the plan of my perfect happiness, with all the chosen in the everlasting enjoyment of God, of Christ, of one another, in forms of devotion and glory ; of glory and felicity which *eye has not seen, nor ear heard, neither hath entered into the heart of man.* And shall not all be taken well from a hand which will do all this ? a hand which, even while it afflicts, has this great end of all in view, that *the light afflictions, which are but for a moment, may work out a far more exceeding and an eternal weight of glory.*"

Whatever it may please God to work, there is something not only quieting but elevating in these considerations : something which may not only silence a Christian's complaint, but engage him to break out into a song of praise.

DODDRIDGE.

SCRIPTURAL SELECTIONS.

SEEING then that we have a great High Priest, that is passed into the heavens, Jesus the Son of God, let us hold fast our profession.

For we have not an high priest which cannot be touched with the feeling of our infirmities: but was in all points tempted like as we are, yet without sin.

Let us therefore come boldly unto the throne of grace, that we may obtain mercy, and find grace to help in time of need.—*Heb.* iv. 14—16.

Behold, the Lord God will come with strong hand, and his arm shall rule for him: behold, his reward is with him, and his work before him.

He shall feed his flock like a shepherd: he shall gather the lambs with his arm, and carry them in his bosom, and shall gently lead those that are with young.—*Is.* xl. 10, 11.

Hast thou not known? hast thou not heard, that the everlasting God, the Lord, the Creator of the ends of the earth, fainteth not, neither is weary? there is no searching of his understanding.

He giveth power to the faint; and to them that have no might he increaseth strength.

Even the youth shall faint and be weary, and the young men shall utterly fall:

But they that wait upon the Lord shall renew their strength; they shall mount up with wings *as* eagles; they shall run, and not be weary; and they shall walk and not faint.—*Is.* xl. 28—31.

The Weaned Child.

Quiet, Lord, my froward heart,
  Make me teachable and mild,
Upright, simple, free from art;
  Make me as a weaned child.
    From distrust and envy free,
    Pleased with all that pleases Thee.

What thou shalt to-day provide,
  Let me as a child receive;
What to-morrow may betide,
  Calmly to Thy wisdom leave.
    'Tis enough that Thou wilt care,
    Why should I the burden bear?

As a little child relies
  On a care beyond its own;
Knows he's neither strong nor wise—
  Fears to stir a step alone—
    Let me thus with Thee abide,
    As my Father, Guard, and Guide.

Thus preserved from Satan's wiles,
  Safe from dangers, free from fears,
May I live upon thy smiles
  Till the promised hour appears;
    When the sons of God shall prove
    All their Father's boundless love.

II.

Songs in the Night Season.

" But none saith, where is God my Maker, who giveth songs in the night?"—Job, xxxv. 10.

THE night is proverbially a time of festivity and song. The cares and business of the day are then over; the taxed mind and the wearied muscles seek relaxation; the stillness of the evening invites to those pleasures which cannot be enjoyed amidst the bustle and din of business; and the darkness calling off the mind from the outdoor duties and gayeties, turns it to those domestic or social or festive gatherings, where the gladness of the heart testifies its existence by singing and the voice of melody.

But the vast majority of these songs are earth-born, and designed only for earthly ends. The bacchanalian chorus, the moonlight serenade, the orchestral concert, the parlour melody, the love-lorn ditty, and the trumpet-rousing strains of martial music, are each of terrestrial birth; and though they may deeply affect the heart, rousing it to wildest joy or sinking it to pensive sadness, yet are they evanescent, and soon are among the things of a forgotten past.

No such songs, though sung with unrivalled art, though swelling with delicious melody, though rich in

"And at midnight Paul and Silas prayed
and sang praises unto God and the prisoners
heard them."   Acts XVI. 25.

tones of " linked sweetness long drawn out," satisfy
the soul.   Who that has listened to the most rapturous
songs, to those which in our imagination come nearest
to angelic harmony, has not, as its last cadence fell on
the ear, and its last echo died away, felt a pang of
sorrow that such tones must die as fast as they are
uttered? that, with a soul fitted to enjoy such vocal
richness, we can obtain it so seldom and so briefly?   And
to all this has there not often been joined the wish, Oh!
that there were songs that would never ceasę to thrill!
Oh! that there were voices that would never lose their
tone and compass by age!   Oh! that there were places
where we might ever abide, and listen at will to the
treasured melodies of tongue and harp in their loftiest
manifestation!

There are such places—there are such voices—there
are such songs.   Yet when I tell you of them, the very
hearts that profess most to desire them will turn away
with scornful looks, and perhaps deride them as the out-
bursts of hot-brained enthusiasm or of canting hypo-
crisy.   But sneer as you may—curl your lip until it
becomes rigid with scorn—mock until you have exhausted the vocabulary of obloquy, and defame until
you are startled by your own blasphemy, I tell you in
a freedom that invites investigation, and with a boldness that challenges denial, that *the religion of Jesus
Christ furnishes such songs, tunes such voices, and opens
such places of perpetual and sublimest melody ;* for the
mansions of glory for ever resound with saintly voices
14

singing the songs of Moses and the Lamb. But you may say this is all true, but what I want is a present gladness of heart—a present song of joy—amidst the daily cares, trials, perplexities, and bereavements of this mortal life; and where can I find such? My answer still is, *in the gospel of the Son of God, and there alone!*

The time when these songs are mostly needed and desired is in the night season; not the period of physical darkness, but the moral night season—the night season of humiliation—the night season of adversity—the night season of sorrow—the night season of sickness—the night season of death; and it is just in these times that the true Christian rejoices in God his Maker, who giveth him songs in the night.

In the life of every individual there are periods of humiliation which take down his pride and bend his spirit to the dust. It may be that the person has occupied some post of honour or profit from which he has been removed—it may be that some unexpected blot has marred and stained his family name—it may be that failure in business has injuriously affected his character, and required him to take a lowly social position, and that in consequence, the gay and the fashionable, who flutter only around the candle of the prosperous, turn their heads at his approach, renounce his society, and cast themselves loose from his family circle—it may be that he is visited by some sore and noisome disease, or by some unexpected deformity that clings to him like a thorn in the flesh, and ever humbles him by a consciousness of its presence—it may be that false reports have tarnished his fair name, and caused him to be marked and avoided,—indeed, there are so many causes of humility actively at work, that it would be in vain to attempt to enumerate them.   Some one of these, however, occasionally affects each person, and makes him bow his head in humiliation.   Does the Bible furnish us any songs for such a night season, when the darkness of adversity, of desertion, of reproach, and of deep self-loathing, stretches over us a black and starless firmament? Yes, it does.   It is furnished in the beautiful words of the prophet Habakkuk, who, as if himself suffering under just such trials, dictates to the chief singer upon his stringed instrument the following exquisite ode : " Although the fig tree shall not blossom, neither shall fruit be in the vines ; the labour of the olive shall fail, and the fields shall yield no meat: the flock shall be cut off from the fold, and there shall be no herd in the stalls : Yet I will rejoice in the Lord, I will joy in the God of my salvation."   What a precious song is this for the night season of humiliation and adversity !   It teaches that no earthly changes should ever shake our confidence in God ; that His favour is not dispensed to us according to our worldly advantages and position ; that His ways of dealing are disciplinary, and will, if rightly improved, work out for us an exceeding weight of glory. What though the honours you once wore are taken from you ? if you are Christ's, there is reserved for you " a crown of life."   What though your earthly reputation

is unjustly stained! there is laid up for you in heaven
a robe of spotless white, with which to array your ransomed spirit. What though you have, through circumstances beyond your control, failed in your business and
shattered your fortune? You have in store for you
above, treasures that never fail—the treasures of Divine
redeeming grace. What though you know not whence
shall come the next supply of daily bread, or where at
night you shall find a place of rest; or how, when one
change of raiment is worn, you shall obtain another?
Your Saviour passed through just such trials. He was
often an hungered; he had not what the foxes and the
birds had—a place where to lay his head—and his
raiment was the gift of poor but loving friends. You
cannot in any condition of adversity go into lower depths
than Jesus went; and no Christian should be unwilling
to follow his steps, though they pass through the lowly
and rugged places of life. Only take his hand in the
strong clasp of faith, and never relax your hold, and
Jesus will make the vale of humiliation radiant with
the light of his own countenance—will put into your
mouth songs of praise, and guide you into final and unending joy. Most forcibly was this illustrated in the
case of Paul and Silas. They had been arrested in
Philippi, a Roman colony, for boldly preaching in the
name of the Lord Jesus; and having by the orders of the
magistrates been severely scourged, were thrust into the
inner cells of the prison, and, lest they should by any
means escape, their feet were made fast in the stocks.

This was to them a deep humiliation. Paul was a Roman citizen, and so was Silas; and yet, though the Porcian law, in the language of Cicero, "had removed the rod from the body of every Roman citizen," so that none claiming such citizenship could be beaten, yet they had had "many stripes laid upon them;" they had been hooted and reviled by the rabble of the town—they had been traduced and vilified by lying and malicious tongues—they had been imprisoned in the lowest, darkest, filthiest cell of the Philippi jail, and they had received the still further indignity of having their feet cruelly fastened in the stocks. What deep affliction! you say; what barbarous treatment!—how it must have chafed and humbled their spirits!—how it must have suggested in them plans of deep and far-reaching revenge! Could there be joy for them? Behold them; their clothes have been so torn by the multitude that they hang in tatters about them. Their backs have been cruelly torn to the quick by the lictor's thongs, and the open unwashed wounds still smart with pain. Their feet are confined in such a manner as to give them no possibility of rest; and the cold, damp, inner dungeon wraps around their half naked, bleeding, exhausted bodies its chilling and unhealthy air. Can there be joy for them? The city of Philippi is asleep—the excited populace are at rest—the thronged streets are empty, and the two strangers who had so engrossed the public mind are now forgotten in the deep slumbers of darkness. But Paul and Silas sleep not. Their pains and their constrained position will not suffer them to close their eyes. And how are they employed in these wakeful hours? Hark! It is midnight! but its stillness is broken by the voice of singing. Listen! It is no Orphic song to Bacchus—no Salian hymn to Diana—no Sapphic ode to Venus—nor yet do these sounds proceed from the halls of revelry or the abodes of wealth: they issue from the prison walls; it is the voice of strange melody struggling upwards from the inner cell —it is Paul and Silas, the beaten, imprisoned, bleeding servants of God, praying and singing praises unto God. They had found and were then rejoicing in "God their Maker," who had given them "songs in the night."

The season of bereavement is emphatically a night season to the human heart. The joys that once gave it delight are withdrawn; the scenes in which it once revelled with pleasure are vanished; a beloved one has been removed from the chambers of life to the chambers of death; and the eye, the voice, the hand, the form that ministered so much to its joy and comfort, is closed and hushed, and palsied, and cold, in the silent grave. You sit in darkness in your darkened dwellings —you feel that one of the great lights that ruled the day of your life has been put out, and there are deep shadows resting upon your spirit, which time and grace can alone remove. To some these night seasons recur with distressing frequency. The bright days of prosperity are short, and the dark hours of sorrow are as long and dreary as the nights of an Arctic winter. To

others, there is a long and sunny period of gladness,
and years pass without a sorrow to cloud the sky;
when suddenly, perhaps, there steals in between your
heart and the sun, the black form of death, and lo, for
a time the darkness of a total eclipse shrouds your soul;
or, in the more expressive language of the Bible, your
" sun has gone down while it was yet day."

And when these night seasons of sorrow come over
the soul; when, tossed upon the billows of affliction, you
can say with imperilled and shipwrecked Paul, that
" neither sun nor stars in many days appeared, and no
small tempest lay on us," what can give you relief?
What can give light in your darkness?   What can draw
aside the curtains of your night season, and let in the
bright and genial light of day?   Friends cannot do it,
though their sympathy is indeed grateful to the mind.
Society cannot do it, for you shun it as something dis-
cordant to your soul.   Worldly pleasures cannot do it,
for you see them in their vanity as you never before
saw them, and loathe them as nauseous to your taste.
At such times nothing can stay and comfort you but a
living faith in Jesus Christ, and an abiding trust and
confidence in the promises of Almighty God.   And when
your soul looks away for its comfort from everything
of an earthly character, and turns its wistful eye of
faith to God, then is it, that He " giveth songs in the
night."

What a night of bereavement was that which afflicted
Job, when all his children, ten in number, were suddenly

cut off at a blow; and when in addition to this he was as suddenly stripped of his riches and his honours, broken up in his family, robbed of his flocks and herds, and blasted in all his possessions! and yet what a song in the night did God his maker put in his mouth when, instead of sinning and charging God foolishly, he caused him to say in the confidence of a lofty and unwavering faith, "the Lord gave and the Lord hath taken away; blessed be the name of the Lord."

What darkness brooded over David in his manifold afflictions and bereavements! yet though he says "the waters are come in unto my soul," though he was "weary with crying"—his "throat was dried"—his "eyes failed," and he was "altogether poor and sorrowful," yet he says in the same Psalm which records this deep distress, "I will praise the name of God with a song, and will magnify him with thanksgiving."

And this is the language of all the true children of God, because they know that "affliction cometh not forth of the dust, neither doth trouble spring out of the ground:" that it is their heavenly Father who takes away their relatives and friends, and that in thus chastening them he is showing his love and interest in them, and so shaping his dealings as to develop in them the graces of the spirit, bring out in them the highest polish of Christian character, and prepare them in the most perfect manner for the rewards of grace in heaven. If we could so rise above our momentary feelings and our narrow relations to the persons and things around us,

as to take in, in one broad view, the whole compass of
our lives, and the future as well as present bearings of
these afflictive dispensations—could we, in fact, survey
them from the point of view which God occupies, or
even from that one which we shall stand at in the
eternal world, then, instead of murmuring and repining,
instead of charging God with harshness, and stigma-
tizing his dealings as unkind, we should the rather rejoice
at the occurrence of afflictions.   We should see how indis-
pensable they were to the perfecting of the work of the
Holy Ghost; how without them we should perhaps lose
our souls—how with them and by them as a necessary
instrumentality, we are fitted for higher and holier joys
in glory.   Such considerations would put songs into our
mouths, and cause us in every hour of sorrow's night
season to sing aloud with gladness, and to rejoice in
spirit, even while the iron was gashing its painful way
into the deepest recesses of our affections.   Stricken
and mourning Christian, remember that there is no season of sorrow so dark that God cannot find his way to
your soul, and no night so black with grief that he cannot
and will not light it up with " the pillar of his presence,"
to guide your feet, and to fill you with comfort.

Sickness is emphatically, in the estimation of the
world, a night season.   Suffering, restlessness, anxiety,
seclusion, days of weariness and nights of anguish, are
the sad and sin-engendered accompaniments of the lot
of nearly every child of Adam.   Few have reached adult
age, over whose life sickness has not passed; whose
15

clayey tabernacle has not been shaken by the earth-
quake commotions of disease, and rent by the shakings
of frequent sickness. We have been made to feel the
frailty of flesh and blood—the folly of earthly joys—
the uncertainty of human schemes. We have been
borne, as it were, upon the sick litter, to the very brink
of the grave; been made, perhaps, to look down into its
narrow depths, and then returned again to friends and
health, to teach us the slenderness of our hold on life,
the nearness of the tomb, the daily advances of an
opening eternity.

Yet, distressing as the period of illness is, the Bible
furnishes for it songs set to heavenly music, melodious
with angelic harmony. It assures the sick that "the
Lord will strengthen him upon the bed of languishing;"
that "he will make all his bed in his sickness;" that
"he will be merciful unto him, and heal his soul;" and
it points the sufferer to Jesus the Great Physician, who
has balm for every pain, and healing medicines for every
sickness. What a song in the night season of disease
did Hezekiah find, when, having turned his face to the
wall and prayed, God granted him length of years
instead of cutting off his days in his strength; and
what a joyful prayer does David put into the mouths
of the sore distressed, when he teaches us to say, "O
Lord my God, I cried unto thee, and thou hast healed
me. O Lord, thou hast brought up my soul from the
grave: thou hast kept me alive, that I should not go
down to the pit. Sing unto the Lord, O ye saints

of his, and give thanks for a remembrance of his holiness. For his anger endureth but a moment; in his favour is life: weeping may endure (or, as the original more forcibly declares, *may lodge*) for a night, but joy cometh in the morning." As if sorrow was only a wayfarer who turned in for a night's lodging, to arise up and depart when the sun of the morning shone in at the casement. There are no solaces for hours of sickness like those found in the Bible; there is no comforter in disease like the presence of Jesus Christ; there is no light that can shine into and dissipate the darkness of the chamber of afflictive illness like the light of divine truth; and nothing can furnish the heart with gladness, or fill the mouth with a song, but the sweet words and inbreathings of the Holy Spirit.

And now we come to the last night season that visits us on earth—the night season of death. There may be those who have never known the darkness of adversity, of sorrow, of affliction, of disease, but all will know the night time of death. Though your sun of life from its rising hour has rolled through an unclouded sky, yet, however bright its morning, however dazzling its meridian, the hour of its setting must come—the evening of life, the night time of death is at hand. Friends dear as your own life must be parted from—scenes precious with a hundred fond associations must be abandoned—objects of interest in which the mind has long been absorbed must be given up—the cherished hopes of years must be thrown away, and everything that fastened down your hearts to earthly scenes and objects must be sundered, and for ever. Will God our Maker, the same God who takes away our breath, will he give songs in the night season of death? Yes, for he has promised, "Behold at even time it shall be light," and that "the redeemed of the Lord shall return and come to him with songs and everlasting joy upon their heads." Death is to be dreaded only by those who have not made their peace with God; by those who do not receive and believe on the Lord Jesus Christ as the Prophet, Priest, and King of their souls. To those who have truly repented of their sins past, who have made an unreserved surrender of their souls to Jesus Christ, and who are leading "a new life, following the commandments of God and walking daily in his holy ways," death has no terrors. They feel that they deserve eternal punishment, but they know that Christ has borne the curse for them, and that therefore it will not fall upon their heads. They feel that they are utterly unworthy of salvation, and that it is not of themselves, but the free and sovereign gift of God, yet they know also that Christ has wrought it out for them, and will freely bestow it upon their souls. They know that they do not deserve heaven, that after doing all that they have done for Christ, they are but unprofitable servants, yet they know that they shall be received up into glory for Jesus' sake—through Jesus' merits—by virtue of Jesus' intercession. "Father I will that they also whom thou hast given me be with me where I am that they may behold," aye! and that they may share too, "my glory." Hence having loved the Saviour, having lived for the Saviour, having committed the soul into his eternal keeping, the Christian is not afraid of death. His sun as it goes down sinks not to its rest in sorrow. His night of death as it draws on, sends no foreshadowing gloom into the soul. On the contrary, full of the peace of God, rejoicing in hope, strengthened by faith in Christ, he finds himself joyful while all around are sad and weeping; and as the shadows deepen over his mortal life, there rises from his lips the hymn of praise to the abounding grace of God, and there is put into his mouth the song of triumph, "Oh death where is thy sting, oh grave where is thy victory; the sting of death is sin, and the strength of sin is the law, but thanks be unto God who giveth us the victory through Jesus Christ our Lord."

These are some of the "songs in the night" given us by "God our Maker." Who does not desire to learn these songs?—who does not wish to sing them? They can be learned only as we sit at the feet of Jesus and learn of him; they can be sung only as our souls are filled by the Holy Ghost, but all are invited to come to Jesus and learn them; for his language is, "Come unto me all ye that labour and are heavy laden and I will give you rest;" and all are promised the renewing of the Holy Spirit if they will but seek in faith the blessed Saviour, through whom alone they can have peace and acceptance with "God our Maker, who giveth songs in the night."

STEVENS.

SCRIPTURAL SELECTIONS.

I WILL not leave you comfortless: I will come to you.

Peace I leave with you, my peace I give unto you: not as the world giveth give I unto you.   Let not your heart be troubled, neither let it be afraid.—*John*, xiv. 18, 27.

These things I have spoken unto you, that in me ye might have peace.   In the world ye shall have tribulation: but be of good cheer: I have overcome the world.—*John*, xvi. 33.

They that sow in tears shall reap in joy.

He that goeth forth and weepeth, bearing precious seed, shall doubtless come again with rejoicing, bringing his sheaves with him.—*Ps.* cxxvi. 5, 6.

He shall not cry, nor lift up, nor cause his voice to be heard in the street.—*Is.* xlii. 2.

Who raised up the righteous man from the East, called him to his foot, gave the nations before him, and made him rule over kings? he gave them as the dust to his sword, and as driven stubble to his bow.

He pursued them and passed safely; even by the way that he had not gone with his feet.—*Is.* xli. 2, 3.

MIDNIGHT HYMN.

At midnight I will rise to give thanks unto thee, because of thy righteous judgments. —Psalm cxix. 62

In the mid silence of the voiceless night,
When, chased by airy dreams, the slumbers flee;
Whom, in the darkness, doth my spirit seek,
        O God, but thee?

And, if there be a weight upon my breast,
Some vague impression of the day foregone,
Scarce knowing what it is, I fly to thee,
        And lay it down.

Or, if it be the heaviness, that comes
In token of anticipated ill,—
My bosom takes no heed of what it is,
        Since 't is thy will.

For, O, in spite of past or present care,
Or anything beside,—how joyfully
Passes that silent, solitary hour,
        My God, with thee!

More tranquil than the stillness of the night,
More peaceful than the silence of that hour,
More blest than anything, my bosom lies
        Beneath thy power.

For, what is there on earth, that I desire,
Of all that it can give, or take from me?
Or whom, in heaven, doth my spirit seek,
        O God, but thee?

The Well Spring in the Desert.

" This is my comfort in mine affliction."—Ps. cxix. 50.
" Is any among you afflicted? let him pray."—James, v. 13.

THE Bible opens a spring of comfort for the afflicted, by giving them free access to the throne of grace, and inviting them to enjoy the privilege of prayer.

This is, indeed, the Christian's privilege at all seasons; and never will he feel himself to be in a right or comfortable state, whatever may be his outward prosperity, if he allow himself to neglect that blessed ordinance, by which intercourse is maintained betwixt heaven and earth, and fellowship enjoyed by the creature with the Creator. And he who, whether in prosperity or adversity, makes it his daily practice to go to the throne of grace, and in *everything* by prayer and supplication with thanksgiving, makes his request known unto God, will, from his own experience, bear testimony to the truth of the promise, that " the peace of God which passeth all understanding, shall keep his heart and mind through Christ Jesus."

But while prayer is a duty incumbent at all seasons, and a privilege which the highest prosperity affords no reason for neglecting, it is, in many respects, peculiarly seasonable in the time of affliction.

Affliction is *favourable to the spirit of prayer.* For, wherein does the true nature of prayer consist? It consists in the *desire of the heart,* offered up to God; and what better fitted to awaken earnest desire than the pressure of affliction? In the day of prosperity, when every want or appetite of our nature is supplied, we may not be conscious of any very strong desire, and are too apt to forget the fact of our dependence, in respect to the supply of our temporal wants; and even in regard to our spiritual necessities, we are prone, when surfeited with worldly prosperity, to become cold and lukewarm in our desires after the communication of divine grace, by which alone they can be supplied. Is there one Christian who has not experienced the deadening effect of uninterrupted prosperity on the spiritual desires and holiest affections of his nature? And if even Christians are too often lulled asleep by its influence, how much more may those be cradled into profound forgetfulness of God, who have never known the necessity, nor made the deliberate choice, of a better and more enduring portion? But when their prosperous course is broken by severe affliction, the minds of both classes are brought into a new state; the Christian is then thrown back on the inward resources of his religion, and will then feel their necessity and value; and even in an unsanctified bosom, such strong natural longings will spring up, as may, under the blessing of God, lead the worldling himself to seek after a better portion than the world. In so far as affliction is

11

the means of awakening earnest desire, and exciting a *sincere* feeling in the heart, it is favourable to the spirit of prayer; for that feeling, or that desire, if directed towards God, is prayer.

Again, prayer is an *expression of our dependence on God;* and it is in affliction that we are most sensible of our helplessness,—it is by affliction that we are made to feel how little of what most nearly concerns our happiness is under our own control, and how absolutely our interests are at the disposal of a higher power. What, for instance, can impress the mind with so deep a sense of helplessness, as the pressure of disease in our own persons, which no human skill can arrest or cure; or the gradual decay and final dissolution of a beloved friend, at whose couch we watch by day and by night, and are only more and more confirmed in the conviction, that unless God interpose, vain is the help of man? In so far as affliction teaches us our dependence on God, it is favourable to the spirit of prayer; for why, in such circumstances, should we refrain from expressing that dependence which we feel, and acknowledging that helplessness which we cannot deny, especially when we know that God has a sovereign control over all events, and that, if we procure his aid, we obtain the benefit of unerring wisdom and almighty power?

Again, affliction is favourable to the spirit of prayer, because, when it is either sudden or severe, it is usually associated in the minds of men *with a sense of guilt, and an apprehension of divine displeasure.* We insist

not on the reasons of it, but on the bare fact that such
an apprehension is universally felt by those who are exposed to imminent danger, or plunged in deep distress;
and that, by the constitution of our nature, such a connexion is established betwixt suffering and sin, as that
the former cannot be, to any great extent, endured,
without being accompanied with a deep sense of personal
demerit and guilt. That such a connexion does exist,
is evident from the dreadful apprehensions which are
experienced and expressed by the most ungodly and
careless, when they are suddenly brought into imminent
danger. Many will then *tremble*, and think of God,
who cared nothing for religion before. Have we not
seen a family, enjoying a long course of prosperity, and
as unmindful of God and religion, as if they were
ignorant that they had a God to worship, and souls to
be saved; but when one of their number was suddenly
seized by the hand of death, the whole of that gay
household were also seized with religious fear, and none
more anxious than they to procure the aid of a minister's consolations, and a minister's prayers! Have we
not known a rude and thoughtless sailor, spending every
hour of fair weather and prosperous winds in jovial
mirth,—night after night retiring to his cot without
thinking of the God above, or of the hell beneath him,
—and even, when the first gale arose that was to founder
his ship, reckless of the coming storm; but when the
crash was heard, and when, from the force of habit, the
first word upon his lip was an oath, that oath died away

into a prayer, when the foaming waters burst across
the deck, and lashed him into the mighty deep! In
the 107th Psalm, we find the tendency of affliction to
produce prayer illustrated by many beautiful examples,
—as in the case of the Jews wandering in the wilderness, in a solitary way, hungry and thirsty, and their
souls fainting within them; or in the case of those who,
by reason of personal distress, "sit in darkness and in
the shadow of death, being bound in affliction and iron,
because they rebelled against the words of God;" or in
the case of those who go down to the sea in ships,
whose soul is melted because of trouble;—in each case,
it is added, "they cried unto the Lord in their trouble,
and he delivered them out of their distresses."

It is true, that in all these cases, prayer may, in the
first instance, be nothing more than the cry of nature
in distress; the desires of such persons may not, at the
outset, be purely spiritual; and the sense of guilt which
they experience, may be characterized more by the terrors
of remorse, than by the tenderness of true repentance.
Be it so; this does not hinder the usefulness of affliction,
as a means in God's hand, of leading them to pray.
God acts on the minds of men by rational inducements;
and seeing that, in their natural state, they are dead to
the influence of higher and more spiritual motives, he
has recourse to their sentient nature; their hopes and
their fears are addressed in the promises and threaten-
ings of Scripture, and their love of happiness, and aversion to suffering, are appealed to in the absence of

holier principles. When he sends affliction, he appeals to their natural feelings; and the lessons which it is fitted to teach, are so many motives to a religious life, —motives which, although, in the first instance, addressed to the mere natural feelings, and hopes, and fears of the sufferer, may, nevertheless, through these, arrest the attention, and reach the conscience, and ultimately renew the heart. The impressions which are made during a season of affliction, may be the result, in a great measure, of mere natural feeling; but they may, nevertheless, be the means which the Holy Spirit has chosen for the commencement of a saving change; and if they lead the sufferer *to pray*, they bring him under a new influence, whereby the sentient feelings which at first prompted him, may gradually and imperceptibly rise into gracious and devout affections. At all events, let no sufferer be debarred from the throne of grace, because he is in doubt as to the spirituality of his affections, or depressed by a sense of guilt; let him remember, that *as a sinner* he is invited, and that his present affliction is designed to induce him to pray; and should he still question his warrant or his prospect of acceptance, let him remember the words of the apostle to Simon Magus,—"Thou art in the gall of bitterness and the bond of iniquity; but pray to God if perhaps the thought of thy heart may be forgiven thee."

As affliction prepares the mind for prayer, *so prayer relieves the mind in affliction.*

Prayer is often the means of averting the evils with

which we are threatened, and of delivering us from those under which we labour. Its *efficacy*, both for defence and delivery, is frequently stated in express terms, and illustrated by striking examples in the Sacred Writings.

It is recorded of Hezekiah, that when he heard the message of God by the mouth of Isaiah the prophet, saying, "Set thine house in order: for thou shalt die, and not live," he "turned his face toward the wall, and prayed unto the Lord, and said, Remember now, O Lord, I beseech thee, how I have walked before thee in truth, and with a perfect heart, and have done that which is good in thy sight: and Hezekiah wept sore. Then came the word of the Lord to Isaiah, saying, Go and say to Hezekiah, Thus saith the Lord, the God of David thy father, I have heard thy prayer, I have seen thy tears: behold, I will add to thy days fifteen years." "And Isaiah said, Take a lump of figs; and they took and laid it on the boil, and he recovered." Thus was a sore disease removed, and early death prevented by the efficacy of prayer; and Hezekiah had reason to sing for joy: "Thou hast, in love to my soul, delivered it from the pit of corruption, for thou hast cast all my sins behind my back; the Lord *was ready to save me,* therefore we will sing my songs to the stringed instruments, all the days of our life, in the house of the Lord."

The history of the people of Israel affords many interesting examples of the effect of prayer in delivering from outward trouble, as well as of the tendency of affliction to impress the most careless with the necessity and value of prayer. These examples are thus beautifully referred to in the 107th Psalm: "O give thanks unto the Lord, for he is good; for his mercy endureth for ever. Let the redeemed of the Lord say so, whom he hath redeemed from the hand of the enemy. They wandered in the wilderness in a solitary way; they found no city to dwell in. Hungry and thirsty, their souls fainted in them. Then they cried unto the Lord in their trouble, and he delivered them out of their distresses. For he satisfieth the longing soul, and filleth the hungry soul with goodness."

Nor was the efficacy of prayer, in preventing or removing trouble, confined to the Jewish people, although they lived under a dispensation which was in many respects supernatural and miraculous; we are taught, on the contrary, to regard the examples which their history presents, as so many indications of the unalterable principles on which the general government of the world is conducted; and in so far as the point now before us is concerned, the same principle is recognised and embodied in a promise in the New Testament itself: "If any man is afflicted, let him call for the elders of the church; and let them pray over him, anointing him with oil in the name of the Lord: and the prayer of faith shall save the sick, and the Lord shall raise him up; and if he have committed sin, it shall be forgiven him." And in more general terms, our Lord has said to all his disciples, "Ask and ye shall receive, seek and ye shall find, knock and it shall be opened unto you." "Whatsoever ye ask in my name, believing, ye shall receive."

To this, many may be ready to oppose their own experience, and may be unwilling to admit the efficacy of prayer in preventing or removing outward calamity, when they remember with what frequency and earnestness they supplicated for mercies which were, nevertheless, withheld, and deprecated trials which were, nevertheless, sent or continued with them. They may remember that, when threatened with bereavement, they wept sore, and besought the Lord to spare and restore the object of their fond affections; and yet, that he allowed disease to take its course, until it terminated in death. These facts, which no Christian minister will seek either to deny or to conceal, may have had the effect of staggering the belief of many in the efficacy of prayer; and where they have not had this effect, they may occasionally embarrass even the minds of believers, and overwhelm them with deep anxiety, by suggesting the awful thought, that, since their prayers have received no direct answer, they must either not be of the number of God's people at all, or they must "have prayed amiss."

But these conclusions are not warranted by Scripture, and they arise from a misapprehension, not so much of the promise annexed to prayer, as of the very nature of prayer itself. No prayer is scriptural which does not express a desire in unison with the will of God; and where the purpose of God is, as in most cases it must be, secret or unknown to us, no prayer is scriptural in which the expression of our own desire is not limited by a holy acquiescence in his will. We are not entitled, for example, to pray absolutely that God's chastening hand may be withdrawn from us, or that the life of a relative may be spared, or that we may be blessed with worldly prosperity;—all these desires, however natural and however strong, must be limited by, and subordinated to, the will of Him who knoweth what is best for us, and who has graciously taken the management of our case into His own hands. This is strikingly implied in the very structure of that form of prayer which our Lord himself gave to his disciples; for it is a very remarkable fact, that the three first petitions of that prayer are expressive of a desire for God's glory, acquiescence in God's will, and zeal for the extension of His kingdom; and it is not till after we have thus ascribed sovereignty to Jehovah, and cast ourselves absolutely into His hands, that we are permitted to broach one petition for our own particular interest, even to the extent of daily bread!

It is only, therefore, when our desires are in unison with the divine will, that we have reason to expect a direct fulfilment of our requests. And this consideration is fraught with much interesting instruction, and with great practical comfort in regard to the efficacy of prayer; for it assures us, that if we should happen

17

to pray in a right spirit, but, from ignorance, should ask what is not really good for us, God will not take advantage of our ignorance or weakness, so as to visit us with a curse when we are seeking a blessing. There can be no doubt that, were every desire which we express in prayer to meet with a direct and literal fulfilment, the efficacy of prayer might, through our ignorance of what is really for our good, become a source of calamity rather than of comfort. As it is related of one who, being possessed of great wealth, and having an only son, and that son labouring under a very sore disease, and being repeatedly counselled to resign him into God's hand, and to acquiesce in his appointment, even should he be pleased to take him away, did, nevertheless, so far yield to his natural affections, as resolutely to refuse any act of submission, and could not bring himself to utter one word of acquiescence in such a result, and who, many years after, was seen dishonoured and beaten in his old age, by that very son whom he was so loath to lose, and mourning, in the bitterness of his heart, over filial ingratitude and disobedience, as the heaviest curse of his gray hairs! But when our petition is limited by acquiescence in the sovereign disposal of Almighty God, even should we ask amiss, God will neither withhold what is truly good for us, nor give what he knows to be bad. And thus the omniscient wisdom of God is our security against the effect of our own ignorance, or weakness in prayer.

It is chiefly in reference to external comforts or

privileges that we are ignorant of God's will and our own interest, for, on that subject, we have no revelation to guide us; but for spiritual blessings, in so far as these are necessary for the safety of the soul, we have a stronger assurance of an answer, in proportion as we have better evidence both of its being God's will to bestow, and of its being our interest to receive them. It may be doubtful how far God will be pleased to grant, or how far it would be for our real welfare to obtain, exemption from outward trials or the uninterrupted enjoyment of worldly prosperity; but we know, from Scripture, that the blessings of God's grace are of such a nature, that we must at all times be willing to dispense them, and that we cannot pray for, or receive them, without being substantially benefited. We have greater confidence, therefore, of a literal fulfilment of our petitions, when we supplicate the grace of a penitent spirit, than when we pray for a prosperous outward estate, since the former must, at all times, be an object of complacency to God, and a real blessing to ourselves, whereas the latter may be fraught with danger to our higher interests, and may, therefore, by unerring wisdom, be withheld.

In this view, also, our prayers may be really answered, although the special evil which we deprecate is, nevertheless, inflicted, and the good which we supplicate is, nevertheless, withheld. For what is our prayer? Why, that God would deal with us according to the counsels of unerring wisdom, and give or withhold according to

his sovereign will. That being our prayer, it is answered, even though it should be by crosses. And, in
this, God magnifies his grace, by bringing the substan-
tial blessings which we need out of the unlikeliest means,
nay, out of those very evils which we are most eager to
avoid. We see, hence, not only that the prayers of his
people are answered, but that they cannot fail to have
their fulfilment. For the desires of their hearts are
going forth in unison with the divine will, and that will
is omnipotent!

In these circumstances, however, the unbelieving
mind will be ready to reason against the utility of
prayer altogether, and to say that God's will, being
omnipotent, must have its effect, whether we pray or
no. But, by those who can entertain this idea, it is
not duly considered, that prayer is in the moral, what
any other ordinary cause is in the physical world,—a
means established by God himself,—a link in the grand
chain of cause and effect, which not only comprehends
both the physical and moral departments of his government, but combines the two, and establishes a very intimate relation betwixt their several parts,—a cause, in
fact, which is not less regarded by God than any other
secondary agent in nature. It might, therefore, with
the same propriety be affirmed, that God's omnipotent
will must cause the pre-determined harvest to spring up
from the earth, without the agency of manual labour,
as that God's will must cause the fulfilment of such of
our desires as are in unison therewith, without the

agency of prayer. And, be it observed, that even were we unable to obviate the difficulty, we cannot fail, at least, to perceive, that it is founded on a principle directly the reverse of that on which our Lord argued; for, so far from regarding the infinite knowledge, or the sovereign will, or the almighty power of God, as superseding the necessity of prayer on the part of man, he refers to these as the very ground and reason, nay, as the strongest motive and encouragement of prayer: "For your heavenly Father knoweth that ye have need of these things." Were we to act on any other principle, we must virtually declare that we will not pray, unless we are allowed to dictate to God, or assured that our desires shall overrule the decision of omniscient wisdom!

Even when prayer is not effectual in averting or removing the evil which we fear or endure, yet it imparts to the believing mind the strongest of all consolation,—that which arises from the persuasion that God's will is answered by the event, and that any other result would have been, in the judgment of unerring wisdom, neither so good in itself, nor so beneficial to our real interest.

Besides its effect in averting threatened calamity, or procuring positive blessings at the hand of God, prayer exercises a *beneficial influence* on the mind, and thus fits it for suffering, and relieves it when calamity comes.

The degree of sorrow that is occasioned by affliction depends a great deal more on the state of mind in which it finds the sufferer, than on the amount of the calamity itself. The same trial which overwhelms one, may be sustained with composure and comfort by another, and that, too, although both are equally sensitive in their feelings. This difference depends on the preparation which they have respectively made for the event. If the one has been careless, while the other was thoughtful, and, above all, if the one has been negligent in fortifying his mind by prayer and supplication, while the other, under a deep sense of his liability to affliction, and his dependence on God, has betaken himself, in the exercise of humble trust and confidence, to the throne of grace, and has been enabled there to repose the burden of his anxieties on the Lord, it cannot but be that the latter will feel very differently from the former, when the event occurs. And that event, however calamitous in itself, will be the less overwhelming to him, in proportion as he was the better prepared to meet it, and the more accustomed to regard it in connexion with the will of Him, who is at once the God of Providence, and the hearer of prayer.

And as prayer, offered up in anticipation of suffering, puts the soul in a right state of preparation, so, by virtue of its natural influence, it has the effect of relieving the mind of those feelings, which severe calamity, when it does come, must, in all cases, in a greater or less degree, awaken. Prayer before affliction, fits the mind for suffering; prayer under affliction, relieves the mind of its sorrow. So long as the feelings of the sufferer are restrained and pent up within his own bosom, they prey upon his internal peace; but when they find a channel through which they obtain utterance and expansion, their depressing power is mitigated, and the heart is, in part at least, relieved of its burden. Hence excessive grief is often mitigated by copious weeping,— much more by communion with a dear and confidential friend,—but most of all by prayer, which is *the heart's communion* with God, the best and nearest of friends. Those who have witnessed the strong agony of grief, occasioned by some sudden and unexpected calamity, and have watched, with intense anxiety, its progress and results, can best appreciate the benefit of such outlets to human feeling, and they will testify, that so soon as the grief of their friend found vent in tears or in free conversation, they felt that the worst was already past. And, above all, if the sufferer retired to his chamber, and, on his bended knees, poured out his soul to God in the confidence of prayer, a calm serenity and composure ensued, which showed that the crisis was over, and that, too, although he may have prayed with strong crying and tears.   It may be difficult to account for the relief which a suffering spirit derives from the gushing of tears, unless it be resolved into a natural harmony between the physiology of the body, and the deep emotions of the mind.   It may be difficult, also, in some cases, to account for the relief that is derived from the mere utterance of the heart's fulness into the ear of another, unless it be referred to the principle of sympathy, whose law seems to be, " that it redoubleth joys, and cutteth griefs in halves; for, as there is no man that imparteth his joys to his friend, but he joyeth the more, so there is no man that imparteth his griefs to his friend, but he grieveth the less."* But, whatever difficulty may be felt in ascertaining the reason why such outlets of feeling are so proverbially the means of relieving sorrow, surely there can be none in accounting for the relief which a pious mind experiences in unbosoming its sorrows in the very presence and ear of its God. For there, at his footstool, who dare arraign the wisdom, or blame the rectitude, or question the sovereignty of Him from whom affliction comes? In prayer, the mind is brought into immediate contact with the Supreme Will; the sovereignty of God is recognised and felt; the wisdom of his dispensations acknowledged; and the very misery which leads the sufferer to the throne of grace, is the means of placing him in a position in which he feels that he must adore the divine goodness, and trust in it still, notwithstanding all that has occurred, otherwise he has neither help nor hope. By the very act of bending the knee before his footstool, the Christian makes all these acknowledgments, and gives a practical expression of his confidence in God's faithfulness and love,—he repairs to God as his friend—a friend that will not leave him nor forsake him. And if such acknowledgments be made, and such feelings awakened, in the hour of prayer, is not his spirit thereby placed

* Lord Bacon.

in the best condition for at once procuring the mitigation of his sorrow, and improving by the calamity which has called it forth? It is, indeed, wonderful, how the mind clears up its views of God's dispensations, while engaged in prayer. At first, thick clouds may seem to darken his prospect, but, as he proceeds, streaks of light break through, and shine in upon his spirit, and, "while he sits in darkness, the Lord is a light to him." "While David kept silence, his bones waxed old, through his roaring all the day long;" while "he restrained prayer, his spirit was straitened;" but no sooner did he pour out his heart before God, than he "was compassed about with songs of deliverance." In such a case, much sorrow may still remain, but the bitterness of grief is past. The subdued and humble feeling which affliction is designed to produce, and by which it operates, in part, its beneficial results, will characterize the sufferer, long after the agony of grief has subsided into calm resignation. His soul will no longer resemble the troubled sea which cannot rest, but will be like "a weaned child." And this wholesome conversion of the excitement of violent sorrow into the mild virtue of suffering affliction with patience, is best produced by the agency of prayer.

BUCHANAN.

SCRIPTURAL SELECTIONS.

FOR a small moment have I forsaken thee; but with great mercies will I gather thee.

In a little wrath I hid my face from thee for a moment; but with everlasting kindness will I have mercy on thee, saith the Lord thy Redeemer.

For this is as the waters of Noah unto me: for as I have sworn that the waters of Noah should no more go over the earth; so have I sworn that I would not be wroth with thee, nor rebuke thee.—*Is.* lvi. 7—10.

Sing unto the Lord, O ye saints of his, and give thanks at the remembrance of his holiness.

For his anger endureth but a moment; in his favour is life: weeping may endure for a night, but joy cometh in the morning.—*Ps.* xxx. 4, 5

The Fountain.

In that day there shall be a fountain opened to the house of David and to the inhabitants of Jerusalem for sin and uncleanness.—Zech. xiii. 1.

Come to Calvary's holy mountain,
　Sinners! ruined by the fall;
Here a pure and healing fountain
　Flows to you, to me, to all,—
In a full, perpetual tide,
Opened when the Saviour died.

Come, in poverty and meanness,
　Come, defiled without, within;
From infection and uncleanness,
　From the leprosy of sin,
Wash your robes and make them white;
Ye shall walk with God in light.

Come, in sorrow and contrition,
　Wounded, impotent, and blind;
Here the guilty, free remission,
　Here the troubled peace may find:
Health this fountain will restore;
He that drinks will thirst no more.

He that drinks shall live for ever:
　'T is a soul-renewing flood:
God is faithful—God will never
　Break his covenant in blood,
Signed when our Redeemer died,
Sealed when he was glorified!

IV

THE WEANED CHILD.

Surely I have behaved and quieted myself as a child that is weaned of his mother: my soul is even as a weaned child."—PSALM CXXXI. 2.

THERE are few lessons taught in God's school more difficult to learn, and yet, when really learned, more blessed and holy, than the lesson of *weanedness*. The heart resembles the vine, which, as it grows, grasps and unites its feeble tendrils to every support within its reach. Or, it is like the ivy, which climbs and wraps itself around some beautiful but decayed and crumbling ruin. As our social affections develop and expand, they naturally seek a resting place. Travelling, as it were, beyond themselves, breathing love and yearning for friendship, they go forth seeking some kindred spirit, some "second self," upon which they may repose, and around which they may entwine. To detach from this inordinate, idolatrous clinging to the animate and the inanimate creatures and objects of sense, is one grand end of God's disciplinary dealings with us in the present life. The discovery which we make, in the process of his dealings, of the insufficiency and insecurity of the things upon which we set our affections, is often acutely painful. Like that vine, we find that we grasped a support at the root of which the canker-worm was secretly feeding,—and presently it fell! Or, like that ivy, we discover that we have been spreading our affections around an object which, even while we clung to and adored it, was crumbling and falling into dust,— and presently it became a ruin! And what is the grand lesson which, by this process, God would teach us? The lesson of *weanedness* from all and everything of an earthly and a created nature. Thus was David instructed, and this was the result: "Surely I have behaved and quieted myself as a child that is weaned of his mother: my soul is even as a weaned child." It may be profitable, tried and suffering reader, briefly to contemplate this holy state, and then the way by which the Lord frequently brings his people into its experience.

Every true believer, whatever may be the degree of his grace, is an adopted child of God. It is not the amount of his faith, nor the closeness of his resemblance to the family, that constitutes his relationship; it is the act of adoption by which his heavenly Father has made him his own. If he can only lisp his Father's name, or bears but a single feature of likeness to the Divine image, he is as much and as really a child of God as those in whose souls the lineaments are deeply and broadly drawn, and who, with an unfaltering faith, can cry, "Abba, Father!" Doubtless there were many of feeble faith, of limited experience, and of defective knowledge—mere babes in Christ—in the church to which the apostle inscribed his letter; and yet, addressing them all, he says, "Behold what manner of love, that we should be called the sons of God." But it is the character of the *weaned* child we are now to contemplate. All believers are children, but are all believers *weaned* children? From what is the child of God thus weaned?

The first object from which our heavenly Father weans his child, is—*himself*. Of all idols, this he finds the hardest to abandon. When man in paradise aspired to be as God, God was dethroned from his soul, and the creature became as a deity to itself. From that moment, the idolatry of self has been the great and universal crime of our race, and will continue to be until Christ comes to restore all things. In the soul of the regenerate, divine grace has done much to dethrone this idol, and to reinstate God. The work, however, is but partially accomplished. The dishonoured and rejected rival is loath to relinquish his throne, and yield to the supreme control and sway of another. There is much yet to be achieved before this still indwelling and unconquered foe lays down his weapons in entire subjection to the will and the authority of that Saviour whose throne and rights he has usurped. Thus, much still lingers in the heart which the Spirit has renewed and inhabits, of self-esteem, self-confidence, self-seeking, and self-love. From all this, our Father seeks to wean us. From our own wisdom, which is but folly; from our own strength, which is but weakness; from our own wills, which are often as an uncurbed steed; from our own

ways, which are crooked; from our own hearts, which
are deceitful; from our own judgments, which are dark;
from our own ends, which are narrow and selfish, he
would wean and detach us, that our souls may get more
and more back to their original centre of repose—God
himself. In view of this mournful exhibition of fallen
and corrupt self, how necessary the discipline of our
heavenly Father that extorts from us the Psalmist's
language: "Surely I have behaved and quieted myself
as a child that is weaned of his mother." *Self* did
seem to be our mother—the fruitful parent of so much
in our plans and aims and spirit that was dishonouring
to our God. From this he would gently and tenderly,
but effectually, wean us, that we may learn to rely upon
his wisdom, to repose in his strength, to consult his
honour, and to seek his glory and smile supremely and
alone. And O how effectually is this blessed state attained when God, by setting us aside in the season of
solitude and sorrow, teaches us that he can do without us. We, perhaps, thought that our rank, or our
talents, or our influence, or our very presence were
essential to the advancement of his cause, and that
some parts-of it could not proceed without us! The
Lord knew otherwise. And so he laid his hand upon
us, and withdrew us from the scene of our labours, and
duties, and engagements, and ambition, that he might
hide pride from our hearts—the pride of self-importance.
And O, is it no mighty attainment in the Christian life
to be thus weaned from ourselves? Beloved, it forms

the root of all other blessings. The moment we learn to cease from ourselves—from our own wisdom, and power, and importance—the Lord appears and takes us up. Then his wisdom is displayed, and his power is put forth, and his glory is developed, and his great name gets to itself all the praise. It was not until God had placed Moses in the cleft of the rock that his glory passed by. Moses must be hid, that God might be all.

Our heavenly Father would also wean us *from this poor, perishing world*. It is true Christ has taken the child of God out of, and separated him from, the world; assailed by all its evils, and exposed to all its corrupting influences. The intercessory prayer of our Lord seems to imply this : " They are not of the world, even as I am not of the world. I pray not that thou shouldst take them out of the world, but that thou shouldst keep them from the evil." And O what an evil does the Christian find this world to be ! In consequence of the earthward tendency of his affections, and the deep carnality with which the mind is imbued, things which God designed as blessings to soothe, and soften, and cheer, become, by their absorbing and idolatrous influence, powerful snares. Rank is a snare, wealth is a snare, talent is a snare, friendship is a snare. Rank may foster pride and ambition ; wealth may increase the thirst for worldly show ; talent may inspire a love of human applause ; and friendship may wean the heart from Christ, and betray us into a base and unholy compromise of Christian professson. Now from this endangering world our heavenly Father would shield, by withdrawing us. It is not our rest, and he agitates it; it is not our portion, and he embitters it; it is not our friend, and he sometimes arms it with a sword. It changes, it disappoints, it wounds; and then, thankful to expand our wings, we take another and a bolder flight above it. Ah! beloved, how truly may the Lord be now sickening thine heart to the world, to which that heart has too long and too closely clung. It has been thy peculiar snare; thy Father saw it, and wisely and graciously laid his loving, gentle hand upon thee, and led thee away from it, that from a bed of sickness, or from a chamber of grief, or from some position of painful vicissitude, thou mightest see its sinfulness, learn its hollowness, and return as a wanderer to thy Father's bosom, exclaiming with David, "My soul is even as a *weaned* child."

This weanedness, of which we speak, often involves *the surrender of some endeared object of creature affection.* The human heart is naturally idolatrous. Its affections, as we have previously remarked, once supremely centered in God. But now, disjoined from him, they go in quest of other objects of attachment, and we love and worship the creature rather than the Creator. The circle which our affections traverse may not indeed be a large one; there are perchance but few to whom we fully surrender our heart; nay, so circumscribed may the circle be, that *one* object alone shall attract, absorb, and concentrate in itself our entire and undivided love—that one object to us as a universe of

19

beings, and all others comparatively indifferent and in-
sipid.   Who cannot see that in a case like this, the
danger is imminent of transforming the heart—Christ's
own sanctuary—into an idol's temple, where the creature is loved and reverenced and served more than He
who gave it?   But from all idolatry our God will
cleanse us, and from all our idols Christ will wean us.
The Lord is jealous, with a holy jealousy, of our love.
Poor as our affection is, he asks its supreme surrender.
That he requires our love at the expense of all creature
attachment, the Bible nowhere intimates.   He created
our affections, and he it is who provides for their proper
and pleasant indulgence.   There is not a single precept
or command in the Scriptures that forbids their exercise, or that discourages their intensity.   Husbands are
exhorted to " love their wives, even as Christ loved his
church."   Parents are to cherish a like affection towards
their children, and children are bound to render back a
filial love not less intense to their parents.   And we
are to " love our neighbours as ourselves."   Nor does
the word of God furnish examples of Christian friendship less interested and devoted.   One of the choicest
and tenderest blessings with which God can enrich us,
next to himself, is such a friend as Paul had in Epaphro-
ditus, a " brother and companion in labour, and fellow-
soldier ;" and such an affectionate friendship as John,
the loving disciple, cherished for his well beloved Gaius,
whom he loved in the truth, and to whom, in the season
of his sickness, he thus touchingly poured out his heart's

affectionate sympathy: "Beloved, I wish above all things that thou mayest prosper and be in health, even as thy soul prospereth." Count such a friend, and such friendship, amongst God's sweetest and holiest bestowments. The blessings of which it may be to you the sanctifying channel, are immense. The tender sympathy—the jealous watchfulness—the confidential repose —the faithful admonition—above all, the intercessory prayer, connected with Christian friendship, may be placed in the inventory of our most inestimable and precious blessings. It is not therefore the use, but the abuse, of our affections—not their legitimate exercise, but their idolatrous tendency——over which we have need to exercise the greatest vigilance. It is not our love to the creature against which God contends, but it is in not allowing our love to himself to subordinate all other love. We may love the creature, but we may not love the creature more than the Creator. When the Giver is lost sight of and forgotten in the gift, then comes the painful process of weaning! When the heart burns its incense before some human shrine, and the cloud as it ascends veils from the eye the beauty and the excellence of Jesus,—then comes the painful process of weaning! When the absorbing claims and the engrossing attentions of some loved one are placed in competition, and are allowed to clash with the claims of God, and the attentions due from us personally to his cause and truth, —then comes the painful process of weaning! When creature devotion deadens our heart to the Lord, lessens our interest in his cause, congeals our zeal and love and liberality, detaches us from the public means of grace, withdraws from the closet, and from the Bible, and from the communion of the saints, thus superinducing leanness of soul, and robbing God of his glory,—then comes the painful process of weaning! Christ will be the first in our affections—God will be supreme in our service—and his kingdom and righteousness must take precedence of all other things. In this light, beloved, read the present mournful page in your history. The noble oak that stood so firm and stately at thy side, is smitten,—the tender and beautiful vine that wound itself around thee, is fallen,—the lowly and delicate flower that lay upon thy bosom, is withered—the olive branches that clustered around thy table, are removed —and the "strong staff is broken and the beautiful rod;" not because thy God did not love thee, but because he desired thine heart. He saw that heart ensnared and enslaved by a too fond and idolatrous affection,—he saw his beauty eclipsed and himself rivalled by a faint and imperfect copy of his own image, and he breathed upon it, and it withered away! "The day of the Lord of hosts shall be upon all . . . *pleasant pictures.*" When an eminent artist, who had concentrated all the powers of his genius upon a painting of our Lord celebrating the last supper, observed that the holy vessels arranged in the foreground were admired to the exclusion of the chief object of the picture, he seized his brush and dashed them from the canvass, and left the image of Jesus standing in its own solitary and unrivalled beauty. Thus deals our God oftentimes with us. O solemn words! "The day of the Lord of hosts shall be upon all . . . . PLEASANT PICTURES,"—all pictures that veil and eclipse the beauties of him who is the "brightness of the Father's glory, and the express image of his person," God will obliterate.

Filial submission to God's will, is, perhaps, one of the most essential features in this holy state of weanedness of which we speak. "Surely I have *behaved* and *quieted* myself as a child that is weaned of his mother." There are some beautiful examples of this in God's word. "And Aaron held his peace." Since God was "sanctified and glorified," terrible as was the judgment, the holy priest mourned not at the way, nor complained of its severity, patient and resigned to the will of God. He "behaved and quieted himself as a child that is weaned of his mother." Thus, too, was it with Eli, when passing under the heavy hand of God: "It is the Lord; let him do what seemeth him good." He bowed in deep submission to the will of his God. Job could exclaim, as the last sad tidings brimmed his cup of woe, "The Lord gave, and the Lord hath taken away; blessed be the name of the Lord." And David was "dumb and opened not his mouth, because God did it." But how do all these instances of filial and holy submis sion to the Divine will—beautiful and touching as they are·—fade before the illustrious example of our adorable and blessed Lord: "O my Father, if this cup may not

pass away from me, except I drink it, *thy will be done.*"
Ah! how did Jesus, in the deepest depth of his unuttera-
ble sorrow, " behave and quiet himself as a child that is
weaned of his mother? his soul was even as a weaned
child." Such, beloved, be the posture of thy soul at
this moment. " Be still." Rest in thy Father's hands,
calm and tranquil, quiet and submissive, weaned from
all but himself. O the blessedness of so reposing!

> " Sweet to lie passive in his hands,
>   And know no will but his."

" *God's love!*" It is written upon your dark cloud
—it breathes from the lips of your bleeding wound—it
is reflected in every fragment of your ruined treasure—
it is pencilled upon every leaf of your blighted flower—
" GOD IS LOVE." Adversity may have impoverished
you—bereavement may have saddened you—calamity
may have crushed you—sickness may have laid you low
—but, " GOD IS LOVE." Gently falls the rod in its
heaviest stroke—tenderly pierces the sword in its deepest thrust—smilingly bends the cloud in its darkest hues
—for, " GOD IS LOVE." Does the infant, weaned from
its wonted and pleasant fount, cease from its restlessness and sorrow, reposing calmly and meekly upon its
mother's arms?—so let thy soul calmly, submissively
rest in God. How sweet the music which then will
breathe from thy lips in the midnight of grief: " Surely
I have behaved and quieted myself as a child that is
weaned of his mother : my soul is even as a weaned child."

And who can bring you into this holy position ? The

Holy Spirit alone can. It is his office to lead you to
Jesus—to reveal to you Jesus—to exhibit to your eye the
cross of Jesus—to pour into your heart the grace and love
and sympathy of Jesus—to bend your will and bow your
heart to the government of Jesus, and thus make you as a
weaned child. The work infinitely transcends a power
merely human. It is the office and the prerogative of the
Divine Spirit—the "Spirit of holiness"—who only can
sever between flesh and spirit, to bring you into the
condition of one whose will in all things is completely
merged in God's. And what is his grand instrument
of effecting this? *The cross of Christ!* Ah! this is it.
THE CROSS OF CHRIST! Not the cross as it appeared
to the imagination of the Mahomedan Chief, leading the
imperial army to battle and to conquest; not the cross
pictured—the cross engraved—the cross carved—the
cross embroidered—the cross embossed upon the prayer-
book, pendant from the maiden's neck, glittering on the
cathedral's spire, and springing from its altar: not the
cross as blended with a religion of Gothic architecture,
and painted windows, and flaming candles, and waving
incense, and gorgeous pictures, and melting music, and
fluttering surplices: O no! but the cross—the naked,
rugged cross—which Calvary reared, which Paul
preached, and of which he wrote, "God forbid that I
should glory save in the cross of our Lord Jesus Christ,
by which* the world is crucified unto me, and I unto

* "*Whereby.*" See versions of Tyndale, Cranmer, and Geneva, as
collated in Bagster's English Hexapla.

the world." Faith, picturing to its view this cross, the
Holy Spirit engraving it on the heart in spiritual
regeneration, the whole soul receiving him whom it lifts
up, as its "wisdom, and righteousness, and sanctification, and redemption," gently and effectually transforms
the spirit, that was chafened and restless, into the
"meekness and gentleness of Christ." O what calm-
ness steals over his ruffled soul! O what peace flows
into his troubled heart! O what sunshine bathes in its
bright beams, his dark spirit, who from the scenes of
his conflict and his sorrow, flees beneath the shadow
and the shelter of the cross. The storm ceases—the
deluge of his grief subsides—the Spirit, dove-like, brings
the message of hope and love—the soul, tempest-tossed,
rests on the green mount, and one unbounded spring
clothes and encircles the landscape with its verdure and
its beauty. Child, chastened by the Father's love, look
to the cross of your crucified Saviour. And as you fix
upon it your believing, ardent, adoring gaze, exclaim—

> "Wearily for me thou soughtest,
>   On the cross my soul thou boughtest;
>   Lose not all for which thou wroughtest."

What is thy sorrow compared with Christ's? What
is thy grief gauged by the Lord's? Thy Master has
passed before thee, flinging the curse and the sin from
thy path, paving it with promises, carpeting it with
love, and fencing it around with the hedge of his divine
perfections. Press onward, then, resisting thy foe

resolutely, bearing thy cross patiently, drinking thy cup submissively, and learning, while sitting at the Saviour's feet, or leaning upon his bosom, to be like him, "meek and lowly in heart." Then, indeed, shall " I have behaved and quieted myself as a child that is weaned of his mother: my soul is even as a weaned child."

WINSLOW.

SCRIPTURAL SELECTIONS.

BLESSED is the man that endureth temptation: for when he is tried he shall receive the crown of life, which the Lord hath promised to them that love him.—*James*, i. 12.

But the God of all grace, who hath called us unto his eternal glory by Christ Jesus, after that ye have suffered a while, make you perfect, stablish, strengthen, settle you:

To him be glory and dominion for ever and ever. Amen.—1 *Pet.* v. 10, 11.

So then they that are in the flesh cannot please God.—*Rom.* viii. 8.

For which cause we faint not; but though our outward man perish, yet the inward man is renewed day by day.

For our light affliction, which is but for a moment, worketh for us a far more exceeding and eternal weight of glory;

While we look not at the things which are seen, but at the things which are not seen: for the things which are seen are temporal; but the things which are not seen are eternal.—2 *Cor.* iv. 16—18.

Glory in Affliction.

Jesus, I my cross have taken,
　　All to leave and follow thee;
Naked, poor, despised, forsaken,
　　Thou, from hence, my all shalt be:
Perish every fond ambition,
　　All I've sought, or hoped, or known,
Yet how rich is my condition,
　　God and heaven are still my own.

Let the world despise and leave me,
　　They have left my Saviour too;
Human hearts and looks deceive me,
　　Thou art not, like them, untrue:
And whilst thou shalt smile upon me,
　　God of wisdom, love, and might,
Foes may hate, and friends may scorn me,
　　Show thy face, and all is bright.

Go, then, earthly fame and treasure,
　　Come disaster, scorn, and pain,
In thy service pain is pleasure,
　　With thy favour loss is gain:
I have called thee, Abba, Father,
　　I have set my heart on thee,
Storms may howl, and clouds may gather,
　　All must work for good to me.

Man may trouble and distress me.
    'Twill but drive me to thy breast,
Life with trials hard may press me,
    Heaven will bring me sweeter rest:
Oh! 'tis not in grief to harm me,
    While thy love is left to me,
Oh! 'twere not in joy to charm me,
    Were that joy unmixed with thee.

Soul, then know thy full salvation,
    Rise o'er sin, and fear, and care,
Joy to find in every station,
    Something still to do and bear:
Think what spirit dwells within thee;
    Think what Father's smiles are thine,
Think that Jesus died to save thee:
    Child of heaven, canst thou repine?

Haste thee on from grace to glory,
    Armed by faith, and winged by prayer,
Heaven's eternal days before thee;
    God's own hand shall guide thee there:
Soon shall close thy earthly mission,
    Soon shall pass thy pilgrim days,
Hope shall change to glad fruition,
    Faith to sight, and prayer to praise.

Comfort.

COMFORT.

THE REFUGE FROM THE STORM.

MEN, in great straits, when they are not able to make defence against pursuing enemies, run to their hiding place, as the Israelites did from the Philistines. "When the men of Israel saw that they were distressed, they hid themselves in caves, in thickets, in rocks, in high places, and in pits," 1 Sam. xiii. 6; and so God's children, when they are too weak for their enemies, seek a safe and sure hiding place: "A prudent man foreseeth the evil, and hideth himself," Prov. xxii. 3; certainly there is a hiding place for God's children, if we had but the wisdom to find it out—and where is it but in God? "Lord, thou art my hiding place, thou shalt preserve me from trouble." So again—"In the time of trouble he shall hide me in his pavilion; in the secret of his tabernacle shall he hide me: he shall set me upon a rock," Psalm xxvii. 5. God's protection of his people is a secret, hidden mystery, as everything that pertains

unto God is to the carnal man.   The person hidden is
seen abroad every day following his business—serving
his generation—doing that work which God hath given
him to do, yet is he hidden, while he is seen, by the
secret power and love of God dispensing all things for
his protection, the man is kept safe by ways which the
world knows not of.   "Thou shalt hide him in the
secret of thy presence from the pride of man," Psalm
xxxi. 20.   There is a secret power of God by which his
people are upheld and maintained by one means or
another, which they see not, and cannot find out.   So
there is that in God, that we may trust him with our
souls, with our bodies, with our peace, with our goods,
with our good name, with our all; all that concerns us
between this and the day of judgment, as St. Paul did
—"I know whom I have believed, and I am persuaded
that he is able to keep that which I have committed
unto him against that day."   His soul and all the concerns of it he durst trust in the hands of God.   Our
soul is much sought after; Satan, that hath lost the
favour of God himself, envies that others should enjoy
it, therefore he pursues God's people with great malice
and power; but let them put it into the hands of God,
he is able to keep it.   And so for outward things this
hiding place is large enough for all we have.   "Thou
shalt keep them secretly as in a pavilion, from the strife
of tongues."   As the hearts of men are in the hands
of God, so are their tongues, Exod. xi. 7.   There is
the same reason why we should trust God in all things,

as when we trust him for one thing.   And indeed, did
we truly, and on scripture grounds, trust him for one
thing, we should trust him for all.   If we did trust him
with our souls, we should without anxious care trust
him with our bodies, our secular interests and concerns
also.   There is safety till the trouble is over, and we
may be kept as quiet in God, as if there was no danger.
" Under the shadow of thy wings will I make my refuge
until these calamities are overpast," Psalm lvii. 1. '
There is an allusion to the chicken under the hen's wing:
—when hawks or birds of prey are abroad, that are
ready to seize upon them with their talons, they run to
the hen's wings, and there they are safe.   " Come, my
people, enter thou into thy chambers, and shut the
doors about thee: hide thyself as it were for a little
moment, until the indignation be overpast," Isaiah xxvi.
20.   Here we have an allusion to a storm which is soon
over ; it is as a little cloud, that will easily be blown
over ; but in the mean time here is a covert and defence.
The use of God's protection and love is best known in
a time of straits and difficulties.   There is not only
safety, but comfort also.   Christians, it is not a dead
refuge or hiding place, but, as the Psalmist says, " None
of them who trust in God shall be desolate," Psalm
xxxiv. 22.   There are sweet support, spiritual experience, and inward comforts ; so that a believer, that is
hidden in the secret of God's presence, fares better than
all those who have the world at their command, and go
on in ease and plenty, if we judge of his condition by

21

spiritual considerations. And not only will He be his protection, but He will be a sun, as well as a shield, Psalm lxxxiv. 11. As a "shield," he will keep off all dangers from us; as a "sun," he will give all things that belong to our blessedness; "He will give grace and glory." The word of God shows not only what God CAN do herein, but what he WILL do for our sakes. To Abraham, God said, "I am thy shield and thy exceeding great reward," Gen. xv. 1. Abraham might be under some dread that the kings he had lately vanquished would work him some trouble, and then God comes and appears to him and comforts him, and says to him, "Fear not, I am thy shield." Here then we may rest; for where else can we hope to find a resting place but in the arms of God's protection—in his attributes, promises, and providences? His word invites us so to make use of God—to enter into Him as a covert from the storm, while it seems to rage, and be likely to overwhelm us. "He that dwelleth in the secret place of the Most High shall abide under the shadow of the Almighty," Psalm cxi. 1. He that committeth himself to God shall not be thrust out, but shall be suffered to dwell there, and enjoy the benefit of a covert and defence; we have this assurance repeated again and again in Scripture. "Every word of God is pure; he is a shield unto them that put their trust in him," Prov. xxx. 5. Do not think these are careless expressions, dropped into the word of God by chance, Oh no! they are the sure and pure words of the Lord himself, that will yield comfort, peace, and happiness, to them that flee unto him :—it is only to trust and to have. If you will glorify God by trusting him, and depend upon him according to his word, you will find it to be so. We miss of our protection and defence by our doubts, unbelief, and distrust of God. All those that in time of danger are duly sensible of it, and make use of God as their refuge and hiding place, shall find him to be that to them, which their faith expects from him. There is à keeping of the outward man, and a keeping of the inward man. As to the outward man, "all things come alike to all," Eccles. ix. 2 ; the Christian is safe, whatever becomes of the man; the Lord will keep him to his heavenly kingdom, 2 Tim. iv. 17, 18. What the Christian desires mainly to be kept is his soul, that he may not miscarry—blemish his profession, and dishonour God. I say, we cannot absolutely expect temporal safety. The righteous are liable to many troubles, Psalm xxxiv. 19, therefore, in temporal things, God will not keep off the temporal stroke, but leave us to many uncertainties, or at least hold us in doubt about it, that we may trust his goodness. When we trust God we may trust all his attributes, not only his power, that he is able to preserve, but his goodness, that he will do what is best for us, that there may be a submission and a referring all to his will. God will certainly make good his promise, but this trust lies not in an absolute certainty of success as to temporal things. However, this should not discourage us from making

God our refuge, because promises of better things are
sure enough, and God's keeping us in suspense about
other things is no evidence he will not afford them to
us; it is his usual course (and few instances can be
given to the contrary) to have a special regard to his
trusting servants, and to hide them secretly. They, that
know His name, will find that he hath never forsaken
them that put their trust in him, Psalm ix. 10.   It is
the only sure way to be safe; whereas, to perplex our
souls with distrust, even about these outward things,
dishonours God's faithfulness, and is the way to bring
ruin upon ourselves.   You see then what respect the
word hath to this privilege, that God is a shield and
a hiding place.   The word discovers God under these
figures, the word invites and encourages us to put God
to this use, the word assures us of his divine protection,
it directs us to the qualification of the persons that shall
enjoy this privilege, "They that can trust God;" and
it directeth us to expect the blessing, not with absolute
confidence of success, but in humble submission to his
will.   This quiets the heart in waiting God's leisure.
"Our soul waiteth for the Lord, he is our help and
our shield," Psalm xxxiii. 26.   If so, then faith is
quietly to wait God's leisure; till he send deliverance,
his promise must bear up our hearts, and we must be
contented to tarry his time,—our impatience must not
make us outrun God.   This will fortify the heart against
present difficulties.   When all visible helps are cut off, yet
may we encourage ourselves in the Lord.   When Israel

were wandering in the wilderness, and had neither house
nor home, then Moses, that man of God, pens that Psalm,
"Lord, thou hast been our dwelling place in all generations," Psalm cx. 1. What was wanting to sense, they
saw made up in the all-sufficiency of God. And here is
the use of faith, when in defiance of all difficulties, we
can see an all-sufficiency in God to counterbalance that
which is wanting to sense. "Lord, thou art my shield
and glory, and the lifter up of my head," Psalm iii. 3.
David wrote this psalm when he was driven from his
palace by his son Absalom; when he was in danger,
God was his shield; when his kingdom and honour were
laid in the dust, God was his glory; when he was under
sorrow and shame, and enemies insulting over him;
when the people rose against him, and he was in great
dejection of spirit, "God was the lifter up of his head."
This is getting under the covert of this shield, or within
the compass of this hiding place: "Into thy hands I
commit my spirit, for thou hast redeemed me, O Lord
God of truth," Psalm xxxi. 5. David was then in
great danger, the net was laid for him, as he said in a
former verse, and when he was likely to perish, what
does he do? he casts all his care upon God, and trusts
him with his life, his safety: "Into thy hands I commit
my spirit."

The use of faith is to quicken us to go on cheerfully
in our path, and with a quiet heart resting on God's
love, power, and truth. To persuade us to contentment
in a time of trouble, though our condition be not what

we desire, yet if we have but a hiding place, if God vouchsafe us a little liberty in our service, we ought to be content, if he will give us safety though not plenty, —for here is not our rest.　God never undertook in his covenant to maintain us in such a state, nor thus to enlarge our earthly portion; if he will vouchsafe a little peace and safety to us during the time of our pilgrimage, we ought to be content.　And unless God be our hiding place, the strongest defences in the world are not enough to keep us from danger.　All the shifts we run into will only entangle us the more, drive us farther from God, and to greater suffering.　Many thus run away from God's protection, and seek out means of safety for themselves; thus they do but plunge themselves into troubles so much the more; there is much sin and danger in departing from God; he can soon blast our confidences.　God will blast our carnal shifts, Jer. xvii. 15—18.　No hurt can come to us without God's leave. No creature can move or stir, not only but by God's permission, but by his influence: others may have a will to hurt us, but not the power, unless given them from above, as Christ told Pilate.　Satan is a raging adversary against the people of God, but he is forced to ask leave before he can touch either Job's goods or his person; he could not touch his skin, nor anything that belonged to him, without permission from God, Job, i. Nay, he must ask leave to enter into the herd of swine, Matt. viii. 31.　Constantly then, make use of God.　You may think this advice not needed by you, because you are at present out of fears and dangers; but what saith the scripture? "Be not high-minded but fear,"—and again, "Blessed is the man that feareth always." Are you not constantly to make use of God, whether your state be well or ill, and to live upon God at all times? All our comforts are from God, as well as our support in trouble. Certainly, he that lives upon God in prosperity, will live upon him in adversity. Oh! when you are at ease and abound in all things, and consider Him as the author of all your happiness, and the giver of all your gifts, you will learn better to make Him your refuge when all things fail. But he that lives upon the creature in prosperity, when the creature fails will be in utter distress, and know not which way to turn for comfort, Jer. xvii. 13, 14.

LEIGHTON.

SCRIPTURAL SELECTIONS.

THE eternal God is thy refuge, and underneath are the everlasting arms.—*Deut.* xxxiii. 27.

And he said, The Lord is my rock, and my fortress, and my deliverer;

The God of my rock; in him will I trust: he is my shield, and the horn of my salvation, my high tower, and my refuge, my saviour; thou savest me from violence.

I will call on the Lord, who is worthy to be praised: so shall I be saved from mine enemies.

When the waves of death compass me, the floods of ungodly men made me afraid;

The sorrows of hell compassed me about; the snares of death prevented me.

In my distress I called upon the Lord, and cried to my God; and he did hear my voice out of his temple, and my cry did enter into his ears.—2 *Saml.* xxii. 2–7.

The Lord also will be a refuge for the oppressed, a refuge in times of trouble.

And they that know thy name will put their trust in thee: for thou, Lord, hast not forsaken them that seek thee.—*Ps.* ix. 9, 10.

Be merciful unto me, O God, be merciful unto me; for my soul trusteth in thee: yea, in the shadow of thy wings will I make my refuge, until these calamities be overpast.—*Ps.* lvii. 1.

In God is my salvation and my glory: the rock of my strength, and my refuge is in God.—*Ps.* lxii. 7.

O Lord, my strength, and my fortress, and my refuge in the day of affliction, the Gentiles shall come unto thee from the ends of the earth.—*Jer.* xvi. 19.

JESUS OUR HIDING PLACE.

WHEN God's right arm is bared for war,
And thunders clothe his cloudy car,
Where, where, oh where! shall man retire,
To escape the horrors of his ire?

'Tis he, the Lamb, to whom we fly,
While the dread tempest passes by;
God sees his well-beloved's face,
And spares us in our hiding place.

Thus, while we dwell in this low scene,
The Lamb is our unfailing screen;
To him, though guilty, still we run,
And God still spares us for his Son.

While yet we sojourn here below,
Pollutions still our hearts o'erflow;
Fallen, abject, mean, a sentenced race,
We deeply need a hiding place.

Yet courage—days and years will glide,
And we shall lay these clods aside;
Shall be baptized in Jordan's flood,
And washed in Jesus' cleansing blood.

Then pure, immortal, sinless, freed,
We, through the Lamb, shall be decreed;
Shall meet the Father face to face,
And need no more a hiding place.

II.

The Rainbow; or, Covenant Promises Seen
through Tears.

"I do set my Bow in the cloud."—Genesis, ix. 13.
"And there was a Rainbow round about the Throne."—Rev. iv. 3.

WE have joined together the two extremes of Holy
Writ—yoked in one text passages from Genesis
and from Revelations—placed beside each other as
kindred truths, sentences written by Moses and by
John ; one, relating to the old world more than forty-
three centuries ago, and the other, referring to a scene
in that "new heavens and new earth wherein dwelleth
righteousness," which is yet to be revealed.

Thus beautifully harmonizes the whole Word of God.
Thus are its beginning and ending made to meet and
form one circle of truth, having Christ for its centre,
and Infinitude for its circumference. Nor need we
wonder at this unity of purpose, thought, language, and
doctrine : it was all dictated by the same Divine Spirit,
it is all occupied with the same Divine salvation, and
its united aim is to advance the glory of God, and the
redemption of man.

The passages quoted at the head of this chapter,
introduce to our notice two striking, sublime, and at

(170)

the same time symbolical scenes, in each of which we have a personal interest, and both commend themselves to our earnest attention.

The first carries us back to the morning of the post-diluvial world.

The Deluge had ceased, "The fountains also of the deep and the windows of heaven were stopped, and the rain from heaven was restrained."

The ark containing the eight survivors of the old world rested on Mount Ararat, the dove had been sent forth, and, after returning with an olive leaf in her beak, was again let go, and came back no more. The land became dry, the covering of the ark was removed, and Noah and his family went out of their floating habitation, and stood once more on the firm dry earth, the *fons et origo* of a new generation. The pious patriarch built an altar to the Lord, and the sweet savour of his sacrifice rose up acceptably to heaven, and God returned to the worshippers promises of rest and peace.

But God did more than merely give a promise. He entered into a formal covenant with Noah and his sons, the purport of which was, that "all flesh should not be cut off any more by the waters of a flood; neither shall there any more be a flood to destroy the earth." This covenant was ratified by a seal of signal beauty and expressiveness: "And God said, This is the token of the covenant which I make between me and you, and every living creature that is with you, for perpetual

generations. I do set my bow in the cloud, and it shall
be for a token of a covenant between me and the earth.
And it shall come to pass, when I bring a cloud over
the earth, that the bow shall be seen in the cloud
* * * * and I will look upon it, that I may remember
the everlasting covenant."

A few days, perhaps, after this solemn transaction,
there is seen a gathering of clouds in the heavens, the
sky is quite overcast, the dark masses roll in inter-
mingling convolutions, the wind rises and sweeps down
the mountain gorges—the big drops of rain fall with a
heavy patter, the thunder mutters its distant warnings,
and all conspire to fill their minds with terror and
alarm. They recall the scene a few months back, when
the first waters of the deluge fell, and the first of the
fountains of the great deep was broken up; and a secret
and unwillingly-admitted fear steals into their minds,
lest perchance another storm may sweep them from
the earth. But it is only for a moment; they think of
God's promise, they remember his covenant, and, lo! as
they gaze upon the dark clouds, they discern delicate tints
and particoloured stripes, acquiring each moment more
perfect brilliancy and form, until the whole eastern sky
is spanned by the seven-listed bow of promise; and, as
they look upon the beautiful arch, they recall the covenant of God, and rejoice in the assurance of safety
thus vouchsafed, beholding, as they do, upon the very
storm which created alarm, the seal and signet-ring
of a covenant-keeping God.

'I do set my bow in the cloud, and
it shall be for a token of a covenant between
me and the earth'.

Gen. IX 13.

C Schuessle

J. C. Mc Rae

As a token of God's gracious assurance it is very peculiar. It never appears but at the time when the rain is falling, and hence, viewed in itself, is rather a ground of apprehension than of peace. But God has chosen that to be a pledge of our security, which is, in itself, an intimation of our danger, that our trust might be, not in any change of terrestrial arrangements, but in the simple word of God, a pledge repeated to us by each new-born rainbow, as it carries our thoughts back to the days of Noah, and the covenant token then first pointed out. Look then upon the rainbow, whenever it appears in its particoloured glory, and praise Him who set it in the clouds as the perpetual token of his covenant love. "Very beautiful is it in the brightness thereof, it compasseth the whole heaven with glory, and the hands of the Most High have bended it."

But another rainbow is spoken of in the Bible. St. John opens his Apocalypse with the announcement " I was in the Spirit : and, behold a throne was set in heaven, and one sat on the throne. And he that sat was to look upon like a jasper and a sardine stone : and there was a rainbow round about the throne, in sight like unto an emerald." The rainbow is not introduced here as a mere ornament, but as a most expressive emblem. Our eye is first directed to the throne, that habitation, as the Psalmist terms it, of justice and judgment, and to the majestic appearance of Him who sat upon it, compared here to two precious stones, the jasper and the sardius, or carnelian ; the jasper, as we gather from other passages, representing the essential holiness, and the sardius, or blood-red carnelian, the punitive justice of God, which declares "without the shedding of blood there is no remission of sin."

Lest, however, we should be repelled by this holiness of God, and overawed by his retributive justice, there is also seen, overarching this throne and Him who sits upon it, a rainbow, the symbol of grace returning after wrath, to testify of God's covenant of mercy in Christ Jesus. It is said to be a rainbow in sight like unto an emerald, because to the eye of the holy apostle green was the predominating colour, and green is of all colours the most refreshing and agreeable.

We may not, we cannot, look with unblinking eye upon the jasper-like holiness of Jehovah, for it is that dazzling glory which, filling heaven with its effulgence, causes it to have "no need of the sun or the moon to lighten it." We may not, we cannot, gaze upon the blood-red sardius-like justice of the Almighty, for the lurid glare would scorch the eyeballs of the mind with its scenes of burning and deserved wrath. But we may and can look upon the heavenly bow, "in sight like unto an emerald," and the great sign and seal of this covenant of grace, hung up over the throne of heaven, where "He who sitteth upon the throne" can ever look at it, and ever repeat to his children the promise, "For the mountains shall depart and the hills be removed, but my kindness shall not depart from thee, neither shall

the covenant of my peace be removed, saith the Lord
that hath mercy on thee."

What beautiful imagery Scripture employs in ex-
hibiting the truths of God! Were we so familiar with
the figurative language of the Bible, as to be reminded
of blissful truths every time we beheld those objects,
which have been employed to illustrate sacred ideas,
how would it invest the material world with new beauty,
and paint every picture of nature in the hues of heaven!
The sun, would then ever tell us of Christ, " the light of
the world;" and the moon, of the Church, deriving all her
brightness from " the sun of righteousness:" the well
spring would speak in sparkling language of the "fountain of cleansing" set open in Jerusalem; and the river
of that stream of "living water, clear as crystal, flowing
out from the throne of God and the Lamb:" the grass
would preach to us of the frailty of man, " to-day grow-
ing up, to-morrow cut down and withered;" and the
" lily of the field," beautifully set forth the protecting
care of the Almighty.

Our Lord drew illustrations of his doctrine from the
stars, the sea, the birds, the fishes, the clouds, the
fields; and the Holy Ghost has used the forms and
changes of the visible world to body forth eternal
truths; so that we may truly say that God has made
nature the eloquent expounder and advocate of revelation. When, therefore, we employ such a striking
emblem as the rainbow to set forth some of the precious
truths of God, we are but following in the track of

Scripture, and using God's own covenant seal to illustrate God's own promises.

The rainbow is made up of seven colours, caused by the
different angles at which the light is refracted and reflected from the falling drops of rain. The conditions under
which it can be seen are, that there must be rain falling
at the time; that there must be sunlight at the time;
and that the beholder must be between the two. Let
us look, then, if we can see on the dark and showery
cloud of sorrow, the rays of the Sun of Righteousness so
refracted as to form the iris of mercy, at once inspiring
hope and exciting thanksgiving.

We turn to Isaiah, the evangelical prophet, and find
the first of these prismatic promises in the comforting
words, "But now thus saith the Lord that created
thee, O Jacob, and he that formed thee, O Israel, Fear
not, for I have redeemed thee, I have called thee by
thy name: thou art mine. When thou passest through
the waters I will be with thee; and through the rivers,
they shall not overflow thee; when thou walkest
through the fire thou shalt not be burned, neither shall
the flame kindle upon thee. For I am the Lord thy
God, the Holy One of Israel, thy Saviour." How
much and how beautiful the light refracted from this
glowing passage! As if God had said, Fear not, for
He who created thee out of nothing, He who formed
thee in the shape and fashion of humanity, He who
redeemed thee from the dominion of death, He who so
knows thee as to call thee by name, and to grave thee

on the palms of his hands, and to make thee unto him a chosen peculiar people, will not forsake thee in any emergency or trial; but "when thou passest through the waters" of affliction, "I, the Lord thy God, the Holy One of Israel, thy Saviour," will be with thee; when thou goest through "rivers" of sorrow, "I, the Lord thy God, the Holy One of Israel, thy Saviour," will not suffer them to overflow thee; when "thou walkest through the fire" and along the flame-enkindled pathway of persecution, "I, the Lord thy God, the Holy One of Israel, thy Saviour," will not suffer thee to burn, but will protect thee from the fiery trial. What wide promises, what divine assurance! How full of hope and comfort to the sorrowful and the persecuted!

A few pages on, and we find another promise for our covenant bow; one, too, that has specific relations to the rainbow of the deluge, for that token was evidently present to the mind of God when the words were uttered: "For a small moment," says Jehovah, speaking to his ancient people, "for a small moment have I forsaken thee, but with great mercies will I gather thee. In a little wrath I hid my face from thee for a moment: but with everlasting kindness will I have mercy on thee, saith the Lord thy Redeemer." "For," he continues, "this is as the waters of Noah unto me: for as I have sworn that the waters of Noah should no more go over the earth, so have I sworn that I would not be wroth with thee, nor rebuke thee, for the mountains shall depart and the hills be removed, but my

23

kindness shall not depart from thee, neither shall the covenant of my peace be removed, saith the Lord that hath mercy on thee." This strong promise, made originally to the Israelites, is reaffirmed to each individual believer; for each child of God experiences moments when God seems to forsake him, and periods of darkness when his face seems hidden from him by intervening wrath or sorrow, and at such times we are tempted to murmur, as if we had a right to perpetual sunshine, forgetting that it is our iniquities which have separated between us and God, and our sins which have hid his face from us, that he cannot hear. Yet if we are in truth his children, and do seek to honour and glorify him, he will let it be but a small moment that he forsakes us, and but a passing gush of wrath in which he hides his face from us. The cloud between us may for a little while be black, angry, tempestuous, electrical; but when the gust is over and the Sun of Righteousness again shines out, then will the bright arch of hope span the vanishing cloud; for God declares that, as when he looks upon the rainbow, he remembers his covenant with Noah never again to bring the waters of the deluge upon the earth, so this promise that He would not for ever be wroth with thee nor rebuke thee, shall be to him a token never finally to remove his covenant of peace. Sooner far shall the everlasting hills depart; sooner far the deep foundations of the earth be moved, than God's promise fail or his covenant of peace be removed.

Sitting with our Saviour upon the grassy mount, and listening to the sermon he delivered there, we find another tinted promise of a dye so heavenly that it at once finds its place as one of the septenary colours in this rainbow of hope. The words are few but condensed, the promise is brief but of intensive force, of infinite expansibility—it is the verse " Blessed are they that mourn, for they shall be comforted." But how comforted ? Not with earthly sympathy, for that gives but little solace ; not with worldly succour, for the world has no balm for a broken heart ; but comforted with the choice blessings of the Divine Comforter, by which strength is imparted to the weak, light to the darkened, joy to the saddened, peace to the troubled, and hope to the sinking spirit.

I know that this passage refers not so much to the mourning for the various afflictions of life as to mourning over indwelling corruption and remaining sin. But then what sorrow is greater to bear than a sin-burdened spirit ? What grief more heavy than the weight of an oppressed and fainting soul just waking up to a consciousness of its danger ? These are sorrows that the world knows nothing of ; they lie out of the range of earthly vision, hidden away in the heart, pondered over in secret, confessed perhaps to none, yet how deep and poignant they are ; they drink up the spirit, they weary the heart, they at times crush the soul. Yet though so dark and stormy, the slanting light reflected from the face of Jesus draws out of this angry cloud a ray of bright and gladdening hope, adding another stripe to the covenant bow of promise as it is seen through the tears of a godly, penitential sorrow.

But our Saviour furnishes another prismatic colour for our covenant arch in the invitation, " Come unto me, all ye that labour and are heavy laden, and I will give you rest." There is here no restriction as to the persons invited, none as to the rest promised : whether then you labour under the cares, trials, and perplexities of life ; whether you are burdened by the crushing weight of poverty, sorrow, and sickness ; whether you labour under the sharp convictions of sin from which you struggle to free yourself, or whether you are burdened by a sense of weighty guilt and a conscious deserving of eternal woe ; in each case you are invited to Jesus with the promise of heavenly rest. There is no mind labouring under any of the burdens of life, there is no soul overworked and exhausted by the pressing cares of this mortal state, there is no heart aiming to work out its own righteousness under the taskmasters of formalism and morality, that will not be at once relieved of its burden and find rest in Christ. Sooner can you find in the Bible instances of the sick and the blind going to Him for healing and sent away uncured, than you can produce an instance of a labouring, burdened soul, accepting the invitation which calls him to the Saviour, and not finding the rest which the Saviour covenants to give. You may search the Evangelists through, and not find an instance of rejection to the petitioners for Christ's mercy when he was on earth; and were the records of the inner experience of all Christians since the day of Pentecost open to our inspection, we should be equally unsuccessful in noting any instance of a labouring, burdened soul being turned away from Jesus and deprived of his promised rest. And such rest! The rest of one who has found what he has long sought and deeply needs. The rest of one who has been wearied and overborne with ineffectual seekings after peace and hope; a rest from the dominion of sin, from the harrowing assaults of the adversary, from the restless wanderings of unbelief; a rest in the assured confidence of faith; a rest not of passive indifference, or inactive repose, but full of lively emotions, of holy zeal, of outgoing love; the forecast shadow of that eternal rest which remaineth for the people of God.

When, then, we reflect upon the person who issues the invitation, Jesus Christ, proving his large-hearted love by giving his life for the ransom of his enemies; when we consider the nature of the rest which he offers, spiritual, holy, rejoicing, unending; and when we mark the broadness of his invitation—*all* ye who labour and are heavy laden—thus covering the whole human race, for there is no man that liveth and hath not some labouring care, and some burdening sorrow; and when, to all these precious facts, we add the individual experience of the truth of this promise by each disciple of Jesus for nearly two thousand years, we cannot fail to observe how glowingly such a promise shines on the sorrow-clouds of earth, bending over the labouring and heavy laden child of sin at least one of the colours of the Christian bow of hope.

In the last interview of our Saviour with the apostles before his crucifixion, he gave them many and peculiar consolations in view of his near removal from them. But though those precious chapters in St. John's gospel beginning with the cheering words, "Let not your heart be troubled," were originally addressed to the sorrowing band that clustered around Him on that night of His agony and arrest, yet are they also appropriate and even designed for believers in all ages, for they form an important part of that Scripture which, at all times, and to all people, "is profitable for doctrine, for reproof, for correction, for instruction in righteousness." Among the many thrilling sentences uttered on that memorable night there is one so terse, so full of thought, so rich in comfort, that we may well claim for it a place in Mercy's triumphal arch. It is the passage "I will not leave you comfortless, I will come unto you." The original is, I will not leave you "Orphans:" accordingly Wiclyffe, in his translation, renders it, "I will not leave you Fatherless;" while the Rhiems version, following more closely the Greek word, reads, "I will not leave you Orphans." An orphan is indeed sad and comfortless; his earthly props and counsellors have been taken away, a painful void is made in his life, and his heart is stricken and desolate.

It is not, however, of natural orphanage that the words of Jesus apply, it is of that spiritual desertion, that loss of the props and supports of the Christian life, which too often occurs with the careless, unwatching, and prayer-restraining professor. In those days when doubt perplexes the mind and shadows of earthiness fall upon the spirit, when there is no comfort in devotion, and zeal smoulders in the ashes of a once blazing activity, when there is the first relenting of sorrow for such a cold or lukewarm state, and the awakening soul begins to feel the great lapse which it has made, and the grievous errors which it has committed; when the sense of deserved desertion and spiritual destitution gains ground and almost oppresses the heart, and the Christian feels that he is well nigh fatherless in the moral universe, an abandoned orphan with no spiritual parentage to which he can cling; then it is that there is seen stretching across this dark cloud, that hue of glory which streams from the words of Jesus, "I will not leave you orphans." You may seem to be forsaken and disinherited; you may think from the severity of God's dealings that your Heavenly Father has forgotten you or cast you out from his presence, and you may feel as homeless, parentless, portionless orphans. Yet it is only in the seeming thereof. Christ's promise stands out in full prismatic beauty, the sign of that covenant of grace which assures you, with lips of peace and truth, I will not leave you orphans; I will come to you—come to you in the cheering influences of

my love; come to you in the precious outpourings of my
spirit; come to you in the imparted strength and comfort of the Holy Ghost; come to you in sickness, in
suffering, in sorrow; come to you with the oil and wine
of gospel truth; come to you in the light of my own
countenance, making your dark soul radiant with joy,
and painting upon the lowering vapour, whose showers
have but just discharged themselves upon your head,
the overarching bow of covenant peace, and hope.

The sixth colour of this " bow in the cloud" is added
by the pencil of St. Paul. No one of the apostles endured more persecution and affliction, or had richer
experience of sustaining grace under them, than this
holy martyr. His estimate of sorrow, therefore, is the
more valuable, because it is evolved by the deep experience of his own life, and is the deliberate judgment
of one who had tried the world and Christ, and thus
was prevented from giving ex parte evidence in the
matter. This judgment he has recorded in his second
letter to the Corinthians; and, while it expresses his
personal experience, is yet a type of all affliction en
dured for Christ's sake, or so borne as to be subservient
to His glory. His words are, " Our light affliction,
which is but for a moment, worketh for us a far more
exceeding and eternal weight of glory; while we look
not at the things which are seen, but at the things
which are not seen: for the things which are seen are
temporal, but the things which are not seen are eternal " It will perhaps increase our idea of the inten-

sive force of this passage, if we place beside it that brief catalogue of the Apostle's sufferings which he has drawn up in this same epistle. "Of the Jews five times received I forty stripes, save one. Thrice was I beaten with rods, once was I stoned, thrice I suffered shipwreck, a night and a day have I been in the deep; in journeyings often, in perils of waters, in perils of robbers, in perils by mine own countrymen, in perils by the heathen, in perils in the city, in perils in the wilderness, in perils in the sea, in perils amongst false brethren, in weariness and painfulness, in watchings often, in hunger and thirst, in fastings often, in cold and nakedness."

Few of us could run up such a catalogue of personal sorrow as this; yet how does he speak of it? as a *light* affliction, *but for a moment.* And not only so, but an affliction which is an instrument of working out for us a far more exceeding and eternal weight of glory. Mark the two scales under the respective heads of affliction and glory; observe the diminuendo of the former, and the crescendo of the latter. The "AFFLICTION," "*light*" as to its character; "*but for a moment*" as to its duration; while the "GLORY" has "weight" as being heavy with blessing; is "*eternal*" as to its permanence; is "*exceeding*," as passing human conception; is "*far more* exceeding," as expressive of its unspeakable excellence. So intense was the feeling of the Apostle here, that the usual superlatives could not body forth his thought, and he was forced to make a

24

new word to give utterance to his emotion : it is *glory*,
it is a *weight* of glory, it is an *eternal* weight of glory,
it is an *exceeding* and eternal weight of glory, it is a
far more exceeding and eternal weight of glory. What
a climax ! like the rainbow, its foot, indeed, rests on
earth, but it arches upward to heaven, spanning the
dark cloud of affliction with a list of beauty. And if
the Apostle could say this of himself, so persecuted,
afflicted, tormented, ought not each child of sorrow to
look at his own trials as light and momentary ? We
can do thus, if we have such a lively faith in Christ
that we cling solely to his atoning blood, and hence
regard all the adversities of life as the chastenings of
parental love, designed to fit us to enjoy the far more
exceeding and eternal weight of glory, which shall be
ours when the light affliction, which is but for a
moment, shall be done away for ever. We are too
much disposed to shroud ourselves with our sorrows,
to dwell in the settlings down of the cloud, and have
our hearts ever kept wet by its weeping showers. So
long as we do this we cannot have peace or comfort,
we must go towards the sunshine, and just in proportion as we get into the fuller light of Jesus' face, is the
bow more clearly seen in the cloud, and the covenant
promise of Jehovah more rejoicingly believed. It is
only " while we look not at the things which are seen,
but at the things which are not seen," that we are enabled to lift up ourselves above surrounding and often
depressing influences. The " things seen" are the

present sorrows, with their accompanying trials and sadness, and upon these we morbidly look, and as we look, we magnify, distort, add weight to them, and thus increase the burden; while, would we but look away, and open wide the lids of faith's eye towards the unseen and the eternal, gazing by this spiritual vision upon the future glories and blessedness of those who through much tribulation enter into the kingdom of heaven, we should be so ravished with delight that every sorrow would be cheerfully borne, and not a cloud of affliction could skirt the horizon of our life, upon which we could not discern the rainbow of the covenant.

The last colour in this prismatic arch is furnished by "the Beloved Disciple," and is drawn from a revelation to him of some of these very "things which are unseen and eternal." The Apostle, in his vision at Patmos, had "beheld, and, lo, a great multitude which no man could number, of all nations, and kindreds, and people, and tongues, stood before the throne and before the Lamb, clothed with white robes, and palms in their hands." While he listened to their ascriptions of praise, one of the celestial host approached and asked him, by way of calling his attention to the scene, "Who are these which are arrayed in white robes? and whence came they?" The surprised Apostle answered, "Sir, thou knowest." In reply to this the heavenly visitant said unto him, "These are they which came out of great tribulation, and have washed their robes and made them white in the blood of the Lamb. Therefore are they before the throne of God, and serve him day and night in his temple; and he that sitteth on the throne shall dwell among them. They shall hunger no more, neither thirst any more, neither shall the sun light on them, nor any heat, for the Lamb which is in the midst of the throne shall feed them, and shall lead them unto living fountains of waters, and God shall wipe away all tears from their eyes." Can human thought add aught to this picture? No. All that we can do is to ponder word by word over the terms of this description, to strive to take in one by one the ideas which they convey: the white robe, the branch of palm, the cleansing blood, the posture before the throne, the mighty chorus, the Lamb in the midst of the throne, the absence of hunger and thirst, the feeding in green pastures, the drinking from living fountains, and the wiping away from our eyes all tears, by the very Father's hand, whose chastening rod had caused their flow. Did we dwell more upon these terms, we should realize more than we now do that they are designed to assure us of what will be our state when we pass the vale of tears, and stand upon the Mount Zion above. Yes, every one of these blessings shall be ours, if we have been washed in the blood of the Lamb. If tribulations are the necessary preparative, if there can be no weight of glory unless there has been previously the light affliction, then let us welcome sorrow, welcome suffering which endures but a moment here, but which brings eternal joy hereafter.

And now we have laid side by side seven rich and precious promises, as the seven colours of the rainbow, each lovely in itself, but combined, forming that arch of covenant glory which God has equally "set in the cloud" of sorrow on earth, and "around the throne" in heaven. Behold it in its varied but exquisite hues! Is it not beautiful as it springs upward—as it swells heavenward—as it bends downward, curving over our sorrow-drenched hearts, with assurances of present sunshine and of future bliss?

Having thus far looked upon the "cloud" and the "bow in the cloud," let us now cast one glance at the Sun whose refracted and reflected rays make this arch of glory.

Many are the passages in the Bible which represent Christ as the light of the world; and Malachi especially designates him as the "Sun of Righteousness." Striking and appropriate comparison! Christ is a "*Sun*"—the great light-producing, light-imparting centre of the moral universe. Christ is a "Sun *of Righteousness*," whether we regard Him as infinitely righteous in Himself, or as shedding abroad righteousness upon a dark and sinful world. Christ is a Sun of Righteousness *that casts no shadow.* The material sun casts shadows—nay, more, has dark spots and immense maculæ on its bright disc—but the Sun of Righteousness is immaculate—unblemished in Himself, and like a vertical sun makes no shadow. Christ is a Sun of Righteousness that cast no shadow and *that never sets.* The

earthly sun has its risings, its meridians, its setting
and the light of midday is soon succeeded by the dark
of midnight.   Not so with Christ; He shines out from
the zenith of the spiritual firmament, and there is no
going down of His light—no evening to shroud his
departed rays.   Once shining—for ever shining—without a shadow—without an eclipse—without a sunset.

Such is the Sun whose refracted rays paint the iris
of hope on the cloud of sorrow.   For though the
promises which I have adduced, like the different
stripes of the rainbow, are of different hues, yet the
light which produces them is the pure and colourless
essence of Divine glory.

In this light it is our privilege, as Christians, to
dwell.   Abiding in this light, we have peace, hope, joy,
and prove ourselves to be "the children of light" through
faith in Christ Jesus.   Hence unrenewed men have no
comfort or solace in any of the trials and afflictions of
life.   The heart must be surrendered to Jesus Christ,
it must be washed in His atoning blood, it must be
sanctified by His holy Spirit, before we can become
"children of light and of the day;" but when through the
sovereign grace of God we receive this "adoption of sons,"
then is it our peculiar privilege to see God's love in
every dispensation of His hand, and to see His bow of
covenant promise in every cloud of sorrow.

                                        STEVENS.

SCRIPTURAL SELECTIONS.

FEAR not: for I have redeemed thee, I have called thee by thy name ; thou art mine.

When thou passest through the waters, I will be with thee; and through the rivers, they shall not overflow thee: when thou walkest through the fire, thou shalt not be burned; neither shall the flame kindle upon thee.

For I am the Lord thy God, the Holy One of Israel, thy Saviour.— *Is.* xliii. 1, 2, 3.

For a small moment have I forsaken thee, but with great mercies will I gather thee.

In a little wrath I hid my face from thee for a moment: but with everlasting kindness will I have mercy on thee, saith the Lord thy Redeemer.

For this is as the waters of Noah unto me: for as I have sworn that the waters of Noah should no more go over the earth; so have I sworn that I would not be wroth with thee, nor rebuke thee.

For the mountains shall depart, and the hills be removed; but my kindness shall not depart from thee, neither shall the covenant of my peace be removed, saith the Lord that hath mercy on thee.—*Is.* liv. 7–10.

Blessed are they that mourn: for they shall be comforted.—*Matt.* v. 4.

I will not leave you comfortless: I will come to you.—*John* xiv. 18.

For our light affliction, which is but for a moment, worketh for us a far more exceeding and eternal weight of glory ;

While we look not at the things which are seen, but at the things which are not seen: for the things which are seen are temporal; but the things which are not seen are eternal.—2 *Cor.* 17, 18.

God shall wipe away all tears from their eyes.—*Rev.* vii. 17

THE RAINBOW.

WHEN the sun with cheerful beams
  Smiles upon a lowering sky,
Soon its aspect softened seems,
  And a rainbow meets the eye;
While the sky remains serene,
This bright arch is never seen.

Thus the Lord's supporting power
  Brightest to the saints appears,
When affliction's threatening hour
  Fills their sky with clouds and fears;
He can wonders then perform,
Paint a rainbow on the storm.

All their graces doubly shine,
  When their troubles press them sore;
And the promises divine
  Give them joys unknown before,
As the colours of the bow
To the cloud their brightness owe.

III.

ENTERING THE GATE.

" And he led them forth by the right way, that they might go to a city of habitation."—Ps. CVII. 7.
' Blessed are they that do his commandments, that they may have right to the tree of life, and may enter in through the gates into the city."—REV. XXII. 14.

THIS present world through which we are passing may justly be called a wilderness; it is a solitary, and a barren way. It is a lonely and a dreary way we are travelling in; the path is strait and narrow, and few there are that walk therein. This world is no more our friend, than it is our home; the true Christian, therefore, who is born from above, whose conversation is in heaven, and who is daily travelling thitherward, is the object of its malice, or else the subject of its ridicule. The soil of this present evil world is barren and unfruitful; it presents before our eyes many objects which are an hinderance to us in our way; but it is entirely desert and barren with respect to any help it affords us in our progress. It produces little else but briers and thorns, which have a tendency only to entangle and wound the feet of those who pass through it. The many afflictions with which the people of God are exercised in the present life, are as a constant clog to the wheels of their souls, which makes them drag on heavily: and were they not sometimes favoured with a view of the rest which remains for them, they would be almost ready to despair of getting safe out of this vale of tears, which they have, therefore, too great occasion to call a waste howling wilderness—a solitary and a barren land.

This present world through which we are passing is also properly compared to a wilderness, as it is likewise a dangerous way. A wilderness is a place not only barren and unfrequented, but is generally full of pits and wild beasts, which render it exceeding dangerous. For this reason it is styled in Scripture " a terrible wilderness, wherein are fiery serpents, and scorpions, and drought, where there is no water," Deut. viii. 15. We are called to pass through an enemy's country; this world is under the influence of our greatest and most inveterate enemy. The Devil is styled the prince of the power of the air, and the generality of this world's inhabitants are his willing slaves and vassals. Whilst therefore we are passing through his territories, he will be sure to gain all the advantages he can against us. No sooner do we enlist ourselves under the banner of Christ Jesus, but Satan and the world immediately join in a league against us; as though they were re-solved to rob the Redeemer of his spoil, and pluck those who are the purchase of his blood out of his hands. There is a rooted enmity between the seed of the woman and the seed of the serpent. Satan has an inveteracy against every one that bears the image of Jesus; and " as a roaring lion walketh about seeking whom he may devour," 1 Peter v. 8. And, like an old serpent, he conceals his wiles that he may get the better advantage over us. We are, in this life, never free from his temptations : he is always contriving some temptation against us, or presenting it to us. And that we do not oftener fall into the snares which he lays to entrap us, is only owing to the care and vigilance of our Great Leader, and the grace which he is pleased to communicate to us out of his fulness.

As for the world; "the lust of the flesh, the lust of the eyes, and the pride of life," how prevalent have these been to draw aside the believer from the God and guide of his youth! these Philistines are often upon us before we are aware of them, and there is an unbelieving heart always within, which is as constant fuel to the fire of temptations from without. So that were not God pleased at particular times to open our eyes, and let us see that, "they who are for us are more than they which are against us," we should be ready to give up all in despair.

On these accounts the present state is compared to a wilderness. We wander here in the wilderness, in a solitary way, "we can find no city to dwell in, hungry and thirsty, our souls faint within us." But herein God leads his people by the right way, to the city of habitation. They are dear to him every one as the apple of his eye—as near to him as his right hand. His love was fixed from everlasting upon them, and therefore his care and loving kindness are ever exercised towards them. He may bring his people into the wilderness, but he cannot, in consistency with the perfections of his nature, or the promise of his grace, ever leave them there. They may, and often do seem to lose their hold of him; but he never does, he never can lose his hold of them. "For the Lord's portion is his people; Jacob is the lot of his inheritance. He found him in a desert land, and in the waste howling wilderness; he led him about, he instructed him, he kept him as the apple of his eye," Deut. xxxii. 9, 10. There is no getting to Immanuel's land, but by the way of the wilderness; which though it is not our rest itself, yet it leads us to our rest; it fits and prepares us for it; and the afflictions which we meet with therein, serve also to make the heavenly blessedness the more desirable now, and delightful hereafter. God may therefore often lead us in a rough and unpleasant way, but he always leads us in a right way. Let us only take a view of these particular seasons, wherein we are most apt to question the loving kindness of our God, and we may determine the happy issue of all the rest.

Let us begin with the melancholy state and condition of those from whom God hides the light of his countenance. These are often ready to object against themselves, that they shall never "see the goodness of the Lord in the land of the living." Methinks I hear them complaining with the church of old, "My way is hid from the Lord, and my judgment is passed from my God." And condemning themselves for hypocrites, and mere professors, because of the uncertainty of their frames, and the unfruitfulness of their lives. They are for the present bewildered, as those that have lost their way. They have no sensible communion with Christ— no present discovery of the love of God, to take comfort in : but notwithstanding their fears, "this is the right way, wherein God leads us to the city of habitation." Were the reconciled countenance of a covenant God and Father always to be lift up on us, we should be apt to prize the comforts we receive immediately from him more than the glorious person who was the purchaser, and is the bestower of them. Were he never to hide his face, we should live upon the streams, rather than the fountains; we should be too ready to say with the three disciples, "Lord, it is good for us to be here;" we should be ready to make a stop at the banks of Jordan ; or at least, we should pass that river with reluctance, indifferent in our desires after what remaineth to be received by us in the heavenly world. In a word, God is pleased to give us at some times, a glimpse of our future glory, that he may excite our desires after the farther enjoyments thereof; and at other times is pleased wisely to withhold his hand in this respect, that we may be willing when he calls us, "to depart, and be with Christ." This, then, though it be a way less pleasant for us to walk in, is nevertheless the right way to the place where our hearts and treasure are both lodged; by this means, we are made to long after, and then are led to the city of habitation.

The same may be said, concerning the various outward afflictions with which the believer is exercised. They are all of them, let them arise from what quarter soever, useful to us, and necessary for us. God never sends an affliction to us but when he sees it needful for us; and he never removes it from us, before it has answered the end for which he at first sent it. Outward afflictions are not accidental things, they come not by chance, but are sent to us by a wise and merciful Father, who causes them to answer the end for which he sends them. By them we are purged from our dross and tin; grace is tried and refined in the furnace of affliction, and they, who have tasted that the Lord is gracious, are hereby conformed to his heavenly image—made partakers of his holiness, Heb. xii. 10, and more prepared for his heavenly kingdom. Afflictions are a furtherance to us in our way heavenward—not an hinderance to us; though when we are exercised therewith we often conclude ourselves to be in a desert and desolate land. We must be first of all prepared for glory, before we can, in consistency with the perfections of our God, be received into it: and this is the end, and proves the blessed issue of our present afflictions, 2 Cor. iv. 17. Hereby, then, it further appears, that God leads his people the right way, though it may be a rough way, to the city of habitation.

The temptations of Satan every one of them answer the same general end. He is, indeed, styled, with an emphasis, "our adversary," 1 Peter v. 8. But he oftentimes proves, contrary to his own design and our expectation, our great friend. The powers of darkness are suffered to dwell amongst us for the same reason that some of the Canaanites were left among the people of Israel; that is, to try us, and show us how weak we are without Christ; and how strong we are when we depend upon that grace which is treasured up in him. By all the advantages they gain against us, they only render us the more distrustful of ourselves; and the grace which we have already received, makes us the more in love with Christ Jesus, our glorious head, in whose strength we overcome them—and more desirous of that city of habitation, which God has prepared for his people ; where we shall join the heavenly host, in saying with a loud voice, "Now is come salvation, and strength, and the kingdom of our God, and the power of his Christ : for the accuser of our brethren is cast down, who accused them before our God day and night," Rev. xii. 10. Thus we see how God leads his people by the right way, that they may go to a city of habitation.

If then God has prepared for his people a city of habitation; how great is that grace, how free and sovereign is that love, to which this was originally owing! All that we have in time, and all that we expect to enjoy to eternity, proceed alone from this spring; this is the original fountain from which they all flow. The vessels of mercy were prepared from all eternity TO glory, though they are prepared FOR it only in time. And to what can this unspeakable privilege be owing, or into what can it be resolved, short of the sovereign and distinguishing grace of God ? This it is alone that makes us differ from others : considered in ourselves, we were equally the objects of the anger and resentment

of an holy God, with those "who are reserved in chains
of darkness, to the judgment of the great day;" and
had not the free grace of God found out an expedient
for our salvation, we must equally with them, have
suffered the vengeance of eternal fire. "But God, who
is rich in mercy, for his great love wherewith he loved
us, even when we were dead in sins, hath quickened us
together with Christ (by grace ye are saved); and hath
raised us up together, and made us sit together in
heavenly places in Christ Jesus; That in ages to come,
he might show the exceeding riches of his grace, in his
kindness towards us, through Christ Jesus," Eph. ii.
4–7. Grace acts like itself, it gives all things freely.
God deals with us as the "God of all grace;" for
he gives us both grace here, and glory hereafter,
and "no good thing will he withhold from them that
walk uprightly." He first of all makes us his sons,
takes us into the number of his family, and gives us a
right and title to the privileges of his house in our
justification; and in our sanctification, he gradually
prepares us for the more immediate enjoyment of himself in a better world; and then he calls us home to
the glorious inheritance itself, "the city of habitation,"
which he had settled upon us before all worlds. And
who of us can take but a slight view of these things,
without crying out with the apostle, "Behold what
manner of love the Father hath bestowed upon us, that
we should be called the sons of God," 1 John iii. 1.
Our eternal predestination to glory, and our actual
preparation for it, are both of them owing wholly, and

alone, to his free and sovereign grace; and to this shall we everlastingly ascribe it, when we come "to the general assembly, and church of the first-born, and to the spirits of the just made perfect."

Are we to pass through the wilderness to this city of habitation? How much need have we of a guide to show us the way, and how thankful should we be to Him who has undertaken to perform this kind office for us. Were we left in this wilderness-world without a guide, our condition would be deplorable, and our ruin inevitable; we should then fall into the pits and snares which our enemies have made for the entanglement of our feet, and the destruction of our souls; they, that are more mighty than we, would assuredly prevail against us—we should be led captive by Satan at his will—there would be no withstanding his temptations —no escaping his malice and fury, or resisting those whom he employs against us in this desolate and dangerous way. But through grace, this blessing we have. Christ Jesus is styled the "captain of our salvation," and he faithfully discharges his office, which he has engaged to perform as such. He not only undertook to purchase salvation by his death, but to apply it likewise by his life; he goes before continually as our guide and leader, and marks out the path which we are to take; he communicates to us suitable help and refreshment, while we are in our way; restores our souls when we have gone out of our way, and preserves us from the fury and violence, as well as the craft and subtlety of our many enemies. He is "a pillar of cloud to us for

26

our covering by day, and a pillar of fire for our guidance by night." He is always at our right hand, so that we should not be greatly moved. Here lies our safety, and the strong ground of our hope, that we shall not fall short of our rest, or lose the prize we are so earnestly contending for. Christ himself is our life, and the length of our days; who has graciously promised that He will never fail, nor forsake us. May we, therefore, begin the work of heaven before we come there, daily offering the sacrifices of praise and thanksgiving unto him, even the fruit of our lips. Using the same language here, as we hope to use for ever hereafter. "Unto Him that loved us, and washed us from our sins in his own blood, and hath made us kings and priests unto God and his Father: to Him be glory and dominion for ever and ever. Amen," Rev. i. 5, 6.

Is the way of the wilderness the right way to a city of habitation? How easy should this make us under all the temptations, trials, and afflictions with which we are now exercised. "All things are for your sakes, that the abundant grace might, through the thanksgiving of many, redound to the glory of God," 2 Cor. iv. 15. This should make us willingly submit to the various trials we meet with on our passage. There is a crown of glory reserved in heaven for all those that shall continue faithful unto death—a city of habitation where the weary pilgrim shall rest—rivers of pleasure, where we shall be refreshed and delighted. There he will have an ample amends for all the difficulties he has been exposed to in the present life. The view of this recompense of reward will make death itself pleasant, and hang out a lamp sufficient to enlighten even that dark valley.

Can none get admission into this city of habitation but the "redeemed of the Lord?" Let this lead us to Jesus Christ, the only person "Who is of God, made unto us wisdom, righteousness, sanctification, and redemption," 1 Cor. i. 30. "Him hath God exalted with his right hand to be a Prince and a Saviour, for to give repentance unto Israel, and forgiveness of sins," Acts v. 31. . No one can save us from our sins, but He whom God hath set forth to be a propitiation for our sin, through faith in his blood. Hither, then, must the convinced sinner fly, as his city of refuge; on His righteousness must we all depend for a right and title to life; and his spirit alone can fit and prepare us for it. If we have not on us Christ's perfect righteousness, we are not his people; none but they who are arrayed with this fine linen, clean and white, shall be thought worthy to enter into this city of habitation. Let us, therefore, be importunate with God to lead us unto Christ, and enable us to believe in him to the saving of the soul. Such he has purchased glory for, and he lives to prepare them for it. "There, as their forerunner, he is for them already entered; and thither, as the captain of their salvation, will he at last bring them, and present them faultless before the throne of his Father's glory, with exceeding joy."

EAST.

SCRIPTURAL SELECTIONS.

BE patient therefore, brethren, unto the coming of the Lord. Behold, the husbandman waiteth for the precious fruit of the earth, and hath long patience for it, until he receive the early and latter rain.

Be ye also patient; establish your hearts: for the coming of the Lord draweth nigh.—*James* v. 7, 8.

And a highway shall be there, and a way, and it shall be called, The way of holiness; the unclean shall not pass over it; but it shall be for those: the wayfaring men, though fools, shall not err therein.

No lion shall be there, nor any ravenous beast shall go up thereon, it shall not be found there; but the redeemed shall walk there:

And the ransomed of the Lord shall return, and come to Zion with songs, and everlasting joy upon their heads; they shall obtain joy and gladness, and sorrow and sighing shall flee away.—*Isaiah* xxxv 8–10.

In my Father's house are many mansions: if it were not so, I would have told you. I go to prepare a place for you.

And if I go and prepare a place for you, I will come again, and receive you unto myself; that where I am, there ye may be also.— *John* xiv. 2, 3.

Blessed are they that do his commandments, that they may have right to the tree of life, and may enter in through the gates into the city.—*Rev.* xxii. 14.

Heaven.

" And God shall wipe away all tears from their eyes; and there shall be no more death, neither sorrow, nor crying, neither shall there be any more pain; for the former things have passed away.— Rev. xxi. 4

No sickness there,—
No weary wasting of the frame away,
No fearful shrinking from the midnight air,
No dread of summer's bright and fervid ray.

No hidden grief,
No wild and cheerless vision of despair,
No vain petition for a swift relief,
No tearful eyes, no broken hearts are there.

Care has no home
Within the realm of ceaseless prayer and song:
Its billows break and melt away in foam,
Far from the mansions of the spirit throng.

The storm's black wing
Is never spread athwart celestial skies;
Its wailings blend not with the voice of spring,
As some too tender floweret fades and dies.

No night distils
Its chilling dews upon the tender frame,
No moon is needed there. The light which fills
That land of glory, from its Maker came.

No parted friends
O'er mournful recollections have to weep;
No bed of death enduring love attends,
To watch the coming of a pulseless sleep.

No blasted flower,
Or withered bud celestial gardens know;
No scorching blast, or fierce-descending shower
Scatters destruction like a ruthless foe.

No battle word
Startles the sacred host with fear and dread;
The song of peace creation's morning heard,
Is sung wherever angel minstrels tread.

Let us depart,
If home like this await the weary soul.
Look up, thou stricken one! Thy wounded heart
Shall bleed no more at sorrow's stern control.

With faith our guide,
White-robed and innocent, to lead the way,
Why fear to plunge in Jordan's rolling tide,
And find the ocean of eternal day?

IV

The White-Robed Throng.

*" I beheld, and, lo, a great multitude, which no man could number, of all nations, and kindreds, and people, and tongues, stood before the throne, and before the Lamb, clothed with white robes, and palms in their hands."—*Rev. vii. 9.

WHAT a different scene, what a different world, separated only by a slight veil from that which we inhabit, is here exhibited to our view! a world into which we may enter by a single step, and in a moment of time! Here we see a busy world, eager in vain pursuits, agitated by mere trifles, contending about objects of no moment, and immersed in things which perish with the using. All is noise, and confusion, and vanity, and sorrow, and evil.

But behold another world nigh at hand, composed of different beings, governed by different principles; where all things are as momentous, as here they are frivolous; where all things are as great, as here they are little; where all things are as durable, as here they are transitory; where all things are as fixed, as here they are mutable! That world has also its inhabitants —so numerous, that the population of this world is but as a petty tribe compared to them. It has its employments; but they are of the noblest kind and weightiest import; and compared with them, the whole sum of the concerns of this life is but as a particle of dust. It has its pleasures; but they are pure and spotless, holy and divine. There, perfect happiness, and un-interrupted harmony, and righteousness, and peace, ever prevail. What a contrast to our present state! And is this blessed scene near us? may we be called into it in a moment? With what anxious solicitude, then, should we endeavour to realize it; and how ardently should we desire to be prepared for an admission into it!

The number of the blessed inhabitants of heaven is represented as infinite: "I beheld, and lo! a great multitude which no man could number:"—and if we consider the infinite power and glory of him who created them; the magnificence, and even profusion displayed in the works of his hands; the end and design for which they were created, namely, to manifest his glory; we shall at once feel that their number must be, in the fullest sense of the word, infinite. Let us reflect, that to create a million, or a million of millions of the brightest and most glorious spirits, is as easy to the Almighty, as it was to create our first parents: he has but to will, and it is done. Let us consider that he rejoices in the multitude of his works: that every part of the universe is filled with being—from the immeasurable systems of worlds, to the atom whose minuteness eludes the keenest sight. Let us reflect, that heaven is the perfection of his works, the grand scene of his glory, the immediate place of his residence. There he is to be known, and adored, and glorified; there he is to receive the homage so justly due to his majesty. And shall this part of his works only be scantily peopled? Shall those realms alone, which he made for himself, be without inhabitants? shall heaven alone be a blank in the creation? Our Lord, it is true, hath said, speaking of the race of man, that "narrow is the way which leadeth to life, and few there be that enter in thereat;" but this expression relates solely to the earth we inhabit—one world amidst, perhaps, an innumerable multitude. It relates also, principally, to the time in which our Lord lived. Even this world, we trust, will not ultimately be barren, but produce numerous and faithful witnesses to the glory of the Redeemer. He made this earth the scene of his sufferings, and we may expect it to become the scene of his triumphs. Only allow the Gospel of Christ to prevail, as the prophets lead us to hope that in the latter days it will prevail; allow the world to continue, as there is ground to expect it will continue, to a period of which the infancy is scarcely yet past; and we may conclude, that even from this fallen world shall multitudes, as numerous as the drops of the morning dew, crowd into the realms of light, to ascribe "glory, and praise, and honour, to Him that sitteth on the throne, and to the Lamb for ever."

In considering the multitudes, beyond the power of calculation, which will people the realms of bliss, we must recollect, that, there, multitudes constitute happi-

27

ness. On the earth, where a difficulty of subsistence
is often experienced; where there exists a constant
collision of interests; where one stands in the way of
another; where jealousies and envyings, anger and
revenge, pride and vanity, agitate and deform the
world; numbers may tend to diffuse wretchedness and
to multiply evil. Hence we flee for peace and joy from
the crowded haunts of men, and court the sequestered
habitation and the retired vale. But in heaven, where
there can be no thwarting interests; where the wants
of one are never supplied at the expense of another;
where every bosom glows with love, and every heart
beats with desire to promote the general happiness;
the addition of a fresh individual to the innumerable
throng diffuses a wider joy, and heightens the universal
felicity.

The multitude assembled there is described as composed of all "nations, and kindred, and people, and
tongues." Here, again, we must beware of forming
our judgment from the feelings and views of this fallen
world. There, it will be no cause of jealousy, or
rivalry, or hatred, that one person received his birth on
this, and another on that side of a river or sea. A
man will not despise his brother on account of the
different shade of his complexion; he will not seek his
destruction because he spoke in another language; nor
renounce communion with him because he praised the
same God, with the same spirit of piety, in a house of
a different form. All these petty distinctions will have

either ceased to exist, or will be completely annihilated in the general spirit of love that will then animate every mind. One pursuit will occupy every heart; each will strive to glorify God. There will either be no distinctions, or the distinctions be like the beautiful variety we see in the works of God—like flowers enriched with different colours to delight the eye, or with various perfumes to gratify the smell. Why should distinctions offend, or variety disgust? It is the dark and selfish pride of the heart which considers itself as the only standard of right and excellence, and therefore despises and hates every deviation from itself. Let the pride be removed, and the distinction would become a pleasing variety, instead of a source of hatred.

Alas! alas! what petty differences, engendered by pride, and nursed by the worst passions of the human breast, here separate, with unchristian hatred, those who are brethren, the children of the same God, the members of the same church, taught by the same book, partakers of the same hope, redeemed by the same Saviour, influenced by the same Spirit, travelling along the same road towards the same blessed country!   O religion! our best, our dearest, holiest guide! is thy divine aim to be diverted, to sanction discord, to justify hatred, and to consecrate bigotry?   No; Religion acknowledges nothing as her own work, but union and peace. In heaven, her throne, no odious denominations will parcel out the regenerated church, no frivo-

lous distinctions be suffered to break the unity of the
members of Christ; but people of every nation, and
kindred, and tribe, and tongue, will unite in one worship, will be animated with one spirit, will be actuated
by one principle; and that, the principle of pure and
universal love.

The society of that blessed place is composed of
angels and *saints;* of those, that is, who have never
sinned against God: and those who, having sinned have
been redeemed by the cross of Christ, and have
"washed their robes, and made them white in the blood
of the Lamb"—of those who were created, and have
continued, in the highest order of bright and glorious
spirits; of those who once were "dead in trespasses
and sins," who "walked according to the course of this
world, according to the prince of the power of the air,
the spirit that now worketh in the children of disobedience," but who have been "quickened together with
Christ, and raised up together with him, and made to
sit together" with angels, and with the Lord of angels,
"in heavenly places." Yet the angels scorn not such
society; they reproach not the children of men with
their fall; they refuse not to receive them into their
company. On the contrary, they *rejoice* when any
sinner repenteth; they convey the departed Lazarus
into Abraham's bosom; they become "ministering
spirits to the heirs of salvation;" they worship with
them in the same adorations; they answer in responsive

chorus to their praises. What a model for the conduct and worship of the saints below!

The employment of that innumerable company is represented as that of praise *to God and to the Lamb,* who redeemed them and bought them with his blood. In other parts of the Sacred Writings, where the employments of heaven are described, worship and praise are represented as the chief occupation. We are not, however, to infer from this, that the exclusive employment is religious adoration; for we know that the angels, being of a still higher order and more spiritual nature, are frequently engaged in active commissions to execute the will of God. What are the precise occupations of the *spirits of the just made perfect,* we indeed know not; nor could we, perhaps, comprehend them. It is sufficient for us to rest assured that they are occupied in that work for which they are best qualified. It is sufficient for us to know, that, whatever the employments are which their Creator and Redeemer assigns to them, they are such as must tend to produce the greatest happiness, and to excite new and continual praises to God: for, in every description which is given us of the heavenly world, it is the voice of incessant praise and thanksgiving we hear; it is the overflowing of thankfulness for a state of exquisite enjoyment; it is the universal burst of gratitude, extending from one boundary of heaven to the other. The voice of prayer itself is lost in the exultations of praise; the language of complaint is unknown; the

lamentations of sorrow, and the sighs of grief, are
never heard. The happiness of that innumerable company is described in the most glowing colours : "They
shall hunger no more, nor thirst any more ; the sun
shall not light on them" (to scorch them), "nor any
heat" (molest them). "The Lamb which is in the
midst of the throne, shall feed them, and shall lead
them unto living fountains of water; and God shall
wipe away all tears from their eyes." Here we see
every source of evil, and even of inconvenience,
removed, and every good bestowed, by the unrestrained
bounty of Heaven.

Descriptions of this kind must be figurative : but the
figures are evidently intended to convey to us the
highest possible conception of unqualified good, and the
total absence of all evil. The remaining part of the
description both manifests the nature and the source of
the happiness which they enjoy. They are "before
the throne of God, and serve him day and night in his
temple : and He that sitteth on the throne shall dwell
among them." The happiness which they enjoy is,
then, a refined and holy happiness. It is not the
happiness of a Mahometan paradise, but such as is
suited to spiritual beings of the highest order and most
exalted taste. It is a happiness founded upon religion
and devotion, upon near and intimate access to the
Lord of life and glory. And let not this happiness be
judged of by those who, far from having enjoyed
pleasure arising from such a source, have, on the con-

trary, experienced from it only pain and restraint. They know not what religion is, nor are capable of appreciating its nature and excellence. To others, it will be sufficient to state, that religion is but another word for happiness. I do not mean this merely in the sense in which, without guarding them, the words may be understood, viz. that the effect produced by religion is happiness. I use the words literally; and design to state, that religion itself, the act and exercise of it, is the purest and highest happiness. It may here be necessary to rectify the general definition of religion. Religion is not merely the worship of God, or the exercise of obedience: it is the union of the soul with God; the conformity of the will with his will; the enjoyment of communion with him; and the transformation of every faculty of the soul to his image and likeness. Religion, here, is but the faint outline of this more sublime image of its nature; the outward expression of what it ought to be, and of what it is above. Now happiness arises from a frame of mind harmonizing with the objects which surround us. When the soul, therefore, is moulded into the perfect frame of religion in its most exalted state; when every affection and every faculty are put in perfect tune, and all are in unison with the divine Source of all good; there must be happiness, arising from such a constitution, the most pure and perfect which a creature can enjoy. It is the happiness of God himself—of God, the source of all happiness. It is a state of mind in which that necessarily gives pleasure which gives him pleasure; in which there is a participation of his feelings; in which the soul drinks at the fountain-head of all enjoyment; in which the bliss of the Almighty becomes the bliss of his creatures. Thus religion and happiness are convertible terms. They are, in fact, one and the same thing: and it is not more impossible that God should be unhappy, than that his devout servants, dwelling near his throne, and "serving him day and night in his temple," should taste of misery.

To what an exalted height of happiness and glory, is then that *innumerable company* advanced! With what a glorious society do they hold communion! In what noble employments are they engaged; of what refined enjoyments do they partake! Blessed spirits! your lot is fixed; your happiness is permanent and eternal. You will suffer pain or feel distress no more; your minds are cleansed from every taint of sin; your breasts are the everlasting abode of purity and joy. All around you is peace; everything is concerted, by almighty wisdom and infinite goodness, to banish the very elements of evil; to dispel the slightest shade of misery; to pour around you, in luxuriant profusion—a profusion, designating the infinitely varied power of the Giver—all the richest stores of good. How unlike this is our present state! what a different abode is this world below! Here, fear and terror, danger and violence, pain and suffering, sin and remorse, misery and grief, poverty and labour, the curse and the frown of justice, have fixed their abode. But, though these *days be evil,* give not way to despair.

Let me now present to you this innumerable company under a different aspect. Let me point out to you what was their former, as well as what is their present state. Once, these were "men of like passions with yourselves; they have come out of great tribulation;" they once sighed and groaned under sufferings and sorrows, as deep and grievous as those by which any of you are afflicted. O! what an invaluable and sure source of consolation is it to every pious Christian suffering under the weight of worldly calamities, to direct his contemplation to this glorious host above! Standing before the throne, and before the Lamb, clothed with white robes, and with palms in their hands, methinks they say to him, "We were once as you are; we were assaulted by the same temptations, we were stricken by the same arrows, we drank deep of the same bitter cup, we combated with the same enemies, we felt all the sharpness and bitterness of the Christian warfare. Often were we ready to faint; often we cried to God in an agony of grief, on the point of being swallowed up in despair. We felt all the weakness of our faith, and trembled under the infirmities of our common nature. Faint not therefore in your course. Behold the *cloud of witnesses* surrounding you. With one voice they bid you 'lift up the hands which hang down, and strengthen the weak knees.' Be strong, fear not; your God will come: he will come with a

28

recompense, and save you." Let me conjure every weak, and every afflicted soul to contemplate these blessed inhabitants of heaven. How changed are they from what they once were! praises incessantly occupy their tongues, which once breathed out only complaints, and told of fears and apprehensions. Not a complaint can you make which they have not made: not a temptation can you describe to which they were not exposed. All your weakness they felt: all your trials they endured. Some, like Lazarus, were afflicted with poverty: some, like Job, were plunged from the height of prosperity to the lowest depth of adversity; some, like David, were harassed by severe persecutions; some, like Lot, were vexed by the unrighteousness of those around them; some, like Eli, were cursed with unrighteous children; some, like Peter, were shut up in prison; some, like Manasses, felt all the anguish of remorse! some, like the apostles and the noble army of martyrs, were stoned or sawn asunder; yet, now, their sufferings have been long forgotten, or are remembered only to bless God, who " counted them worthy to suffer for his name's sake." One moment spent in heaven effaces for ever the afflictions endured upon earth. O ! look to them, then, and indulge the delightful hope that one day " God may wipe away all tears from your eyes," and compensate all your sufferings. For the better confirmation of your faith, let me lastly refer you to the means by which this wounderful change was accomplished in them. " They washed their robes, and made them white with the blood of the Lamb." They bear in their hands the *palm*, as an emblem of victory in the good fight of faith; and they are *clothed with white robes*, to denote the purity of their hearts under the regenerating influence of the Holy Spirit. The first point to which our attention is here directed, is that "blood of the Lamb," in which their "robes have been washed and made white." This image is designed to show, that it was to the efficacy of the death of Christ they trusted as the atonement for their sins. Christ was to them the *hope of glory*; that is, they founded all their hope of glory upon him. Their robes were formerly defiled and stained by sin; but they were "washed, they were cleansed, they were justified, they were glorified," by Christ. He it was who gave them heaven, and who gave them the preparation for it. He is the Lord of the world above: he has the "keys of death and hell;" *openeth*, and no man shutteth; he *shutteth*, and no man openeth. To him, trusting in his grace and mercy, they applied, as to the Saviour of mankind; and he heard their cry, and was gracious and merciful unto them. He delivered them out of the "terrible pit and the mire, and set their feet upon a rock."

Behold then, the secret source of the wonderful change wrought in them—this grand translation from earth to heaven, from ruin to glory. The Son of God came down from heaven "to seek and to save those that were lost." They heard of his love; they needed his power; they approached him in faith; they received him as their Lord; and he acknowledged them as his disciples, interceded for them, delivered them out of their distress, and raised them to eternal glory. And is his arm shortened, that it cannot save? Is his ear heavy, that it cannot hear? Has he intermitted his gracious work? Are there no trophies of his power to be suspended in the kingdom of glory? Yes; he is " the same, yesterday, to-day, and for ever." Approach him, then, with true faith and fervent prayer; " fight the good fight of faith," as they did, and you also shall receive the palm of victory. Seek for the sanctifying influence of the Spirit, and you shall receive the robe of *righteousness granted to them.*

VENN.

Scriptural Selections.

AFTER this I beheld, and, lo, a great multitude, which no man could number, of all nations, and kindreds, and people, and tongues, stood before the throne, and before the Lamb, clothed with white robes, and palms in their hands;

And cried with a loud voice, saying, Salvation to our God which sitteth upon the throne, and unto the Lamb.

And all the angels stood round about the throne, and about the elders and the four beasts, and fell before the throne on their faces, and worshipped God,

Saying, Amen: Blessing, and glory, and wisdom, and thanksgiving, and honour, and power, and might, be unto our God for ever and ever. Amen.

And one of the elders answered saying unto me, What are these which are arrayed in white robes? and whence came they?

And I said unto him, Sir, thou knowest. And he said to me, These are they which came out of great tribulation, and have washed their robes, and made them white in the blood of the Lamb.

Therefore are they before the throne of God, and serve him day and night in his temple: and he that sitteth on the throne shall dwell among them.

They shall hunger no more, neither thirst any more; neither shall the sun light on them, nor any heat.

For the Lamb which is in the midst of the throne, shall feed them, and shall lead them unto living fountains of waters: and God shall wipe away all tears from their eyes.—*Rev.* vii. 9–17.

And God shall wipe away all tears from their eyes; and there shall be no more death, neither sorrow, nor crying, neither shall there be any more pain: for the former things are passed away.—*Rev.* xxi. 4.

WHO are these in bright array?
   This innumerable throng,
Round the altar, night and day
   Tuning their triumphant song?
Worthy is the Lamb once slain,
   Blessing, honour, glory, power,
Wisdom, riches, to obtain;
   New dominion every hour.

These through fiery trials trod;
   These from great affliction came;
Now before the throne of God,
   Sealed with his eternal Name:
Clad in raiment pure and white,
   Victor palms in every hand,
Through their great Redeemer's might
   More than conquerors they stand.

Hunger, thirst, disease unknown,
   On immortal fruits they feed;
Then the Lamb amidst the throne
   Shall to living fountains lead;
Joy and gladness banish sighs;
   Perfect love dispels their fears
And, for ever from their eyes
   God shall wipe away their tears.

Leaning on the Beloved.

LEANING ON THE BELOVED.

I.

CHRIST A MAN OF SORROWS.

" He is despised and rejected of men; a man of sorrows, and acquainted with grief: and we hid as it were our faces from him; he was despised, and we esteemed him not. Surely he hath borne our griefs, and carried our sorrows. Yet we did esteem him stricken, smitten of God, and afflicted. But he was wounded for our transgressions, he was bruised for our iniquities; the chastisement of our peace was upon him, and with his stripes we are healed. All we like sheep have gone astray; we have turned every one to his own way; and the Lord hath laid on him the iniquity of us all. He was oppressed, and he was afflicted, yet he opened not his mouth; he is brought as a Lamb to the slaughter; and as a sheep before her shearers is dumb, so he opened not his mouth.—ISAIAH, LIII. 3–7.

IT has been supposed by many, that the sufferings of our Lord were rather apparent than real; or at least that his abundant consolations, and his knowledge of the happy consequences which would result from his death, rendered his sorrows comparatively light, and almost converted them to joys. But never was supposition more erroneous. Jesus Christ was as truly a man as either of us, and, as man, he was as really susceptible of grief, as keenly alive to pain and reproach, and as much averse from shame and suffering, as any of the descendants of Adam. As to divine consolations and supports, they were at all times bestowed on him in a very sparing manner, and in the season of his greatest extremity entirely withheld; and though a knowledge of the happy consequences which would result from his sufferings, rendered

(225)

him willing to endure them, it did not, in the smallest
degree, take off their edge, or render him insensible to
pain. No, his sufferings, instead of being less, were in
comparably greater than they appeared to be. No finite
mind can conceive of their extent; nor was any of the
human race ever so well entitled to the appellation of
the *Man of Sorrows*, as the man Christ Jesus. His sufferings began with his birth, and ended but with his life.

In the first place, it must have been extremely painful
to such a person as Christ, to live in a world like this. He
was perfectly holy, harmless, and undefiled. Of course,
he could not look on sin, but with the deepest abhorrence.
It is that abominable thing which his soul hates. Yet
during the whole period of his residence on earth, he was
continually surrounded by it, and his feelings were every
moment tortured with the hateful sight of human depra-
vity. How much sorrow the sight occasioned him, we may
in some measure learn from the bitter complaints which
similar causes extorted from David, Jeremiah, and other
ancient saints. They described, in the most striking
and pathetic language, the sufferings which they experienced from the prevalency of wickedness around them,
and often wished for death to relieve them from their
sufferings. But the sufferings of Christ from this cause
were incomparably greater than theirs. He was far more
holy than they, his hatred of sin incomparably more intense, and the sight of it proportionably more painful.
In consequence of his power of searching the heart, he saw
unspeakably more sin in the world, than any mere man
could discover. We can discover sin only when it displays

itself in words and actions. But he saw all the hidden wickedness of the heart, the depths of that fountain of iniquity, from which all the bitter streams of vice and misery flow. Every man that approached him was transparent to his eye. In his best friends he saw more sin than we can discover in the most abandoned reprobates. He saw also, in a far clearer light than we can do, the dreadful consequences of sin, the interminable miseries to which it is conducting the sinner; and his feelings of compassion were not blunted by that selfish insensibility which enables us to bear with composure the sight of human distress. On the contrary, he was all sympathy, compassion, and love. He loved others as himself, and therefore felt for the sufferings of others as for his own. If Paul could say, Who is weak, and I am not weak? who is offended, and I burn not? much more might Christ. In this, as well as in a still more important sense, he took upon himself our griefs, and bore our sorrows. As he died for all, so he felt and wept for the sufferings of all. The temporal and eternal calamities of the whole human race, and of every individual among them, all seemed to be collected and laid upon him. He saw at one view the whole mighty aggregate of human guilt and human wretchedness; and his boundless benevolence and compassion made it by sympathy all his own. It has been said by philosophers, that if any man could see all the misery which is daily felt in the world, he would never smile again. We need not wonder then that Christ,

who saw and felt it all, never smiled, though he often
wept. We may add, that the perfect contrast between
the heavens which he had left, and the world into which
he came, rendered a residence in the latter peculiarly
painful to his feelings. In heaven he had seen nothing
but holiness and happiness and love. In this world, on
the contrary, he saw little but wickedness and hatred
and misery, in ten thousand forms. In heaven he was
crowned with glory and honour and majesty, and surrounded by throngs of admiring, adoring angels. On
earth, he found himself plunged in poverty, wretchedness, and contempt, and surrounded by malignant,
implacable enemies. My friends, think of a prince,
educated with care and tenderness in his father's court,
where he heard nothing but sounds of pleasure and
praise, and saw nothing but scenes of honour and
magnificence, sent unattended to labour as a slave in a
rebellious province, where himself and his father were
hated and despised; think of a person of the most
delicate and refined taste, going from the bosom of his
family and the magnificent abodes of a polished city, to
spend his life in the filthy huts of the most degraded
and barbarous savages, and compelled daily to witness
the disgusting scenes of cruelty and brutality which are
there exhibited; think of a man endowed with the
tenderest sensibility, compelled to live on a field of
battle, among the corpses of the dead and the groans
of the dying, or shut up for years in a madhouse with
wretched maniacs, where nothing was to be heard but

the burst of infuriated passions, the wild laugh of
madness, and the shrieks and ravings of despair.
Think of these instances, and you will have some conception, though but a faint one, of the scenes which
this world presented to our Saviour, of the contrast
between it and the heaven he left, of the sorrows which
embittered every moment of his earthly existence, and
of the love which induced him voluntarily to submit to
such sorrows.

Another circumstance which contributed to render
our Saviour a man of sorrows, and his life a life of
grief, was the reception he met with from those whom
he came to save. Had they received him with that
gratitude and respect which he deserved, and permitted
him to rescue them from their miseries, it would have
been some alleviation of his sorrows. But even this
alleviation was in a great measure denied him. Some
few, indeed, received him with affection and respect,
though even they often grieved him by their unkind-
ness and unbelief; but by far the greater part of his
countrymen he was treated with the utmost cruelty and
contempt. Many of them would not allow him even to
remove their bodily diseases, and still greater numbers
were unwilling that he should save them from their
sins. Now to a noble, ingenuous mind, nothing is so
cutting, so torturing as such conduct. To see himself
despised, slandered, and persecuted with implacable
malice, by the very beings whom he was labouring to
save; to see all his endeavours to save them, frustrated

by their own incorrigible folly and wickedness; to see
them by rejecting him filling up to the brim their cup
of criminality and wrath, and sinking into eternal per-
dition within reach of his vainly-offered hand,—to see
this, must have been distressing indeed. Yet this
Christ saw. Thus he endured the contradiction of
sinners against himself; and how deeply it affected him,
we may infer from the fact, that though his own sufferings never wrung from him a tear, he once and again
wept in the bitterness of his soul over rebellious Jerusalem, exclaiming, O that thou hadst known, even thou
at least in this thy day, the things that belong to thy
peace; but now they are hid from thine eyes!

Another circumstance that threw a shade of gloom
and melancholy over our Saviour's life, was his clear
view, and constant anticipation of the dreadful agonies
in which it was to terminate. He was not ignorant, as
we happily are, of the miseries which were before him.
He could not hope, as we do, when wretched to-day, to
be happier to-morrow. Every night, when he lay down
to rest, the scourge, the crown of thorns, and the cross,
were present to his mind; and on these dreadful objects
he every morning opened his eyes, and every morning
saw them nearer than before. Every day was to him
like the day of his death, of such a death too, as no one
ever suffered before or since. How deeply the prospect
affected him, is evident from his own language: I have
a baptism to be baptized with, and how am I straitened
till it be accomplished!

Such are the circumstances which prove that our Saviour was, during life, a man of sorrows. Of the sorrows of his death we shall say nothing. The bitter agonies of that never-to-be-forgotten hour, the torturing scourge, the lacerating nails, and the racking cross, we shall pass in silence. Nor shall we now bring into view the tenfold horrors which overwhelmed his soul, rendering it exceedingly sorrowful, even unto death. These we have often attempted to describe to you, though here description must always fail. Enough has been said to show the justice of that exclamation which the Prophet utters in the person of Christ: " Behold and see, all ye that pass by, if there be any sorrow like my sorrow. Reproach hath broken my heart, and I am full of heaviness. I looked for some to pity, but there was none ; for comforters, but I found none."

What was our Saviour's conduct under the pressure of these sorrows ? " He was oppressed and afflicted, yet he opened not his mouth. He was brought as a lamb to the slaughter, and as a sheep before her shearers is dumb, so he opened not his mouth." Never was language more descriptive of the most perfect meekness and patience ; never was prediction more fully justified by the event than in the case before us. Christ was indeed led as a lamb to the slaughter. Silent, meek, and unrepining, he stood before his butchers, at once innocent and patient as a lamb. No murmurs, no complaints, no angry recriminations escaped from his lips. If they were opened, it was but

to express the most perfect submission to his Father's
will, and to breathe out prayers for his murderers.
Yes, even at that dreadful moment, when they were
nailing him to the cross, when nature, whose voice will
at such a time be heard, was shuddering and convulsed
in the prospect of a speedy and violent death; when his
soul was tortured by the assaults of malignant fiends,
and his Father's face hidden from his view; even then
he possessed his soul in patience to such a degree,
as to be able to pray for his murderers. We
must attempt to bring the scene more fully to your
view. Come with us, a moment, to Calvary. See the
meek sufferer, standing with hands fast bound in the
midst of his enemies; sinking under the weight of his
cross, and lacerated in every part by the thorny rods
with which he had been scourged. See the savage,
ferocious soldiers seizing with rude violence, his sacred
body, forcing it down upon the cross, wresting and
extending his limbs, and with remorseless cruelty
forcing through his hands and feet the ragged spikes
which were to fasten him on it. See the Jewish priests
and rulers watching with looks of malicious pleasure
the horrid scene, and attempting to increase his sufferings by scoffs and blasphemies. Now contemplate
attentively the countenance of the wonderful Sufferer,
which seems like heaven opening in the midst of hell,
and tell me what it expressed. You see it indeed full
of anguish, but it expresses nothing like impatience,
resentment, or revenge. On the contrary, it beams

with pity, benevolence, and forgiveness. It perfectly corresponds with the prayer, which, raising his mild, imploring eye to heaven, he pours forth to God: "Father, forgive them, for they know not what they do!" Christian, look at your Master, and learn how to suffer. Sinner, look at your Saviour, and learn to admire, to imitate, and to forgive. But why, it may be naturally asked, why is this patient innocent sufferer thus afflicted? Why, in his life, in his death, is he thus emphatically a man of sorrows? To this question our text returns an answer, and an answer which ought to sink deep into our hearts; for in it we are all most deeply interested: "He was wounded for our transgressions, he was bruised for our iniquities; the chastisement of our peace was upon him; by his stripes we are healed. We all like sheep have gone astray; we have turned every one to his own way, and the Lord hath laid on him the iniquity of us all." Here, we see the true cause of our Saviour's unparalleled sufferings. He was cut off, says the Prophet, but not for himself. He knew no sin, but he was made sin, made a curse for us. We have all strayed from the path of duty. Yes, you and I, and all our race, have forsaken the God that made us, and chosen the path that leads to hell. God's violated law condemned us to die. Justice demanded the execution of the sentence. There was apparently no remedy. It is true that God, as our Creator and Father, was sufficiently inclined to spare us; but truth and justice for-

30

bade him to do it, unless a suitable atonement could be found. There was but one individual in the universe who could make such an atonement, and that being, prompted by infinite compassion, offered himself for this purpose. The Father, with equal love, accepted the offer. To carry it into effect, the Son assumed our nature, and appeared on earth; and the bitter cup, which the divine law condemned us to drink, was put into his hand, and he drank it to the last drop. We were condemned to live a life of sorrow and pain, and therefore he lived such a life. We were condemned to shame and everlasting contempt; and therefore he hid not his face from shame and spitting. We were condemned to die under the curse; and therefore he died the accursed death of the cross: We were condemned to lose the favour and endure the wrath of God; and therefore Christ was forsaken by his Father in the agonies of death. We were condemned to perish without mercy; and therefore Christ had no mercy, no pity shown him in his last moments. We were condemned to remain under the power of death, till by satisfying divine justice we could restore ourselves to life; and therefore Christ remained in the grave till he had made full satisfaction, and then resumed the life he had laid down. Thus he bore our sins, or, what is the same, the punishment of our sins in his own body on the tree, that we being dead unto sin, might live unto God.

What was the manner in which Christ was treated, when he thus came as a man of sorrows to atone for our sins? He is despised and rejected of men. We hid as it were our faces from him; he was despised, and we esteemed him not. How literally this prediction was fulfilled, we have already seen. Yet who but an inspired prophet would have predicted that such would be the reception of such a person, coming from heaven on such a design? We should naturally expect that he would be received with the most lively emotions and demonstrations of grateful joy, by the beings whom he came to save. Even after we were told that, instead of thus receiving, they rejected and condemned him, we should have expected that when they saw his lamb-like patience and meekness, and heard him praying for his murderers, they would have relented and spared him. And when this could not prevail, we should have hoped that the miracles which attended his crucifixion, and especially his resurrection from the dead, would convince them of their error, and cause them to relent. But none of these things, nor all of them united, could conquer the inveterate malice of his enemies. Living and dying, rising and reigning, he was still despised and rejected of men. Neither his miracles, nor his sorrows, nor his meekness, nor his patience, could shield him from hatred and contempt. But what was his crime? What had he done? I answer, he was good; he dared to speak the truth; he reproved men for their sins, he testified to the world that its deeds were evil; above all, he bore the image of God, of that God whom sinners hate. These were crimes never to be forgiven; crimes, for which nothing but his blood could atone; crimes, which in their view rendered him unworthy of that commiseration which men usually feel for the vilest malefactors when in the agonies of death. Nor were those who treated him in this manner, worse than the rest of mankind. As in water face answereth to face, so the heart of man to man. The truth of this assertion is abundantly proved by the manner in which all succeeding generations have treated Christ. He has always been despised and rejected of men; and he is so still. It is true, he has long since ascended to heaven, and therefore cannot be the immediate object of their attacks. But his gospel and his servants are still in the world; and the manner in which they are treated, is sufficient evidence, that the feelings of the natural heart toward Christ are not materially different from those of the Jews. Every man, who voluntarily neglects to confess Christ before men, and to commemorate his dying love, must say, either that he does not choose to do it, or that he is not prepared to do it. Now if a man says, I do not choose to confess Christ, he certainly rejects him. If he does not choose to remember Christ, he certainly chooses to forget him. If he is unwilling to bind himself to live such a life as a profession of religion requires, he certainly loves sin better than he does his Saviour. On the other hand, if any one shall say, I wish to come to the table of Christ, but am not prepared, he expressly avows himself an enemy of Christ, for all his friends are fully prepared to approach his table; and those who are not his friends are his enemies; for Christ has said, "He that is not with me is against me." For a man to say, I am not prepared to come to Christ's table, is the same as to say, I do not repent of sin, I do not believe in or love Christ; I am not willing to live a prayerful, watchful, religious life. Nor are those who come to Christ's table without obeying his commands, less guilty of rejecting Christ. We find in the parable of the marriage, that he who came in without a wedding garment was excluded, as well as those who refused to come. To sum up all in a word, it is certain that all who do not receive the instructions of Christ with the temper of a little child, reject him, as a prophet. All who do not trust in his merits alone for salvation reject him as a Saviour; and all who do not habitually and sincerely obey his commands, reject him as a king. This being the case, the conduct of multitudes among us fully justifies us in asserting, that Christ is still despised and rejected of men.

Was Christ a man of sorrows and acquainted with grief? Then we need not be surprised or offended, if we are often called to drink of the cup of sorrows; if we find the world a vale of tears. This is one of the ways in which we must be conformed to our glorious Head. Indeed, his example has sanctified grief, and almost made it pleasant to mourn. One would think, that Christians could scarcely wish to go rejoicing through a world which their Master passed through mourning. The path in which we follow him is bedewed with his tears and stained with his blood. It is true, that from the ground thus watered and fertilized many rich flowers and fruits of paradise spring up to refresh us, in which we may and ought to rejoice. But still our joy should be softened and sanctified by godly sorrow. When we are partaking of the banquet which his love has spread for us, we should never forget how dearly it was purchased.

> "There's not a gift his hand bestows,
> But cost his heart a groan."

The joy, the honour, the glory through eternity shall be ours; but the sorrows, the sufferings, the agonies which purchased them were all his own.

Was Christ wounded for our transgressions; were the iniquities of all his people laid upon him; then, surely, our iniquities shall never be laid upon us. He has borne and carried them away. He was made sin for us, that we might be made the righteousness of God in him. Away then with all guilty unbelieving fears. Whatever your sorrows or trials may be, he knows by experience how to sympathize with you. Has your Heavenly Father forsaken you, so that you walk in darkness and see no light? He well remembers what he felt, when he cried, "My God, my God, why hast thou forsaken me?" Has Satan wounded you with his fiery darts? He remembers how sorely his own heart was bruised when he wrestled with principalities and powers, and crushed the head of the prince of darkness. Are you pressed down with a complication of sorrows, so as to despair even of life? The soul of Christ was once exceeding sorrowful, even unto death. Are you mourning for the danger of unbelieving friends? Christ's own brethren did not believe in him. Does the world persecute and despise you, or are your enemies those of your own household? Christ was despised and rejected of men, and his own relations stigmatized him as a madman. Are you suffering under slanderous and unjust accusations? Christ was called a man gluttonous, and a wine-bibber, a friend of publicans and sinners. Are you struggling with the evils of poverty? Jesus had not where to lay his head. Do Christian friends forsake or treat you unkindly? Christ was denied and forsaken by his own disciples. Are you distressed with fears of death? Christ has entered the dark valley that he might destroy death. O, then, banish all your fears. Look at your merciful High Priest who is passed unto the heavens, and triumphantly exclaim with the apostle, Who shall separate us from the love of Christ?

PAYSON

Scriptural Selections.

Who hath believed our report? and to whom is the arm of the Lord revealed?

For he shall grow up before him as a tender plant and as a root out of a dry ground: he hath no form nor comeliness; and when we shall see him, there is no beauty that we should desire him.

He is despised and rejected of men; a man of sorrows, and acquainted with grief; and we hid as it were our faces from him: he was despised, and we esteemed him not.

Surely he hath borne our griefs, and carried our sorrows; yet we did esteem him stricken, smitten of God, and afflicted.

But he was wounded for our transgressions, he was bruised for our iniquities: the chastisement of our peace was upon him; and with his stripes we are healed.

All we, like sheep, have gone astray; we have turned every one to his own way; and the Lord hath laid on him the iniquity of us all.

He was oppressed, and he was afflicted; yet he opened not his mouth; he is brought as a lamb to the slaughter, and as a sheep before her shearers is dumb, so he opened not his mouth.

He was taken from prison and from judgment: and who shall declare his generation? for he was cut off out of the land of the living; for the transgression of my people was he stricken.

And he made his grave with the wicked, and with the rich in his death; because he had done no violence, neither was any deceit in his mouth.

Yet it pleased the Lord to bruise him; he hath put him to grief: when thou shalt make his soul an offering for sin, he shall see his seed, he shall prolong his days, and the pleasure of the Lord shall prosper in his hand.

He shall see of the travail of his soul, and shall be satisfied: by his knowledge shall my righteous servant justify many: for he shall bear their iniquities.—*Isaiah* liii. 1–11.

Looking unto Jesus.

Thou who didst stoop below,
To drain the cups of woe,
Wearing the form of frail mortality,—
Thy blessed labours done,
Thy crown of victory won,
Hast passed from earth—passed to thy home on high.

Man may no longer trace,
In thy celestial face,
The image of the bright, the viewless One;
Nor may thy servants hear,
Save with faith's raptured ear,
Thy voice of tenderness, God's holy Son!

Our eyes behold thee not;
Yet hast thou not forgot,
Those who have placed their hope, their trust in thee;
Before thy Father's face
Thou hast prepared a place,
That where thou art, there they may also be.

It was no path of flowers,
Through this dark world of ours,
Beloved of the Father, thou didst tread;
And shall we in dismay
Shrink from the narrow way,
When clouds and darkness are around it spread?

O, thou, who art our life,
Be with us through the strife!
Was not thy head by earth's fierce tempests bowed?
Raise thou our eyes above,
To see a Father's love
Beam, like the bow of promise, through the cloud.

Even through the awful gloom
Which hovers o'er the tomb,
That light of love our guiding star shall be;
Our spirits shall not dread
The shadowy way to tread,
Friend, Guardian, Saviour, which doth lead to thee.

C Schuessle

J. C. McRae

"She goeth unto the grave to weep there"

John XI. 31

II.

CHRIST AT BETHANY.

" Then said Martha unto Jesus, Lord, if thou hadst been here, my brother had not died. . .
Then when Mary was come where Jesus was, and saw him, she fell down at his feet, saying unto him
*Lord, if thou hadst been here, my brother had not died."—*JOHN, XI. 21, 32.

IT is better," says the wise man, "to go to the house of mourning than to go to the house of feasting: for that is the end of all men; and the living will lay it to his heart. Sorrow is better than laughter: for by the sadness of the countenance the heart is made better. The heart of the wise is in the house of mourning: but the heart of fools is in the house of mirth." If this be true generally of the effect which should be produced by familiarizing the heart with the devout contemplation of death, and of the grief which death occasions, it must be especially true when we have Jesus as our companion.

It was our Lord's custom, in his visits to Jerusalem, to retire in the evenings, after the toils and trials of his daily ministry in the temple, to the quiet village of Bethany, and the peaceful abode of Lazarus, that he might there repose amid the holy endearments of a congenial family circle. That house is now the house of mourning. Let us visit it in the company of Jesus, and observe how he is received there, and how his presence cheers the gloom.

The sisters, Martha and Mary, greet him with the same pathetic salutation, "Lord, if thou hadst been here, my brother had not died;" and this might seem to indicate an entire similarity in their sorrow. But if we look a little closer, we see a striking difference of demeanour, corresponding to the marked difference of their characters generally. And this difference is marked in our Lord's different treatment of them. In every view it is an interesting study, from which we may learn, in the first place, How much sameness there is in grief; secondly, How much variety; and, lastly, How much compass there is in the consolation of Christ, as capable of being adapted to all varieties of grief—to grief of every mould and of every mood. We speak chiefly throughout of the grief of true Christians; for we think we are warranted in assuming that, notwithstanding their great contrast in respect of natural temperament, the two sisters were partakers of the same grace.

At present, we advert to the similarity of their common sorrow—the sameness of their grief. For it is remarkable, that two persons so different in their turn of mind, as we shall afterwards see that these sisters were—so apt to view things in different lights, and to be affected by them with different feelings—should both utter the same words on first meeting the Lord Jesus— "Lord, if thou hadst been here, my brother had not died." It shows how natural such a reflection is in such a season—how entirely the heart, when deeply moved, is the same in all—and how much all grief is alike.

The sisters, however otherwise dissimilar, were united
in their fond affection for their departed brother, as well
as in their grateful reliance on that divine friend "who
loved Martha, and her sister, and Lazarus." They had
sat and watched together beside their brother's bed of
sickness. They joined together in sending unto Jesus,
saying, "Lord, behold, he whom thou lovest is sick."
In their distress they both thought of the same remedy,
and applied to the same physician. It was a joint petition that they despatched, and they did not doubt that
it would prevail. Together they waited anxiously for
his coming. They reckoned the very earliest moment
when he could arrive; and as they looked on their brother's languid eye, and saw him sinking every hour and
wasting away, ah! they thought, how soon their benefactor might appear, and all might yet be well. But
moments and hours rolled on, and no Saviour came.
Wearisome days and nights were appointed to them.
Often did they look out and listen; often did they fancy
that they heard the expected sound, and the well-known
accents of kindness seemed to fall upon their ears. But
still he came not. Ah! what were their anxious thoughts,
their earnest communings, their fond prayers, that life
might be prolonged at least for a little longer, to give
one other chance, one other opportunity, for the interposition of Him who was mighty to save even from the
gates of death; and how were their own hearts sickened,
as they whispered to the sick man a faint hope, to which
they could scarcely themselves any longer cling. Still

the time rolls slowly on. The last ray of expectation is extinguished; the dreaded hour is come; it is over; their brother has fallen asleep; Lazarus is dead.

And now four days are past and gone since he has been laid in the silent tomb. The first violence of grief is giving place to the more calm, but far more bitter pain of a desolate and dreary sadness;—the prolonged sense of bereavement which recollection brings along with it, and which everything around serves to aggravate and embitter. The house of mourning, after the usual temporary excitement, is still,—it is the melancholy stillness of the calm, darkly brooding over the wrecks of the recent storm,—and amid the real kindness of sympathizing friends, and the formal attentions of officious strangers, the sisters, as each familiar object recalls the past, are soothing, or suppressing, as best they may, those bitter feelings which their own hearts alone can know—when suddenly they are told that Jesus is at hand.

He is come at last, but he is come too late. His having come at all, however, is a comfort. He is welcome as their own and their brother's friend; he is welcome as their Lord. They never doubt his friendship; they question not his willingness, or his power, to do them good. But still, as they meet him, they cannot but look back on the few days that are gone; and as all their anxieties and alarms, their longing hopes and cruel disappointments, rush again upon their minds, they are constrained to give utterance to the crowded emotions of their hearts in the irrepressible exclamation—"Lord, if thou hadst been here, my brother had not died."

It is the voice of nature that speaks in these words—the voice of our common nature mingling its vain regrets with the resignation of sincere and simple faith.

There is here, first, the feeling that the event might have been otherwise;—"If thou hadst been here, my brother had not died." We know not what has detained thee. Some call of duty may have prevented thee from coming; or, perhaps, our message did not reach thee in time; or it may have been some merely casual circumstance that hindered thee. If this sickness had happened but a little sooner, when thou wast in Jerusalem at the feast;—or if we had taken alarm early enough, so as to send for thee before our brother was so ill;—or if our messenger had been more expeditious, and had used more despatch;—or if we had but been able to lengthen out, by our care, our brother's sickness for a single week;—had we not been so unfortunate in the occurrence of this evil just when it did occur; or had we, when it occurred, used more diligence, and taken better precautions;—then thou mightst have been here, and "if thou hadst been here, our brother had not died."

Is it not thus that the heart speaks under every trying dispensation? Is it not thus that an excited imagination whispers to the forlorn soul? Who has ever met with any affliction—who has ever lost any beloved brother or dear friend,—without cherishing some such reflection as this? If such or such a measure had been

adopted ; if such or such an accident had not happened ;
if it had not been for this unaccountable oversight, or
that unforeseen and unavoidable mischance ; so grievous
a calamity would not have befallen me ;—my brother
would not have died.

Alas ! and is not the reflection, however natural, a
sinful and sad delusion,—proceeding upon a very limited
view of the power and the providence of God our Saviour ?
How did these sisters know that, if Jesus had been there,
their brother would not have died ? How could they
tell whether he might not have ends to serve, which
would have required that, even though he had been
there, he must have permitted him to die ? And were
they not aware that, though he was not there, yet, if
he had so chosen and so ordered it, their brother would
not have died ? Had they not heard of his being able,
at the distance of many a long mile, to effect an immediate and complete cure ? Did they not believe that he
had but to speak, and it would be done ; he had but to
say the word, and, however far off he was, his friend
and their brother would be healed ? Ah ! they had forgotten who it was to whom they made this most touching and pathetic appeal ; that he was one who, though
not actually present, could have restored their brother
if it had been consistent with his wise and holy will ;
and who, even if he had been present, might have seen
fit, for the best reasons, to suffer him to die.

And are not these the very truths concerning him
which you in your distress are tempted to forget, when

you dwell so much on secondary circumstances and causes, instead of at once and immediately recognising his will as supreme? You are overtaken by misfortune; you are overwhelmed in the depths of sorrow. You ascribe your suffering to what seems to be its direct occasion;—whether it be your own neglect of some precaution which you might have taken, had you thought of it in time; or the fault of others, with whose skill or diligence your dearest hopes were inseparably connected; or something perhaps, in the course of events, over which neither you nor they could have any control. You fix upon the very date, the very scene, when and where your brother's doom seems to have been sealed; and you think that, if you had but suspected what was about to be the issue, or if the help which you now see would have been available had then been within your reach; if you had been warned in time, or had taken the warning, or had been able to employ the right means of escape,—you might not now have been left disconsolate; your beloved one might still have been spared to cheer you with his smiles, and share with you all your cares;—your brother might not have died.

So you are apt to think and feel. But however natural the thought—is it not in reality the very folly of unbelief—the dream of a soul forgetting that the Lord reigneth? What! is it come to this, that you conceive of Him as limited by events which he himself ordains—as the slave of his own laws? You think that if a certain obstacle had not come in to prevent relief, the calamity you bewail might not have happened. But, notwithstanding that obstacle, might he not, if he had seen fit, have found means to avert the calamity? And are you sure that, even if the obstacle had been removed, he might not have seen fit still to let the calamity come? "If thou hadst been here," say the mourning sisters, "our brother had not died." Nay, he might have answered, I could have been here if it had seemed good to me; and, though I was not here, I might have kept your brother alive; and, though I had been here, I might have allowed him to die.

Look, ye afflicted ones, beyond second causes, to Him who is the first cause of all things! Believe, and be sure that the circumstances which you regret as the occasion of your misfortune, are but the appointed means of bringing about what he determines. If evil come upon you, if your brother die, it is not because this or that accident prevented relief; it is not because He was not with you in sufficient time, but because it was his will. Be still, and know that he is God!

But farther, secondly, there may be in this address of the sisters somewhat of the feeling, that the event not only might, but should have been otherwise. There is at least an intimation of their having expected that the event would have been otherwise. "If thou hadst been here, our brother had not died." And why wert thou not here? We sent to thee—we sent a special message—a special prayer—and surely thou mightest have been persuaded to come. Ah! why didst thou linger for two whole days after tidings of our threatened loss reached thee? Why didst thou not make haste to help us? We could not believe that thou wouldst have treated us thus. Thou wast not unmindful of us before. Thou didst regard us as friends. Thou didst bless our house with thy presence; making it thy resting-place, thy home. Thou didst choose us before thine own kinsmen. Thou didst select our brother as the object of thine especial affection. And we thought it would have been enough to touch thy heart simply to send to thee, saying, "He whom thou lovest is sick,"—that thou hadst but to hear of his illness to rush at once to his relief. True, we had no right to dictate to thee, and now we have no right to complain. But we cannot help feeling that if thou hadst been here our brother had not died; and that surely thou mightest have been here. It was not so very great a favour that was asked of thee; and was he not worthy for whom thou shouldst do this? He loved thee—he trusted in thee; and thou mightest have come, if not to preserve his life, at least to soothe and satisfy his dying hours. He looked for thee, and thou didst not appear. To the very last he waited for thee, and thou didst hide thyself. He missed thee, and he was not comforted.

Such are the instinctive complaints of nature in a season of sore trial, of bitter bereavement. Thus does the wounded soul rise against the stroke that pierces it, and turn round upon the hand that smites it. It is very hard for flesh and blood to believe, in regard to any crushing load of woe, that it is God who directly and immediately ordains it. It is far harder to believe, that in ordaining it he does not do wrong. Simply to be still, and know that he is God, is no easy exercise of resignation. To be sure that he doeth right, that he doeth well, is even more difficult still. You fancy that, if he had really been here, it would have happened otherwise—your brother would not have died. And you feel as if you had had some right to expect that he should have been here—that it should have happened otherwise—that your brother should not have died. And you can give, perhaps, many reasons. You can point out many ends which might have been served had your brother been spared—how faithful and successful he might have been—how noble a course he might have run. He was just prepared for entering into active life; he was just newly fitted for the service of God in the world; and it does seem strange and unaccountable, that at the very time when his life seemed to have become most valuable—when his character was ripening for increased usefulness—and when the mere word of the great Physician would have brought him back from the gates of death, he should yet have been suffered to die.

Ah! but remember that the Lord may have many purposes in view with which you may be unacquainted, which indeed you could not as yet comprehend. Only wait patiently for a little, and you will see that "this sickness is not" really "unto death, but for the glory

of God, that the Son of God may be glorified thereby"
(ver. 4). Would that thou hadst been here!—thou
surely mightest have been here!—is the natural language of the mourner to his Lord. Nay, says the Lord
himself to his own disciples, "I am glad for your sakes
that I was not there, to the intent ye may believe" (ver.
15). A hard saying this,—who can always hear it?
But consider who it is that speaks. It is your friend,
your Saviour. He might have been here, and might
have taken care that your brother should not die; and
may you not be sure that, if it had been for his glory,
and for your good, he would have been here, and would
have taken care that your brother should not die? He
might have ordered this matter otherwise, you say; and
you almost think that he ought to have ordered it otherwise. But may you not believe that, had it been right
and good, he would have done so; and that, if he has
not, it must be for the best of reasons? What these
may be you cannot tell. He may have need of your
brother's services elsewhere. He may intend to make
his death the occasion of showing forth his glory, and
blessing your soul. Only be patient, and hope unto
the end. What he doeth you may not know now, but
you shall know hereafter. Meantime, as you are tempted
to fancy that he might have interfered—nay, that he
should have interfered—to prevent the calamity under
which you suffer, may not that very feeling, on second
thoughts, suggest the conviction, that if he has not so
interfered, it must be because he intends to make to

you some gracious discovery of himself, and to confer upon you some special benefit? Be not hasty, then, to judge, but rest in the assurance that all things shall work together for good to them that love God. And though he may seem to stand aloof when you would most desire, and most need, his interposition; yet when he does come, be sure that you receive him gladly—as did the sorrowing sisters.

Happy will it be for you who mourn, if in like circumstances you are enabled to feel as these sisters felt, and to meet your Saviour's gracious advances as they did. In the hour of blighted prospects and disappointed hopes, when the evil which you deprecated has befallen you, you may think that consolation comes too late. Like Rachel, you may weep, and refuse to be comforted; like Jonah, when your gourd withers, you may almost be tempted to say that you do well to be angry. You may turn away when your Saviour draws near; you may sit disconsolate when he calls. If he had come for the purpose of averting the calamity;—if he had been here sooner, and had interposed his power to help;—it had been well, for then my brother had not died. But the calamity has overtaken me—my brother is dead; and what avails it that He is here now?

Beware of all such impatience, such natural irritability of grief. Reject not the Saviour's visit of sympathy now, because he did not come to you exactly as you in your ignorance would have had him to come, and do for you exactly what you would have had him to do.

It is enough that He is with you now, to speak comfortably to you—to bind up your broken heart—to fill the aching void in your affections, and be to you instead of all that you have lost.   True, if he had been here before, your brother might not have died, and your brother, alas! is dead.   But He is here now;—he who is better than a thousand brothers—He who hath the words of eternal life; who can speak a word in season to the weary soul, and, when flesh and heart faint, will be the strength of your heart and your portion for ever.

Such might be the feelings common to the two sisters —such are the feelings of nature mingled with grace, common to all sanctified grief—as indicated in the affecting address, "Lord, if thou hadst been here, my brother had not died."

Thus far, we trace in their conduct the working of a common grief.

But the sisters differed in their sorrow, as they did generally in the leading features of their characters, and their manner of thinking and acting in the ordinary affairs of life.   They were persons of very different tempers and dispositions; and this difference is uniformly and strikingly brought out in their treatment of the Lord Jesus.   Both looked up to him with reverence; both regarded him with full confidence and tender affection; and both were equally earnest and eager in testifying their esteem and love.   But each in doing so followed the bent of her own peculiar turn of mind.

Martha was distinguished by a busy, if not bustling activity in the despatch of affairs. She seems to have possessed great quickness, alertness, and energy, together with a certain practical ability and good sense, qualifying her both for taking a lead herself, and for giving an impulse to others; so that she was well fitted for going through with any work to be done, and always awake to the common calls and the common cares of the ordinary domestic routine of life. Mary, again, was evidently characterized by more depth of thought, more devotedness and sensibility of feeling. She was more easily engrossed in any affecting scene, or any spiritual subject; more alive at any time to one single profound impression, and apt to be abstracted from other concerns.

And as their ways of testifying regard to the Lord Jesus in prosperity differed, so also did their demeanour towards him in adversity, (John xi.)

Martha was evidently the first to receive information of his approach (ver. 20), either because to her, as the mistress of the house, the message was brought, or because, going about the house in her usual manner, she was in the way of hearing intelligence. She went out in haste, impatient to meet the Lord, and to render to him the offices of courtesy and respect. She is ready to be up and doing; she can turn at once from the conversation in which her friends from Jerusalem have been seeking to interest her, and disengage her mind for active exertion. Mary again is more absorbed in her grief; her sorrow is of a deeper and more desponding character; for while "Martha, as soon as she heard that Jesus was coming, went and met him, Mary sat still in the house" (ver. 20). This more absorbing intensity of Mary's grief, "the Jews who were with her in the house, and comforted her," seem to have remarked,—when they said of her, as they saw her at last rise hastily and go out, "She goeth unto the grave to weep there" (ver. 31). They had not said this of Martha when she went forth. She might be bent on other errands. Mary could go—only to weep. And at first her feelings so overpower her as to prevent her from going at all. The sudden arrival of her brother's friend is a shock too great for her; it tears the wound open afresh, and recalls bitter thoughts. She is plunged by the tidings into a fresh burst of sorrow, and can only "sit still in the house."

Thus, in different circumstances, the same natural temper may be either an advantage or a snare. Martha was never so much occupied in the emotion of one scene or subject, as not to be on the alert and ready for the call to another. This was a disadvantage to her when she was so hurried, that she could not withdraw herself from household cares to wait upon the word of life. It is an advantage to her now, that she can, with comparative ease, shake off her depression, and hasten of her own accord to meet her Lord. The same profound feeling, again, which made Mary the most attentive listener before, makes her the most helpless sufferer now; and disposes her almost to nurse her grief, until Jesus, her

33

best conforter, sends specially and emphatically to rouse her. Nor is it an insignificant circumstance, that it is the ever-active Martha who carries to her more downcast sister the awakening message;—so ought sisters in Christ to minister to one another, and so may the very difference of their characters make them mutually the more helpful;—"She went her way, and called Mary her sister secretly, saying, The Master is come, and calleth for thee" (ver. 28).

When the two sisters meet Jesus, the difference between them is equally characteristic.

Martha's grief is not so overwhelming as to prevent her utterance. She is calm, and cool, and collected enough to enter into argument. She can give expression to her convictions and her hopes. She can tell that her faith is not shaken even by so severe a disappointment. Having hinted what might seem to imply a doubt (ver. 21), she is in haste to explain her meaning, and to give assurance of her undiminished confidence;—"But I know, that even now, whatsoever thou wilt ask of God, God will give it thee" (ver. 22). And then, as the conversation goes on, she is sufficiently self-possessed to listen to a discourse on the resurrection, and reason with the Lord upon the subject;—as well as to make a formal declaration of her faith in him as the author of eternal life—"the Christ, the Son of God, which should come into the world" (ver. 23–27).

Not so her sister Mary. She indeed, when at last she is emboldened by her Master's kind message, goes forth to meet him, and her reverence, her devotion, her faith, are not less than those of Martha. But her heart is too full for many words. Her emotions, when she sees the Lord, she cannot utter. The passion of her soul she cannot command. She can but cast herself down, weeping, before him, and say, "Lord, if thou hadst been here, my brother had not died." She adds not a word more. She lies prostrate and silent at his feet (ver. 32).

Such are the different aspects which sorrow wears in minds of different stamps, and of different degrees of strength and of sensibility. But if it be the sorrow of a godly heart, it finds in Jesus one who can with the most perfect tenderness and truth adapt his sympathy and consolation to its peculiar character, whatever that may be. For it is most interesting and instructive to observe how the Lord's demeanour towards the two sisters, in his first meeting with them on this occasion, was exactly suited to their respective tempers, and their different kinds of grief.

Martha's distress was of such a nature, that it admitted of discussion and discourse. She was disposed to converse, and to find relief in conversation. Jesus accordingly adapted his treatment to her case. He spoke to her, and led her to speak to him. He talked with her on the subject most interesting and most seasonable—on the resurrection of the body and the life of the soul. Martha had declared her unshaken trust in him as still having power to obtain from God all that he might ask (ver. 22). And a wild idea, perhaps, crossed her mind, that it might not even yet be too late—that the evil might, even now, be repaired. If so, it was but the fancy of a moment—the dreamy notion that sometimes haunts the desolate breast, when it strives in vain to realize the loss which it has sustained. A single sad thought brings the recollection, to which afterwards, as we have seen, in her characteristic spirit of attention to such details, she adverts, that her brother has been now four days in the tomb, and corruption must be doing its horrid work upon his body. When, therefore, she hears her Lord's promise, "Thy brother shall rise again," she applies it to his share in the general resurrection: "I know that he shall rise again in the resurrection at the last day" (ver. 23, 24). Jesus is anxious to explain himself more fully. He speaks not of a resurrection merely, but of a resurrection in Himself;—not of life only, but of life in Himself. "I am the resurrection, and the life: he that believeth in me, though he were dead, yet shall he live: and whosoever liveth and believeth in me shall never die. Believest thou this?" (ver. 25, 26.)

For in fact this is the only true comfort in reference to the future state. He is the only true comforter who can speak, not merely of the immortality of the soul, and of the resurrection of the body, but of Himself as the life of the immortal soul and the quickener of the risen body;—the first-begotten from the dead—the first-fruits of them that sleep. Ah, what consolation is it

that thy brother lives and shall rise again—that he lives
now in the spirit, and that he shall rise again in the
body! The consolation I give is more effectual and
complete by far. He lives in ME. He shall rise with
ME. And what is the life which I continue, even after
death, to sustain? It is the very life which I impart
now—life before God; life in God; the life of a soul
pardoned, justified, reconciled to God, renewed after
the image of God, sanctified and made meet for the
fellowhip of God for ever. And what is the resurrection which I give? Is it not a resurrection to glory—
when these vile bodies shall be changed and fashioned
like unto my glorious body? It is my own life that I
impart to the believer now, and continue to him without
interruption beyond the grave: it is of my own resurrection that I am to make him a partaker when I come
again.

These, or such as these, are the only words which,
spoken by one who has authority, can shed light on the
dark tomb of a lost and buried brother,—or on the
darker sorrow of a surviving sister's heart. So the
apostle felt when he said, "I would not have you to be
ignorant, brethren, concerning them which are asleep,
that ye sorrow not, even as others which have no hope.
For if we believe that Jesus died and rose again, even
so them also which sleep in Jesus will God bring with
him" (1 Thess. iv. 13, 14).

When Mary, on the other hand, draws near in the
anguish of silent woe, Jesus is differently affected, and

his sympathy is shown in a different way. He is much more profoundly moved. He does not reply to her in words, for her own words were few. Sorrow has choked her utterance, and overmastered her soul. But the sight of one so dear to him, lying in such helpless grief at his feet, is an appeal to him far stronger than any supplication. And his own responsive sigh is an answer more comforting than any promise. "When Jesus therefore saw her weeping, and the Jews also weeping which came with her," for it was a melting scene, "he groaned in spirit, and was troubled." And when he had asked of the bystanders, "Where have ye laid him?" and received the reply, "Come and see"—like Joseph, he could not refrain himself—"Jesus wept" (ver. 33–35).

O most blessed mourner, with whose tears thy Saviour mingles his own! O sympathy most unparalleled! To each of the two stricken and afflicted ones the Lord addressed the very consolation that was most congenial. To Martha he gave exceeding great and precious assurances, in words such as never man spake. To Mary he communicated the groanings of his spirit, in language more expressive to the heart than any spoken words could be. With Martha, Jesus discoursed and reasoned. With Mary, Jesus wept.

What a friend is this! What a brother! yea, and far more than a brother! And how confidently may you come to him, ye Christian mourners, in every season of trial! For, surely, he will give you the very cordial, the very refreshment, of which you stand in need. He is a patient hearer if you have anything to say to him; and he will speak to you as you are able to bear it. Your complaints, your regrets, your expostulations, your very remonstrances and upbraidings, may all be expressed to him. He will pity. He will comfort. His Holy Spirit will bring to your remembrance what Christ has said suitable to your case. He will recall to you the Saviour's gracious words of eternal life, and suggest to you considerations fitted to dissipate your gloom, and put a new song in your mouth. And even if you cannot collect your thoughts, and order your words aright—if you are dumb with silence when your sorrow is stirred, and as you muse your heart is hot within you—oh remember, that with these very groanings which cannot be uttered, the Spirit maketh intercession for you! And they are not hid from him who, when he saw Mary weeping, groaned, and was troubled, and wept. There is indeed enough of all varied consolation in that blessed book, which all throughout testifies of Jesus! For the sorrow that seeks vent in words, and desires by words also to be soothed,—there is the Saviour's open ear—there are the Saviour's lips into which grace was poured. For the grief that is dumb and silent,—there are the Saviour's tears.

CANDLISH.

SCRIPTURAL SELECTIONS.

(Now Bethany was nigh unto Jerusalem, about fifteen furlongs off.)

And many of the Jews came to Martha and Mary, to comfort them concerning their brother.

Then Martha, as soon as she heard that Jesus was coming, went and met him: but Mary sat still in the house.

Then said Martha unto Jesus, Lord, if thou hadst been here, my brother had not died.

But I know, that even now, whatsoever thou wilt ask of God, God will give it thee.

Jesus saith unto her, Thy brother shall rise again.

Martha saith unto him, I know that he shall rise again in the resurrection at the last day.

Jesus said unto her, I am the resurrection, and the life: he that believeth in me, though he were dead, yet shall he live:

And whosoever liveth, and believeth in me, shall never die. Believest thou this?

She saith unto him, Yea, Lord: I believe that thou art the Christ, the Son of God, which should come into the world.

And when she had so said, she went her way, and called Mary her sister secretly, saying, The Master is come, and calleth for thee.—*John*, xi. 18–28.

Then when Mary was come where Jesus was, and saw him, she fell down at his feet, saying unto him, Lord, if thou hadst been here, my brother had not died.

When Jesus therefore saw her weeping, and the Jews also weeping which came with her, he groaned in the spirit, and was troubled,

And said, Where have ye laid him? They say unto him, Lord, come and see.

Jesus wept.

Then said the Jews, Behold how he loved him!—*John*, xi. 32–36.

CHRIST'S WORDS TO THE SORROWING.

BROKEN-HEARTED, weep no more!
  Hear what comfort He hath spoken:
Smoking flax who ne'er hath quenched,
  Bruised reed who ne'er hath broken.
    "Ye who wander here below,
      Heavy laden as you go,
      Come with grief, with sin oppressed,
      Come to me and be at rest!"

Lamb of Jesus' blood-bought flock,
  Brought again from sin and straying,
Hear the Shepherd's gentle voice—
  'Tis a true and faithful saying—
    "Greater love how can there be,
      Than to yield up life for thee?
      Bought with pang, and tear, and sigh,
      Turn and live!—Why will ye die?"

Broken-hearted, weep no more,
  Far from consolation flying:
He who calls hath felt thy wound,
  Seen thy weeping, heard thy sighing;—
    "Bring thy broken heart to me,
      Welcome offering it shall be;
      Streaming tears and bursting sighs
      Mine accepted sacrifice."

III.

The Compassionate High Priest.

" Seeing then that we have a great High Priest, that is passed into the heavens, Jesus the Son of God, et us hold fast our profession. For we have not a high priest which cannot be touched with the feeling of our infirmities; but was in all points tempted like as we are, yet without sin. Let us therefore come boldly unto the throne of grace, that we may obtain mercy, and find grace to help in time of need."—Heb. iv. 14-16.

IN the Jewish economy the High Priest occupied solemn and peculiar relations. A descendant of Aaron—anointed with the holy oil—clad in garments made for glory and for beauty—unblemished in person, sacred in office, and standing once each year before the mercy-seat in the Holy of Holies as the mediator between God and his people Israel—he became invested with a sacredness and a majesty of character becoming to him who stood among men as the representative of God.

To this pontifical office the Jews had become much attached, and the design of St. Paul in the Epistle to the Hebrews was to transfer their love of this office as a Mosaic institution, to Christ, a High Priest greater than Aaron, in the new and Christian dispensation. This he does by showing how Christ was in all points equal to the Jewish pontiff, and in many far exceeded him; thus establishing claims to their regard and obedience beyond those which pertained to the Aaronic priesthood. This position we shall better understand by showing wherein they were analogous, and wherein the priestly office of Christ exceeded that of Aaron or his sons.

The Aaronic high priest must be called of God. "No man," says St. Paul, "taketh this honour unto himself, but he that is called of God as was Aaron. So also Christ glorified not himself to be made an High Priest," but God said unto him, "Thou art my Son, this day have I begotten thee."

The Aaronic high priesthood was unchangeable. It could never depart from the family of Aaron. So Christ being made an High Priest, changeth not, "but abideth a priest continually." He "hath an unchangeable priesthood."

The Aaronic high priest was to be anointed with the holy oil. The very name of our Saviour (Christ, or Messiah,) showed that he was anointed by God to execute his mediatorial office; set apart to the office, not with the anointing oil employed in the solemn consecration of Aaron and his sons, but with the antitype of that oil, "the spirit of grace" poured upon him without measure by the hand of God.

The high priest must be without blemish, and holy. He must be sound and healthy in body and mind. Aaron and his sons were also originally sanctified externally by a long series of most solemn offerings and ceremonies; their garments were styled holy, and "Holiness to the Lord" was engraven on a plate, which they were directed to wear upon their mitres. "Such an High Priest," sayeth St. Paul, "is Christ, who is holy, harmless, undefiled, separate from sinners," of whom even his enemies declared they found "no fault in him." His very garments were holy, for the sick and infirm but touched the hem of them and they were made whole.

The Aaronic high priest only could enter into the Holy of Holies once each year, and then only with blood. So Christ entered into the "most holy place" above with the blood wrung from him in Gethsemane and on Calvary. The Aaronic high priest only could make a ceremonial atonement for the sins of the people; and Christ, as the High Priest of our salvation, "by a sacrifice and oblation of himself once offered, made a full, perfect, and sufficient" atonement for the sins of the world. These are some of the more prominent analogies between the priesthood of Christ and the priesthood of Aaron; and, were we to pursue the comparison further, we should find that the symbolical and temporary ministrations of the one had their end and perfection in the spiritual and unchangeable priesthood of the other.

But there are qualities and attributes far above these, which show the superiority of Christ's pontificate. The high priest of the Jews was a sinful being. The High Priest of the gospel was holy. The one, had to make atonement for himself as a sinner; the other, "knew no sin, neither was guile found in his mouth." The high priest of the Jews was a man—weak, frail, mortal man—born of dust to be buried in the dust—naving the pains and sufferings of life about him. But the High Priest Jesus, "is the same yesterday, to-day, and for ever."

The high priest of the Jews was on earth, and only entered into the Holy of Holies once a year to make an annual expiation for the sins of the nation on the great day of atonement. But our High Priest is in heaven, the true Holy of Holies, and there "he ever liveth to make intercession for us;" so that not once a year merely, but at all times; not at Jerusalem only, but in all places, we can have "boldness of access to his mercy-seat."

The Christian dispensation, then, outvies the Levitical in the glory and exaltedness of its great High Priest that is passed into the heavens, Jesus the Son of God; and hence the Apostle subjoins the exhortation to the Hebrews, "let us hold fast our profession," for they were particularly inclined to apostatize from Christianity, and go back to Judaism, being tempted by their unconverted brethren to regard the Mosaic religion and the whole Jewish ritual as far more elevated, splendid, and magnificent than the Christian, in comparison with whose temple, service, and gorgeous ceremonials, the origin and rites of the religion of Jesus appeared mean and insignificant. By therefore showing these Hebrew Christians that we had a High Priest not only equal in office and dignity, but far more exalted than the pontiff of the temple, he urged them to hold fast their profession, not to relinquish their grasp on Christianity, because there was no such external ritual in the primitive

23 *

church—no such altars, sacrifices, offerings, priests, as
in the Jewish—for all these were more than met and
answered by the plenitude of grace in the new dispensation; and, in view of their peculiarly exposed position
to the assaults of the tempter, he brings the touching
argument, "for we have not an High Priest, which cannot be touched with the feeling of our infirmities; but
was in all points tempted like as we are, yet without sin."
Ah, my brethren, this was just such a Priest as man
wanted—a Priest that could feel for him; a High Priest
that was compassionate; a great High Priest who could
be touched with the feeling of our infirmities—one in all
points tempted as we are, yet without sin. There was
nothing like this in the old dispensation. It was reserved for the gospel to introduce to man a High Priest,
who, while exalted in the heavens, could yet be touched
with the feeling of our infirmities—who was tempted
with all the temptations of humanity, yet did not sin,
neither was guile found in his mouth.

Christ, then, our great High Priest, is touched with
the feeling of our infirmities; and O, to creatures so
full of infirmities as ourselves, how delightful to have
a spiritual ruler who understands them, and is touched
with them with an abiding sympathy.

Sin has shorn us of our glory, and strewn the earth
with curses, and planted the path of man with infirmities and sorrows. We are prone to suffering—we are
subject to disease—we are victims of adversity, and we
stagger under the weight of our mental and physical

infirmities, from the tiny footsteps of childhood to the
feeble tread of threescore and ten. Under these infirmities we groan being burdened; we feel the work-
ings of the curse of sin every day of our life, and the
loss of limb and function and strength and health which
is everywhere going on around us, show us the sadness
and misery of man's earthly condition. These infirmities, through the influence of the body on the mind and
soul, often lead us into sin and temptation, become ave-
nues of assault upon the heart, and the means whereby
faith is weakened, and love chilled, and hope repressed,
and the soul bereft of its holy aspirations. In sickness,
how much are we tempted to impatience and repining;
in bereavements, how apt to murmur and complain; in
adversity, how often do we show the restive and un-
tamed spirit of a worldling! No infirmity of mind or
body can overtake us, without begetting some unholy
feelings towards our Creator. Now Jesus, our blessed
Master, suffered the ills of life when on earth; hunger,
thirst, cold, poverty, reproach, buffetings, and all the
infirmities of man. His compassionate heart is therefore touched by our sorrows, and deeply sympathizes
with all our distresses. Frequently was this exhibited
when on earth. He was moved with compassion when
he saw the multitude scattered abroad as sheep having
no shepherd—he had compassion on the multitude without bread—at seeing in the throng sick persons, whom
he healed—at the sight of blind men, whom he restored
to sight—at a leper, whom he cured—at a child pos-

sessed of a dumb spirit, which he cast out—at beholding a mother's grief, whose son he restored to life,
yea, his mission to man was prompted by mercy, and
his life on earth was full of compassion.

We know how delightful it is when suffering under
any sickness or calamity, to have the sympathy and
pity of those we love; to feel that in their bosoms are
kindred emotions of tenderness and regard, causing
them to weep with those who weep. But how much
more cheering is it to the Christian, bowed beneath
some burdensome sorrow, to know that he has the
compassion and sympathy of his Saviour! That Jesus,
the Son of God, our ever-living High Priest in heaven,
is touched with the feeling of his infirmities! That
humanity can know no want, no affliction, no suffering,
which he does not feel, and towards which his com-
passions do not flow out! And this is not a mere in-
operative compassion, expending itself in words and
professions, but it is a sympathy joined to a willingness
to do, and an ability to do, for our relief. For having
been himself tempted, he is able and willing to succour
those who are tempted. Many persons have borne the
same afflictions which befall us, who are not willing to
sympathize with us; many are willing to sympathize
with us, who have not experienced like tribulations; and
many are both able and willing to extend to us their
compassion, who are yet unable to do anything for our
comfort or relief. But our compassionate High Priest
unites all these. He has been a man of sorrows, and

acquainted with griefs, and can therefore sympathize experimentally with us. He is willing and prompted by the benevolence of his heart to tender to us his kind compassion; and, as God in the plenitude of omnipotence, "he is able to save to the uttermost all who come unto God through Him," and to "wipe away all tears from their eyes." The sympathy of Christ to his disciples on earth is a *tender* sympathy; for "as a father pitieth his children, even so pitieth them that hear him." It is an *extensive* sympathy; there is not an infirmity of man which it cannot reach; it is a *proportionable* sympathy, answerable to our peculiar wants, and to every occasion; it is a *perpetual* sympathy, so long as he continues a High Priest, and we remain subject to infirmities, so long will our blessed Jesus be touched with the feeling of them.

Man has no such sympathy as this for his fellow-man. Angels who never wore our nature can have none like it, it is only the man Christ Jesus, both God and man, who centres in himself this plenitude of mercy and this disinterested compassion.

The reason why our great High Priest is so sensibly affected by our suffering condition, is stated by the Apostle to lie in the fact that "He was in all points tempted like as we are, yet without sin." The Greek word here used is more general in its meaning than the English word "tempted." It adverts both to trial by affliction, and temptations to sin; implying no more, however, than that of being susceptible to temptation,

35

resulting from the possession of a human nature. It means then to put to the proof, to try the nature or character; and this proof can be made either by allowing one to fall into temptation, properly so called, where some strong inducement is presented to the mind, and where it becomes thus a trial of virtue, or by subjecting a person to afflictions or sufferings, so that his character is proved, that the principles and motives of conduct may appear. Jesus Christ was subjected to both these in as severe a form as ever was presented to man; his whole life being little else than a long conflict of faith with sense—holiness with sin—virtue with temptation— yet, blessed be God, the tempter was repelled, the sin was overcome, the flesh was nailed to the cross, for he rose from each assault a conqueror—vanquishing every foe, triumphing in every contest. He alone, then, who has conquered sin, and overthrown the tempter, can succour us in the temptations of the one, or the assaults of the other, and enable us to be victor over both.

When thrust at by the enemy of our souls—when attacked by his fiery trials—when seduced by his gilded lures, when teased by the insinuations and cheating whispers of this "father of lies," it is cheering and animating to the half-subdued soul to know, that Jesus was tempted in all points like as we are; and that, having been tempted, he knows what humanity can endure, and will "not suffer us to be tempted above that we are able to bear." In Christ we are invincible—though sin, death, and hell wage war upon the soul; out of Christ we are the victims of the first temptation, and fall an easy prey to the spoiler of our souls.

Such being the nature of our compassionate High Priest, the Apostle argues thence our duty, and urges upon us our peculiar privileges.

Is he thus tender towards our infirmities, and does he thus succour us in our temptations? then should we hold fast our profession. Why should we relax our hold, when He whom we serve is able and willing to sustain us? We serve not an impotent Prince or a weak Sovereign. He under whom we have enlisted is omnipotent. The banner under which we are marshalled is one that never yet was lowered to human foe; and the weapons by which we war are "mighty through God, to the pulling down of the strongholds of sin and Satan." Why, then, should we relax our hold, when " the Lord of hosts is with us, and the God of Jacob is our refuge?" Why should we apostatize and go back to the world? The question there meets us, " What shall it profit a man to gain the whole world and lose his own soul?"

What can the world give in barter for your faith? What will it palm off upon you in lieu of your hopes? What will it sell you for the joys of the Spirit? O, go to its shambles, and its money-changers, and see what trade you can make for the religion of Christ; and when you have learnt the price, decide whether you will hold fast your profession. Shall you give up the contest because it waxes warm? Shall you retreat because of the danger? Does the toil overcome you, and do you faint and grow weary because of the burden and heat of the day ? Had your Saviour been influenced by such motives, what would have become of your soul—when would have been wrought out your salvation ?

Have we such a compassionate High Priest ? then should we confide in him. He knows our infirmities— he is cognisant of our wants—he is touched with our sorrows—he feels for us in our bereavements, and sympathizes in all our adversities. Divine wisdom could not have provided for the soul a more full and perfect counterpart in kind, though in degree infinitely removed above us. It is just such a High Priest as man needs ; and there is no necessity of his moral nature that he does not meet and satisfy. And then, too, he is willing to aid and succour us—more willing than we to ask. And should we not, therefore, confide in his mercy and tenderness ? Look upon his face—do you see there a forbidding aspect ? Are any frowns gathered there ? is repulse expressed there ? or does it not rather beam with a love as infinite as his own perfection, and glow with a smile of compassion, which is the sunlight of the soul ?

If you cannot confide in Christ, in whom can you ? If you fear to go to him with your cares and your sorrows, to whom will you resort ? He suffered for you ; he sorrowed for you ; he bled for you ; he died for you. Shall not his sorrows, his tears, his stripes, his blood, his death, all experienced for you, beget your confidence ? You confide in an earthly friend,—but could all the men of earth combined work out for your soul the ransom which Jesus made for it on Calvary? Oh, is it not, I ask, black ingratitude not to trust him? Is it not an insult to his love to withhold your confidence? Reason it out upon the principles which regulate human friendship, and see in what position it places you to your adorable Redeemer. Yes, confide in Him in all times, in all places, in all circumstances. Are you poor?—he had not where to lay his head. Are you in distress?—he too was afflicted with grief. Are you the object of reproach and scorn?—he was despised and rejected of men. Are you persecuted?—he was reviled, and buffeted, and scourged. Do you weep in silence?—he shed tears as it were great drops of blood falling down to the ground. Are you mourning under bereavement?—he wept at the grave of Lazarus. Do the pains of death take hold?—they were endured by Christ in their highest extremity. You cannot in your most exalted woe exceed his anguish—in your keenest afflictions excel his grief; and the valley of the shadow of death cannot appear darker and more terrible to you than it did to the Crucified, when he cried, "O my Father, if it be possible, let this cup pass from me." All these points are so many guarantees that your confidence is not misplaced—so many invitations to place your hope and trust in his loving kindness. Confide fully in Christ; be not distrustful of his compassion, for "He is faithful that promised."

"Let us therefore come boldly unto the throne of

grace." The mercy-seat of the Jewish temple was inapproachable to the multitude. Only the High Priest could go in before it once each year, and then with blood and incense; but the throne of grace erected in the heavens is accessible to all. It is a *throne*, because occupied by a King, and is the seat of the Majesty on high; but it is named GRACE, because of the clemency and compassion of Him who sits upon it. Approach this throne, and we are sure of an audience. The golden sceptre of mercy is ever held out to us, and we are sure of grace to help in every time of need. Boldly go to that throne, and prefer your request in faith upon the merits of Christ, and in confidence upon the mercy of that great High Priest who is passed unto the heavens, Jesus the Son of God, remembering that he is touched with the feeling of our infirmities, that he succours us in our temptations, and vouchsafes to all who call upon him " grace to help in every time of need."

STEVENS

Scriptural Selections.

For every high priest, taken from among men, is ordained for men in things pertaining to God, that he may offer both gifts and sacrifices for sins:

Who can have compassion on the ignorant, and on them that are out of the way: for that he himself also is compassed with infirmity.

And by reason hereof he ought, as for the people, so also for himself, to offer for sins.

And no man taketh this honour unto himself, but he that is called of God, as was Aaron.

So also Christ glorified not himself to be made a high priest; but he that said unto him, Thou art my Son, to-day have I begotten thee. *Heb.* v. 1–5.

But Christ being come a high priest of good things to come, by a greater and more perfect tabernacle, not made with hands, that is to say, not of this building;

Neither by the blood of goats and calves, but by his own blood, he entered in once into the holy place, having obtained eternal redemption for us.

For if the blood of bulls and of goats, and the ashes of a heifer sprinkling the unclean, sanctifieth to the purifying of the flesh;

How much more shall the blood of Christ, who through the eternal Spirit offered himself without spot to God, purge your conscience from dead works to serve the living God?

And for this cause he is the mediator of the new testament, that by means of death, for the redemption of the transgressions that were under the first testament, they which are called might receive the promise of eternal inheritance.—*Heb.* ix. 11–15.

CLINGING TO JESUS.

" Seeing then we have a great high priest that is passed into the heavens, Jesus, the Son of God, let us hold fast our profession." —HEB. IV. 14.

HOLY SAVIOUR, friend unseen,
Since on thine arm thou bid'st me lean,
Help me throughout life's varying scene,
  By faith to cling to thee!

Blest with this fellowship divine,
Take what thou wilt, I'll ne'er repine;
E'en as the branches to the vine,
   My soul would cling to thee!

Far from her home, fatigued, oppressed,
Here she has found her place of rest;
An exile still, yet not unblest,
   While she can cling to thee!

Oft, when I seem to tread alone
Some barren waste with thorns o'ergrown,
Thy voice of love, in tenderest tone,
   Whispers, "Still cling to me!"

Though faith and hope may oft be tried,
I ask not, need not, aught beside;
How safe, how calm, how satisfied,
   The soul that clings to thee!

Blest is my lot, whate'er befall:
What can disturb me, what appal,
Whilst as my rock, my strength, my all,
   Saviour! I cling to thee?

IV

CHRIST THE KEYHOLDER OF THE ETERNAL WORLD.

"Fear not;" "I am he that liveth, and was dead; and, behold, I am alive for evermore, Amen, and have the keys of hell and of death."—REV. i. 17, 18.

EVERY clause of this sublime declaration, coming as it does from our glorified Redeemer, is pregnant with assurance and consolation to his believing people, and is specially fitted to banish those fearful and anxious forebodings which oppress their minds in the prospect of dissolution.

"*I am he that liveth,*" or rather, "I am THE LIVING ONE," the first and the last, without beginning of days or end of years, self-existent, and, therefore, independent of every outward condition, and incapable of change. He asserts his supreme divinity as a reason why his disciples should "not *fear;*" and, surely, to every Christian mind, the fact, that the Son of Man, in whom they have trusted as their Saviour, is "the Living One," may well furnish a ground of unshaken confidence, since it assures us, that, happen what may, our trust is reposed on one, whose existence, and whose power to affect our welfare, cannot be destroyed by any event whatever, and that our interests for eternity are absolutely safe, being placed in his hands.

36 (281)

But how much greater ought to be our confidence in him, and how much sweeter the consolation which his words impart, when he adds, "I WAS DEAD." He appears to the Apostle not simply as "the Living One," the self-existent Son of God, but as God manifested in the flesh, the Son of God in human nature, and even in his glorified state, "like unto the Son of Man," whom the beloved disciple had ofttimes seen and followed as the "man of sorrows, and acquainted with grief." Let us attempt to conceive of the feelings with which the beloved disciple must have looked on his glorified Master; let us remember that he had companied with him on earth, that he had leaned upon his bosom, and that he knew the sad history of his crucifixion, and we cannot fail to perceive how the mere fact, that the same divine Redeemer now stood before him, and spoke with him of the decease which he had accomplished at Jerusalem, must have served to annihilate in the mind of the Apostle the fear of death, and to open up to his view such a glorious prospect into the invisible world, as would strip the pathway that led to heaven of its terrors, however dark and dismal it might otherwise be.

And to every Christian, the words of our Lord, "I was dead," will suggest reflections that should serve to fortify the mind against the fear of dissolution; or, at all events, to rebuke and mitigate the aversion with which it is usually contemplated.

Did the Redeemer die,—a Being who claims to himself the dignity of "the Living One,"—a Being not only of infinite dignity, but of spotless purity, and who, from the beginning till the end of his existence on earth, was the object of God's supreme complacency and approbation ? And shall we complain that death is allotted as our portion also ? *we*, who, as created beings, are insignificant,—by inheritance, mortal,—by actual guilt, polluted and debased ? To us, death comes as wages earned by guilt ; but even were it otherwise,—did death come to us as an accident of our being, how should we complain of the hardness of our lot, when Christ himself declares, "I was dead ?"

Did the Redeemer die,—as the surety and representative of sinners ? was his death a solemn expiation of our guilt, and an adequate satisfaction to God for the penalty which we had incurred ? Is there no reason, then, to suppose, that dying, as he did, in the room and on behalf of the guilty, death met him in a more formidable shape, and put into his hands a bitterer cup than can now fall to the lot of any of his people ; and that their dissolution will be greatly less terrible than it would have been by reason of his enduring in their room the heaviest part of it ? For what is it that mainly embitters death, and surrounds it, even when viewed at a distance, with innumerable terrors ? Not surely the mere pain with which it is accompanied,—for equal or greater pain we have often endured—not the mere dissolution of the tie betwixt soul and body,—for if that were all, however our sensitive nature might shrink from the shock, our rational nature might enable us to

regard it with composure,—not the mere separation
from the society and business of the present world,—
for that, however it may awaken a feeling of melancholy
regret, can hardly account for the forebodings and
terrors of which every mind is more or less conscious
when it contemplates death.   No; it is something more
than the mere pain of dying, or the mere dissolving of
the elements of our being, or the mere separation from
this world, that embitters the cup of death.   "The
sting of death is *sin*,"—the same sin which gave us
over as a prey to death, makes us also slaves to the
fear of death; for, by the unvarying law of conscience,
sin and fear are bound up together; and it is a conscience burdened with guilt, and apprehensive of punishment, which, in our case, arrays death with terrors
unknown to the inferior and irresponsible creation.
But Christ died to expiate and cancel the guilt of his
people; he has already endured, and by enduring, has
taken away the penalty of their transgression; death
remains, but its sting is taken away; so that we may
"thank God, who hath given us the victory through
Jesus Christ our Lord," and may exclaim with the
Apostle, "Oh! death, where is now thy sting,—Oh!
grave, where is thy victory?"

Did the Redeemer die,—that he might show us an
example of suffering affliction with patience, and be to
us a pattern of faith and hope in our last extremity?
And is there no consolation in the thought, that when
we reach the shore of that dark water which divides

time and eternity, we can fix our eye on one who, for our sakes, crossed it in triumph before us ; and think of the love of our Redeemer, who, in compassion to our fears, became " bone of our bone, and flesh of our flesh," that, by his own example, he might teach us how to die ? Had he returned from earth to heaven in triumph ; had he avoided the dark valley himself, and, summoning his legions of angels, left the world by a direct ascension to glory, then, whatever lessons he might have taught, and whatever commands and encouragements he might have addressed to his followers, respecting their conduct in that last hour of darkness and distress, his instructions would have had little effect in comparison with the charm of his example, when, placing himself in their circumstances, and submitting to their fate, he " bowed his head and gave up the ghost ;" and met death, as he commands his people to meet it, in the exercise of an unshaken confidence in God, and humble submission to his will. Where shall we find such another example of holy fortitude for our imitation ? where such another instance of success for our encouragement ?

Did the Redeemer die,—that he might not only de‑ prive death of its sting, but overcome him that had the power of death, and take it into his own hands ? Let us, then, rejoice in his success ; for once Satan had the power of death, but Christ hath " carried captivity cap‑ tive," and " Satan hath fallen before him as lightning from heaven." In that hour, which he did himself em‑ phatically call " the hour and the power of darkness," when he was in more than mortal agony, travailing in the greatness of his strength, he vanquished death and hell, and he wrested from the hands of our greatest enemy, and took into his own possession, the keys of death and of the invisible world. Death still reigns, but Christ has now the dominion over death.

In token of his victory, the Redeemer adds, " I AM ALIVE FOR EVERMORE." The grave received, but it could not retain him ; and while the fact of his interment may well serve to reconcile us to the peaceful grave, with all its loneliness and darkness, since it was embalmed by the presence of our Lord himself, the fact of his resurrection from the grave should enkindle the bright hope of a glorious morning, after that dark night has passed away.

For, did the Redeemer arise from the tomb ? Then here, at least, is *one* example of restoration to life after the agony of death was past,—one case in which the spell of death was broken, and the cerements of the tomb burst, and the power of Satan vanquished,—one living monument of the immortality of man,—one incontestable proof, that the same body which died, and the same spirit which departed, may meet again after that fearful separation. Christ hath risen, and in his resurrection we find the ground of an eternal hope.

Did the Redeemer arise from the grave in the same character in which he died,—as the head and representative of his people ? Then is his resurrection not only the proof, but the pledge ; not only the evidence, but the earnest of our own. For if the head be risen, shall not the members of his body rise also? If, as our representative, he hath passed into the heavens, shall not we, in whose name, and for whose behoof, he under-took and accomplished his mediatorial work, follow him in our order and time? Did we die with him, and shall we not rise with him? "If we have been planted together in the likeness of his death, we shall be also in the likeness of his resurrection." "If we be dead with Christ, we believe that we shall also live with him." "Because I live, ye shall live also."

Did the Redeemer not only rise from the grave, but does he LIVE FOR EVERMORE? Is he the same yester-day, to-day, and for ever? Not only eternal in his being, but unchangeable in his character, as our Re-deemer? What, then, should cause us to despond, or make us afraid? or "what shall separate us from the love of Christ?" Since Christ hath died, yea, also, and hath risen again, and is now and for ever at the right hand of God, "I am persuaded, that neither death, nor life, nor angels, nor principalities, nor powers, nor things present, nor things to come, nor height, nor depth, nor any other creature, shall separate us from his love." True, we know not what may yet befall us, nor into what untried circumstances, or state of being, we may hereafter be brought; we are sure that one day we must die and enter the invisible world; and we may well be concerned for an event which will have an ever-lasting issue for good or for evil; but placing our trust in the efficacy of the Redeemer's death, and believing in the fact of his resurrection, we may take his own word as the rock of our confidence and hope,—" I am alive for evermore, Amen;" and "because I live, ye shall live also."

If these views of the death and resurrection of our blessed Lord are fitted to banish, or mitigate, the fear of dissolution, and to inspire the hope of a glorious immortality, how much should their impression be aided by the sublime statement in the last clause of the passage,—" I HAVE THE KEYS OF HELL AND OF DEATH !"

The power of the keys is an absolute power,—a royal prerogative. Christ's authority is not confined to the visible Church on earth; it extends to the invisible world, and embraces under its jurisdiction all the disembodied spirits, of whatsoever character: although they have left this world, they are still under the dominion of him, of whom it is said, that "at his name every knee shall bow, of things in heaven, of things on earth, and of things under the earth; and every tongue confess that he is Lord, to the glory of God the Father."

It is *as the Redeemer*, that he asserts his claim to the keys; that claim is founded on the fact, that "he overcame death and him that had the power of death, in order to deliver those who, through fear of death, were all their lifetime subject to bondage;" and it is expressly declared by the Apostle, that, "for this end, Christ both died and rose again, and revived, that he might be Lord both of the dead and of the living."

That he is the *Lord of the dead*, is here asserted— "I have the keys of hell." In the original there are two terms, each of which is rendered by the word " hell" in the English version; the one, however, literally imports the invisible world at large, while the other denotes that department of the invisible world which is specially appropriated to the punishment of the wicked.

In the passage before us, the more comprehensive term is used; and here, as elsewhere, it is to be regarded as signifying not merely the place of future punishment, although that is unquestionably included in it, but, more generally, the world of spirits, the entire state of retribution, whether of reward or punishment. We learn from Scripture, that the whole of that vast world is divided into two departments, and only two—heaven and hell; and that betwixt the two, a great gulf is fixed,— an impassable gulf of separation : but separated as they are, Christ reigns over both; and when he says, " I have the keys of the invisible world," he asserts his dominion over all the spirits that have ever passed from this world, either into heaven or hell; and his absolute control over them in their final destination of happiness or woe.

When it is affirmed, that he has also "the key of death," it is plainly implied that no spirit can pass out of this present world without his permission or appointment; and, more generally, that he is lord of the living not less than of the dead,* and has a thorough control

* See Howe's Redeemer's Dominion over the Invisible World.

over everything that can in any way affect the lives of men. An absolute power over death necessarily presupposes a corresponding power over life and its affairs ; and it is by the exercise of his providence in sustaining life, that he fulfils his purpose as to the time and mode of their departure hence.

So that, combining these several views, we arrive at this grand and comprehensive result, that the Redeemer is possessed of absolute power over the course of our lives on earth, over the time and manner of our departure out of the world, and over that invisible state, in each of its great departments, on which our spirits enter when they quit their mortal tabernacles ; and this noble testimony to the universal power and everlasting presence of Christ with his disciples, is fitted to suggest several reflections, which may be useful in dissipating their anxieties, and in fortifying their courage, when they contemplate either the future course of their pilgrimage here, or the solemn prospect of its termination, or the still more solemn, because untried and eternal, state on which they shall enter hereafter.

Has the Redeemer the *keys of death ?* Then this consideration ought to relieve our minds both of the anxieties and the regrets which we are too apt to feel, in reference to the changes of the present life.

It should mitigate the anxiety which often preys upon the mind when we look forward into futurity, and contemplate the *prospect of our own dissolution.* We should remember, that as the Redeemer alone hath the keys of death, nothing can happen to send us forth from the world before the time which he has appointed for our departure. Neither man nor devils can abridge the term of probation assigned to us by our gracious Master; nor, until he is pleased to call us away, shall any power on earth or in hell prevail against us; no accident, no hostile violence, no insidious snare, no dark conspiracy, can touch our life, but by his command.

The same consideration should prevent or repress the anxiety which is too often felt respecting the *mode* and *circumstances* of our dissolution, not less than respecting the time of its occurrence.

This consideration should repress, not only the anxieties which we feel in regard to the future, but also the regrets which we are too apt to cherish respecting the *bereavements* with which we have already been visited. It is not less instructive and consoling, when viewed in reference to the death of relatives and friends, than when it is considered in respect to our own prospect of dissolution. For it teaches us, that the duration of each man's existence here is determined by the Redeemer; that it belongs to him to appoint a longer or shorter period to each, as he will; and in doing so, we have reason to be satisfied, that he determines according to the dictates of infallible wisdom, although the reasons of his procedure must necessarily be to us, for the present, inscrutable. We cannot tell why one is removed in infancy, another in boyhood, a third in the prime of manly vigour, and a fourth reserved to the period of old age ; and, above all, why the most promising in talent and character, and the most useful in their several sta tions, are taken away, while others of inferior worth are often left behind ; but suffice it for us, that this happens not by chance, neither is it the result of caprice or carelessness, but flows from that unerring wisdom, whose counsels are formed on a view of all possible relations and consequences, whether as to the visible or invisible, the present or the future states of being. The power of death being in the hands of the Redeemer, the duration of human life is, in every instance, determined by him ; and none, therefore, ought to entertain the thought, either that death is, in one case, unduly *premature*, or, in another, unduly *delayed*. None live, either for a longer or for a shorter period than infinite wisdom has assigned to them ; and as reason teaches, that to his appointment we must submit, however unwilling, it being irresistible, and far beyond our control,—so, as Christians, we should learn to acquiesce in it cheerfully, as the appointment of one who cannot err. That the determined hour had arrived, is a reflection that should serve to banish every useless regret,—but that this hour was fixed by one in whose wisdom we confide, and of whose interest in our welfare we have the strongest assurance, is a thought which should not only induce resignation, but inspire comfort and peace.

For, when death does seize any of our friends, whether in the ordinary course of disease and decay, or by violence or accident, how consolatory to the mourning relatives is the thought, that it came at the bidding of the Saviour, and that it has not arrived without his sanction and appointment! Otherwise, we might be apt to reflect, with unavailing regret, on certain needless exposures that might have been avoided, certain remedies whose virtues might have been tried, certain names high in professional reputation, who might have been consulted; or to dwell, with painful self-reproach, on certain accidents that might have been prevented, and injuries which timely care might have cured. The mind will often busy itself with such reflections after the loss of a near and dear friend; but the very intensity of feeling which is thus called forth, is a sufficient proof that any carelessness or negligence that may have been manifested, was far, very far, from being designed or wilful. And although, where criminal negligence has been shown, no doctrine, however consolatory, can prevent regret, or *should* repress feelings of penitential sorrow; yet, in other cases, where the heart bears witness to its own interest in the beloved object, the doctrine of Christ's absolute command over the keys of death, and the consideration that our friend was summoned away by a deliberate act of his sovereign wisdom, may well assuage the grief which such reflections on the commencement, progress, and treatment of the disease, are wont to awaken in the most sensitive and affectionate minds.

While this sublime statement should banish, or at least mitigate, the anxieties and regrets which we some-

times experience, in reference to the events of the
present life, inasmuch as Christ's power over death im-
plies a corresponding power over life and its affairs, it
is equally fitted to fortify our minds for the last struggle
of nature, since it assures us that Christ will *then be
present with us.* In the very article of death, it gives
us comfort. For, hath the Redeemer the keys of death ?
Then he presides over that dark passage which leads
from this world to the next ; his power does not terminate with our present life ; it extends from the world
which is smiling in the cheerful light of day, to that
mysterious passage which lies amidst the sepulchres of
the dead, and which, to our imperfect vision, is shrouded
in impenetrable darkness.   We know not the secrets of
that passage.   We cannot know what it is to die.   The
mind may then have views and feelings of which it is
impossible for us at present to form any conception ;
for who shall attempt to describe what may be passing
in the soul when the tie that binds it to the body is
breaking, and nature is undergoing dissolution ?   And
what renders that scene still more awful is, that *we die
alone,*—alone we enter on the dark valley.   Friends
and family may stand around our couch, and watch the
progress of dissolution ; but they cannot accompany us,
neither are they sensible of what we feel, nor able in
any way to help or deliver us.   The spirit departs
alone ; and in that awful hour of separation from human
fellowship,—in that solitude of death, when, placed on
the verge of the invisible world, we know that all behind

must be forsaken, and are ignorant of what may meet us as we advance, oh! how consolatory to reflect, that death itself is subject to the Redeemer's power,—that he watches over the dissolution of his people, and keeps his eye, not only on the busy scenes of life, but also on the secret mysteries of death. Yes, "*precious in the sight of the Lord is the death of his saints.*" There he is, where most we need a friend and comforter, standing at the gate of death, with absolute power over every enemy that can assail us, and with unquenchable zeal for our welfare. Dark, then, as the passage is, and unknown as are its dangers and pains, surely we may venture to commit ourselves into his hands, and to say with the Psalmist, "Yea, though I walk through the valley of the shadow of death, I will fear no evil: for *thou art with me;* thy rod and thy staff they comfort me;" for, says the Apostle, "all things are yours, whether Paul, or Apollos, or Cephas, or life,—or death."

As Christ has the key of the invisible world at large, so hath he the key of each ward or department—the keys of heaven and of hell.

Hath he the key of hell? Then, knowing as we do, that there are rebellious spirits of great subtlety, and power, and malice, and that they are sometimes permitted to go about as roaring lions, seeking whom they may devour, we might have many an anxious fear, lest, in the dark hour of death, some such should be watching for the spirit, when it ventures alone into the invisible world; but "precious in the sight of the Lord is the

death of his saints,"—to that death-bed the watchful
eye of the Saviour is directed; he can and will restrain
the malice of our enemies; and his promise is, that
"whoso believeth on him shall never come into condemnation," and that "none shall pluck them out of his
Father's hand."

And hath the Redeemer the keys of heaven,—that
blessed asylum of purity and peace, where, in the midst
of his redeemed, the Saviour himself dwells? Then, in
the hands of our best friend, one who is pledged to us
by the sacredness of his word, and by the shedding of
his own blood, in his hands is the power of admitting
us;—and will he shut the door against us?—he who,
for the opening of that door, descended from heaven to
earth, and whose prayer was and is, "Father, I will
that they whom thou hast given me, be with me where
I am, that they may behold my glory?" No; the door
of heaven is thrown open for the reception of his penitent and believing people. Even now is he "preparing
a place for them in his Father's house, where there are
many mansions;" and thus will he receive and welcome
them, on their departure hence: "Come, ye blessed of
my Father, *inherit* the kingdom *prepared for you,*"—
"well done, good and faithful servants, enter ye into
the joy of your Lord."

Buchanan.

SCRIPTURAL SELECTIONS.

HE that is our God is the God of salvation; and unto God the Lord belong the issues from death.—*Ps.* lxviii. 20.

For the Father judgeth no man, but hath committed all judgment unto the Son.—*John,* v. 22.

As thou hast given him power over all flesh, that he should give eternal life to as many as thou hast given him.

Father, I will that they also whom thou hast given me be with me where I am; that they may behold my glory, which thou hast given me: for thou lovedst me before the foundation of the world.—*John,* xvii. 2, 24.

He that hath an ear, let him hear what the Spirit saith unto the churches; To him that overcometh will I give to eat of the tree of life, which is in the midst of the paradise of God.

Fear none of those things which thou shalt suffer: behold, the devil shall cast some of you into prison, that ye may be tried; and ye shall have tribulation ten days: be thou faithful unto death, and I will give thee a crown of life.—*Rev.* ii. 7, 10.

He that overcometh, the same shall be clothed in white raiment; and I will not blot out his name out of the book of life, but I will confess his name before my Father, and before his angels.

Him that overcometh will I make a pillar in the temple of my God, and he shall go no more out: and I will write upon him the name of my God, and the name of the city of my God, which is new Jerusalem, which cometh down out of heaven from my God; and I will write upon him my new name.

To him that overcometh will I grant to sit with me in my throne, even as I also overcame, and am set down with my Father in his throne.—*Rev.* iii. 5, 12, 21.

"I AM THE RESURRECTION AND THE LIFE."

JOHN, XI. 25.

DEAD in sin, and deep in shame,
Kindle, Lord, a vital flame;
Bid the clouds and darkness flee,
Bid me rise and rest in thee—
    Raise me, Saviour,
Raise to all eternity.

Breathe into this soul of mine
Life eternal, life divine;
Slay these passions, fierce and rife,
End, O end this mortal strife—
    Conquering Saviour,
Thou the victory art and life.

Free from sin—from Satan free;
Let my life be hid with thee;
Send thy seraphs from the skies,
Seal this living sacrifice—
    Risen Saviour,
Ceaseless let this incense rise

O'er the silence of the tomb,
May celestial vigour bloom;
When the world dissolves in fire,
Then in robes of light attire—
    Then, O Saviour,
May I join the immortal choir.

The Sleep in Jesus.

C. Schussele.

J.C. McRae

"David said unto his servants
Is the child dead? And they said
he is dead."

II Samuel XII. 19

THE SLEEP IN JESUS.

I.

The Morning Flower Plucked.

" The flower fadeth."—Isaiah, xl. 7.

NO sensitive mind can gaze upon a morning flower, glittering with dewdrops, and not feel that peculiar beauty and peculiar frailty are conjoined in those delicate petals.

Attracted by its colours, pleased with its fragrance, charmed by its form or construction, we are led to seek a more personal enjoyment of it than can be furnished while it abides in the gay parterre, amidst a hundred other specimens of floral beauty ; and therefore we pluck it, for the vase or for our bosom, that we may appropriate to ourselves whatever of fragrance or pleasure it can afford.

Are we selfish in so doing ? No ; God strewed the earth with flowers of various forms, hues, and odours, for the enjoyment of man. He designed that we should use them ; they are the prodigally scattered luxuries of His loving kindness, and we honour Him who made them, and who gave them to us, by turning our thoughts upon their variegated beauty, and rejoicing in the rich evidence they afford of the goodness and mercy of our covenant God. In the Bible, man is frequently compared to a flower, in respect to the frailty and brevity of his life. Job says, of him, " He cometh forth like a flower, and is cut down." The Psalmist declares, " As for man, his days are as grass, as a flower of the field so he flourisheth; for the wind passeth over it and it is gone, and the place thereof shall know it no more." St. James writes, " Let the brother of low degree rejoice in that he is exalted, but the rich in that he is made low : because as the flower of the grass he shall pass away." And St. Peter, compassing in his thought all mankind, exclaims, " For all flesh is as grass, and all the glory of man as the flower of grass : the grass withereth, and the flower thereof falleth away."

If such language may with perfect propriety be used of " all flesh," the old, the robust, the middle-aged, with what peculiar emphasis may we speak of infancy as the morning flower of human life: beautiful, fragrant, lovely, delicate ; yet perhaps to endure but a little while, ere disease breaks it on its stem, or death plucks it for the grave !

It requires but a very casual observation to convince us that a large part of those who are born of woman die in infancy. If we examine the bills of mortality of any city, or district, or nation, we shall be surprised at the vast number of deaths under the age of five years. Nearly one-fourth of the human race thus pass away in the early hours of life's morning. Scarcely a household but what contains a vacant cradle, or an empty crib;

and from nearly every family death has gathered at least one morning flower. The grief which is thus occasioned, the loss thus experienced, the void thus created, are intensely painful; such as a bereaved parent only can understand. For, though these precious babes have been with us but a little season, though they are unable to talk with us, and join in our schemes and hopes; though they are objects of deep solicitude and watchful care; though they are unconscious of the relations which subsist between us, and return but imperfectly the love which is expended in their care and protection,—yet these things only tend to enhance our love; and their helplessness, their frailty, their many little wants, and the unceasing care which they require, bind our hearts to the sweet innocents more closely, and cause the well springs of parental love to gush out with fuller and deeper flow.

The plucking of these morning flowers is, therefore, intensely painful to the parent's heart. If it be the first babe, the one which first opened the fountain of parental love, the one in which the youthful pair first saw their blended image, whose advent brought sunlight and gladness, and awoke emotions of maternal tenderness and paternal care before unknown, oh, how desolating, heart-riving is the bereavement! The cooing voice, the little laugh, the infantile prattle, are hushed; and the chamber echoes no more to the clapping of its hands, or the patter of its tiny feet. The sunlight seems to have passed away; darkness has settled in its place, and there is gloom and woe within that dwelling. Even in cases where other children are left behind, the loss of the infant, the common centre of the household love and care, falls with a deadening weight upon the family circle; a blank, dreary and sad, is made, which, perhaps, may never more be filled. There is much of truth in the touching words of Longfellow:

> " There is no flock, however watched and tended,
>   But one dead lamb is there;
> There is no fireside, howsoe'er defended,
>   But has one vacant chair!"

> " The air is full of farewells to the dying,
>   And mournings for the dead;
> The heart of Rachel for her children crying,
>   Will not be comforted!"

But is there no comfort for such? Is there no hope in the coffin where the infant lies? Is the child's grave rayless with the light of heavenly consolation? The Bible answers these questions for us with a satisfying fulness. It does not indeed tell us in so many words that infants and children dying before they come to the years of responsibility and discretion, are saved; but the whole spirit of Christ's conduct and apostolic teaching leaves upon the candid observer no doubt as to the perfect safety and future happiness of all those who, like the morning flower, are early plucked away.

Infants have committed no overt sin, but they are all "by nature children of wrath;" they inherit a cor-

rupt moral character, and they begin to go astray with
the first dawning of accountability. In Adam's fall,
our entire humanity fell; and all who partake of that
humanity, partake necessarily of that fall and corruption. Hence, infants are subject to all the evils incident to our lapsed condition. They suffer hunger, thirst,
cold, heat; they are assailed by sickness, accidents,
distress of various kinds; and death, the penalty of the
first transgression, ever stands ready to strike them
down. Looking, then, to the state of infants as human
beings, born in sin, and having within them that "fault
and corruption of nature (undeveloped, indeed, but still
there), that naturally is engendered of the offspring of
Adam;" in consequence of which every person born
into this world deserves God's wrath and condemnation,
we should despair of any hope on their behalf. And
so also should we despair if shut up to that other fact,
that salvation is obtained only by the exercise of faith
in Christ Jesus ; for as infants cannot have faith, therefore they cannot believe; therefore they must be lost.
But in the case of infants we have reason to believe
that both these doctrines, true in themselves, and true
in their full applicability to adults, are so modified as
to admit the full salvation of infants, without in the
slightest degree denying the truth of either doctrine
stated, or impeaching the justice and unchangeableness
of God. There is but one Saviour and one salvation;
and infants, if saved, must be saved by that one Saviour
and through that one salvation. What then were the
    39

feelings of Jesus toward children when on earth? This
we readily learn from several striking facts. He invited
them to him; He laid his hands upon them; He took
them up in his arms; He blessed them; He said, "Of
such is the kingdom of heaven."

How significant is all this of Christ's love and tenderness towards "these little ones!" And if by the
term "Kingdom of Heaven" is meant the state of perfect felicity in the world above, and there is no reason
why we should not thus understand it, then "it is an
explicit affirmation by Him who not only knows what
will be, but Himself "holds the keys of death and hell;"
that of them, "even little children, and of those who, by
renewing grace, are made like to them, will the inhabitants of the heavenly world consist." Dr. Doddridge,
commenting on the narration of Christ's interview with
these children, as recorded by St. Matthew, remarks,
"Let parents view this sight with pleasure and thankfulness; let it encourage them to bring their children
to Christ by faith, and to commit them to him by baptism and prayer. And if he who has the keys of death
and the unseen world see fit to remove those dear creatures from us in their early days, let the remembrance
of this story comfort us, and teach us to hope that He
who so graciously received these children, has not forgotten ours; but that they are sweetly fallen asleep in
Him, and will be the everlasting objects of His care
and love, ' For of such is the Kingdom of Heaven.' "

To the same purport are the words of Dr. Scott, who

says, "Indeed the expression may also intimate that the Kingdom of Heavenly Glory is greatly constituted of such as die in infancy. Infants are as capable of regeneration as grown persons; and there is abundant ground to conclude that all those who have not lived to commit actual transgression, though they share in the effect of the first Adam's offence, will also share in the blessings of the second Adam's gracious covenant, without their personal faith and obedience, but not without the regenerating influence of the Spirit of Christ."

The views which we thus deduce from Christ's interview with the little children, are sustained by a further consideration of God's character as revealed to us in the Bible, and His dealings with the children of men. His character is spotlessly holy, just, and good. Nor can He do anything which will at all conflict with this representation of Himself in His blessed word. But to consign one-half of the entire race of men to eternal death because they did not exercise an active faith in Christ, when, by reason of their tender age, they could not either know Him or believe in Him; to cut them thus off before even an opportunity was afforded them for the manifestation of faith; not giving to them a common chance of salvation, but hurrying them away to everlasting woe before their minds opened to a knowledge of themselves or God; such a course of procedure is so abhorrent to all our ideas of divine mercy and justice, that every instinct of our nature shrinks from believing it, and constrains us to say that infants are saved through the abounding grace of God manifested in Christ Jesus our Lord.

"I take it as a fact," says a distinguished writer, "that divine benevolence does not in any case inflict penal evil upon any intelligent creature, nor withhold from them appropriate happiness, unless where the penalty has been incurred and the forfeiture made by sin; in that case divine law and justice must be vindicated. In the case of infants, the vindication has been made, and through Christ they may be saved. That believers may and will be saved is absolutely certain. Infants cannot believe; but will they for that reason perish? May not, will not divine benevolence impart to them the prepared salvation which they need, but which, through natural incompetency, they cannot seek and accept? Under the moral government of God it is a recognised fact, that responsibility is always proportional to the opportunities and means which He has given to men to know and do His will. 'The servant who knew his master's will and did it not, shall be beaten with many stripes; but he who knew not his master's will, and committed things worthy of stripes, shall be beaten with few.' Absolute and invincible ignorance of duty can involve no responsibility; as many as have sinned without the revealed law, will be dealt with accordingly; and they who sin under and with a knowledge of the law, will be judged by the law. The heathen will not be condemned for not believing the gospel which they had never heard, and of which they had no knowledge. No more will be required of them, nor of any, than a faithful improvement of the means of knowledge and obedience which they had. It is their unfaithfulness to what they knew, or might and ought to have known, that leaves them guilty and without excuse. Will infants perish because of their non-acceptance of a Saviour, although their natural imbecility renders such acceptance an absolute impossibility? I admit and believe that they 'are by nature children of wrath;' but, as they do not live to years of moral agency to resist and reject either natural or revealed religion, will they not be saved by grace? Will they not be the objects of the benevolence and mercy of Him who has sworn that He has no pleasure even in the death of those who defy His authority, reject His grace, and die in their sins? God's vindictive displeasure is exercised against wilful sinners only. Where there is no crime he delights in showing favour and conferring happiness. This is true as to holy angels, and all other upright and intelligent creatures; and even on fallen man He delights to bestow happiness where His justice is recognised and His mercy sought; and the grace which reigns through righteousness unto eternal life by Jesus Christ our Lord, does not will that one of these little ones should perish."

When then we behold, as we so often do, these morning flowers plucked by death, what should be our feelings? I well know what *are* our feelings; but what

ought to be their character? The flesh cries out in its
anguish; the heart mourns its removed idol; the spirit
bends and almost breaks beneath its burden of sorrow;
but if we regarded the matter aright, we should find in
this affliction a source of precious consolation. The
child early lost is early saved. Before its tender years
had been made rigid with guilt, while its young mind
had scarcely taken in the meaning of sin, and ere its
little heart had developed the evil principles of a cor
rupt nature, it was removed to a world where sin is not,
where holiness alone abides. And not only so, but it
is taken away from a mass of sin, ignorance, sorrow,
sickness, pain, distress, disappointment, which, as we
look back upon life, almost appals, and which, had we
contemplated it in full at the beginning of our career,
we should have prayed for death to release us from its
burden. To this untold amount of suffering, avoided by
the early removal of children, we must add the equally
untold amount of happiness which they enjoy in heaven.
It is the aim of all parents to remove from their children suffering of every sort, and to bestow upon them
pleasures of every proper kind. To this end they toil,
and watch, and pray; and yet, after all, how imperfectly do they succeed, either in driving away sorrow
or in securing joy; the sad scenes and hours of life
will predominate, and cast dismal shadows over our
devious paths. But death takes from these darlings all
sources of woe and sorrow, and ushers them into full
and perfect bliss; and why should father or mother

mourn when such a priceless boon has been bestowed
upon their precious child?   They may well mourn that
they shall fold the lamb no more in their arms, that its
sweet face will no more smile on them, or its little
tongue no more utter their names; they may sorrow
that so great a blank is made in their household, and
so many tendril-like ties that clasped their babe have
been torn away; but for the dead one they should not
mourn.   They should for it rejoice; and it is a selfish feeling which would bring it back to this world
of sin, and temptation, and misery, and take it
away from that land of holy bliss, simply to fill our
arms again with its form, and cheer our hearts again
with its presence.   The emotions which should be
cherished have been well portrayed and beautifully
illustrated by the following outpouring of a parent's
heart on the second anniversary of the death of the
little lamb of his flock.   Its simplicity must touch the
heart of every reader, while its truth and beauty are
eminently scriptural and comforting:

"Two years ago to-day he went to heaven. With us
they have been long, long years since we heard the sound
of his sweet voice, and the merry laugh that burst from
his glad heart.   He was the youngest of our flock.
Three summers he had been with us, and O! he was
brighter and sunnier than any summer day of them all.
But he died as the third year of his life was closing.
The others were older than he, and all we had of childhood's glee and gladness were buried when we laid him

in the grave. Since then our hearts have been yearning
for the boy that is gone. ‹Gone, but not lost!’ we
have said a thousand times ; and we think of him ever
as living and blessed in another place not far from us.

"Two years in heaven ! They do not measure time
in that world ; there are no weeks, or months, or years ;
but all the time we have been mourning his absence
here, he has been happy there. And when we think
of what he has been enjoying, and the rapid progress
he has been making, we feel that it is well for him that
he has been taken away.

"Two years with angels ! They have been his constant companions, his teachers too ; and from them he
has drawn lessons of knowledge and of love. The
cherubim are said to excel in knowledge, while love
glows more ardently in the breast of seraphim. He
has been two years in the company of both, and must
have become very like them.

"Two years with the redeemed ! They have told
him of the Saviour, in whose blood they wash their
robes, and whose righteousness is their salvation. The
child, while with us, knew little of Jesus and His dying
love ; but he has heard of Him now, and has learned
to love Him who said, ‹Suffer little children to come
unto me.’ There are some among those redeemed who
would have loved him here, had they been living with
us ; but they went to glory before him, and have wel-
comed him now to their company. I am not sure they
know him as our child ; and yet do we love to think

that he is in the arms of those who have gone from our
arms, and thus broken families are reunited around the
throne of God and the Lamb.

"Tᴡᴏ ʏᴇᴀʀs ᴡɪᴛʜ Cʜʀɪsᴛ! It is joy to know that
our child has been two years with the Saviour, in His
immediate presence, learning of Him, and making heaven
vocal with songs of rapture and love. The blessed
Saviour took little children in his arms when he was
here on earth, and he takes them in his bosom there.
Blessed Jesus! blessed children! blessed child!

"He often wept when he was with us; he suffered much
before he died; seven days and nights he was torn with
fierce convulsion ere his soul yielded and fled to heaven.
But now for two years he has not wept! He has known
no pain for two years. That little child who was pleased
with a rattle, now meets with angels, and feels himself
at home. He walks among the tallest spirits that bend
in the presence of the Infinite, and is as free and happy
as any who are there. And when we think of joys that
are his, we are more than willing that he should stay
where he now dwells, though our hope is darkened by
the shadow of his grave, and our hearts are aching all
the time for his return. Long and weary have been the
years without him; but they have been blessed years
to him in heaven. 'Even so, Father.' 'Not our will,
but thine be done.'"

How many kindling, glowing thoughts are suggested
by the plucking of these morning flowers! We call to
mind their number, and imagination revels amidst the

40

myriads of children in the world of glory. We think
of their beauty, perfect in the comeliness which their
God has put upon them. We think of their employ
ments, vying with each other, as did the children in the
temple at Jerusalem, in singing "Hosannas to the Son
of David." We reflect upon their growth, expanding
in soul and mind under the tuition of angels, and away
from the depressing influences of sin and earth, and we
imagine their gladness as they welcome within those
gates of pearl their fathers, mothers, brothers, and sisters, and lead them to "Him who sitteth upon the
throne" of heaven. These, and other kindred thoughts,
press upon the mind as we see death busily gathering
these morning flowers for the Paradise of God. There
is one, however, that should be thrown into bolder
relief than the rest, for it is of deep practical importance. How much ought parents who have lost children
to love the Saviour who has taken them to himself in
glory! Father, whose child was taken from your arms
that it might be folded in the Saviour's arms, and
crowned by Him with unending joy, do you love the
Saviour who thus honoured your child and blessed it
with His grace and His salvation? Mother, whose babe
was removed from your breast that it might rest in
glory on the Saviour's bosom, do you love that Saviour
who thus early took your lamb from the tangled wilderness and dark pitfalls of earth, and made it to dwell a
bright and happy spirit in the world of bliss? You
would love an earthly benefactor, but who of earth

could bestow upon your child the boon of everlasting life? And shall you not love Him by whose death death is conquered; by whose blood sin is pardoned; by whose grace souls are saved; by whose mercy your darling child has been taken from the evil to come, and made "an heir of God and joint heir of Christ to an inheritance that is incorruptible, and undefiled, and that fadeth not away?" Love the Saviour who loved your child, and said "Suffer little children to come unto me, for of such is the Kingdom of Heaven!" Love the Saviour who has transplanted your child into this kingdom! and then, when death shall take you hence, you shall rejoin your child and dwell together in the presence chamber of your God.

STEVENS.

Scriptural Selections.

And it came to pass on the seventh day, that the child died. And the servants of David feared to tell him that the child was dead; for they said, Behold, while the child was yet alive, we spake unto him, and he would not hearken unto our voice: how will he then vex himself, if we tell him that the child is dead?

But when David saw that his servants whispered, David perceived that the child was dead: therefore David said unto his servants, Is the child dead? And they said, He is dead.

Then David arose from the earth, and washed, and anointed himself, and changed his apparel, and came into the house of the Lord and worshipped: then he came to his own house: and when he required, they set bread before him, and he did eat.

Then said his servants unto him, What thing is this that thou hast done? Thou didst fast and weep for the child while it was alive; but when the child was dead, thou didst rise and eat bread.

And he said, While the child was yet alive, I fasted and wept: for I said, Who can tell whether God will be gracious to me, that the child may live?—2 *Samuel*, xii. 18–23.

Then were there brought unto him little children, that he should put his hands on them, and pray: and the disciples rebuked them.

But Jesus said, Suffer little children, and forbid them not to come unto me; for of such is the kingdom of heaven.

And he laid his hands on them, and departed thence.—*Matt.* xix. 13–15.

Verily I say unto you, Whosoever shall not receive the kingdom of God as a little child, he shall not enter therein.—*Mark*, x. 15.

THE GATHERED FLOWER.

AND this is death! how cold and still,
  And yet how lovely it appears!
Too cold to let the gazer smile,
  And yet too beautiful for tears.
The sparkling eye no more is bright,
  The cheek hath lost its rose-like red;
And yet it is with strange delight
  I stand and gaze upon the dead.

But when I see the fair wide brow,
  Half shaded by the silken hair,
That never looked so fair as now,
  When life and health were laughing there,
I wonder not that grief should swell
  So wildly upward in the breast,
And that strong passion once rebel,
  That need not, cannot be suppressed.

And yet why mourn? that deep repose
  Shall never more be broke by pain;
Those lips no more in sighs unclose,
  Those eyes shall never weep again.
For think not that the blushing flower
  Shall wither in the churchyard sod,
'Twas made to gild an angel's bower
  Within the paradise of God.

II.

The Sun going down while yet Day.

" She hath given up the ghost ; her sun is gone down while it was yet day."—Jeremiah, xv. 9.

BEAUTIFULLY illustrative of the words of the weeping Prophet is the following account of the death of Miss Eliza Cuningham, written by her uncle, the Rev. John Newton, rector of St. Mary, Woolnoth, London. It has been slightly abridged, but no important matter has been omitted.

In May. 1782, my sister Cuningham was at Edinburgh, chiefly on account of her eldest daughter, then in the fourteenth year of her age, who was very ill of a consumption. She had already buried an only son, at the age of twelve ; and while all a mother's care and feelings were engaged by the rapid decline of a second amiable child, she was unexpectedly and suddenly bereaved of an affectionate husband. Her trials were great, but the Lord had prepared her for them. She was a believer. Her faith was strong; her graces active ; her conduct exemplary. She walked with God, and he supported her. And though she was a tender and sympathizing friend, she had a happy firmness of temper, so that her character as a Christian, and the propriety of her behaviour in every branch of life,

(318)

appeared with peculiar advantage in the season of affliction. She returned to Anstruther a widow, with her sick child, who languished till October, and then died.

Though my sister had many valuable and pleasing connexions in Scotland, yet her strongest tie being broken, she readily accepted my invitation to come and live with us. She was not only dear to me as Mrs. Newton's sister, but we had lived long in the habits of intimate friendship. I knew her worth, and she was partial to me. She had yet one child remaining, her dear Eliza. We already had a dear orphan niece, whom we had, about seven years before, adopted for our own daughter. My active, fond imagination, anticipated the time of her arrival, and drew a pleasing picture of the addition the company of such a sister, such a friend, would make to the happiness of our family. The children likewise—there was no great disparity between them either in years or stature. From what I had heard of Eliza, I was prepared to love her before I saw her; though she came afterwards into my hands like a heap of untold gold, which, when counted over, proves to be a larger sum than was expected. My fancy paired and united these children; I hoped that the friendship between us and my sister would be perpetuated in them; I seemed to see them like twin sisters, of one heart and mind, habited nearly alike, always together, always with us. Such was my plan —but the Lord's plan was very different, and therefore mine failed.   It is happy for us poor short-sighted creatures, unable as we are to foresee the consequences of our own wishes, that if we know and trust him, he is often pleased to put a merciful negative upon our purposes; and condescends to choose better for us than we can for ourselves.   What might have been the issue of my plan, could it have taken place, I know not; but I can now praise and adore him for the gracious issue of his.   I praise his name, that I can cheerfully comply with his word, which says, "Be still, and know that I am God."   I not only can bow (as it becomes a creature and a sinner to do) to his sovereignty; but I admire his wisdom and goodness, and can say from my heart, "He has done all things well."

My sister had settled her affairs previous to her removal, and nothing remained, but to take leave of her friends, of whom she had many not only in Anstruther, but in different parts of the country.   In February, 1783, I received a letter from her, which before I opened, I expected was to inform me that she was upon the road in her way to London.   But the information was, that in a little journey she had made to bid a friend farewell, she had caught a violent cold, which brought on a fever and a cough, with other symptoms, which though she described as gently as possible, that we might not be alarmed, obliged me to give up instantly the pleasing hope of seeing her.   Succeeding letters confirmed my apprehensions; her malady increased, and she was soon confined to her bed.   Eliza was at school

at Musselburgh. Till then she had enjoyed a perfect
state of health; but while her dear mother was rapidly
declining, she likewise caught a great cold, and her life
was soon thought to be in danger. On this occasion,
that fortitude and resolution which so strongly marked
my sister's character, was remarkably displayed. She
knew that her own race was almost finished; she
earnestly desired that Eliza might live or die with us:
And the physicians advised a speedy removal to the
South. Accordingly, to save time and to save Eliza
from the impressions which the sight of a dying parent
might probably make upon her spirits, and possibly
apprehensive that the interview might make too great
an impression upon her own, she sent this her only
beloved child from Edinburgh directly to London, without letting her come home to take a last leave of her.
She contented herself with committing and bequeathing
her child to our care and love, in a letter, which I
believe was the last she was able to write.

Thus powerfully recommended by the pathetic charge
of a dying parent, the dearest friend we had upon earth,
and by that plea for compassion, which her illness might
have strongly urged even upon strangers, we received
our dear Eliza as a trust, and as a treasure, on the
fifteenth of March. My sister lived long enough to have
the comfort of knowing, not only that she was safely
arrived, but was perfectly pleased with her new situation. She was now freed from all earthly cares. She
suffered much in the remaining part of her illness, but
41

she knew in whom she believed; she possessed a peace
past understanding, and a hope full of glory. She
entered into the joy of her Lord on the tenth of May,
1783, respected and regretted by all who knew her.

I now perceived that the Lord had sent me a treasure
indeed. Eliza's person was agreeable. There was an
ease and elegance in her whole address, and a graceful-
ness, till long illness and great weakness bowed her
down. Her disposition was lively, her genius quick and
inventive, and if she had enjoyed health, she probably
would have excelled in everything she attempted, that
required ingenuity. Her understanding, particularly
her judgment, and her sense of propriety, was far above
her years. There was something in her appearance
which usually procured her favour at first sight. She
was honoured by the notice of several persons of distinction, which, though I thankfully attribute in part to
their kindness to me, I believe was a good deal owing to
something uncommon in her. But her principal endear-
ing qualities, which could be only fully known to us,
who lived with her, were the sweetness of her temper,
and a heart formed for the exercise of affection, gratitude, and friendship. Whether, when at school, she
might have heard sorrowful tales from children, who,
having lost their parents, met with a great difference, in
point of tenderness, when they came under the direction of uncles and aunts, and might think that all
uncles and aunts were alike, I know not; but I have
understood since from herself, that she did not come to

us with any highly raised expectations of the treatment she was to meet with. But as she found (the Lord in mercy to her and to us having opened our hearts to receive her) that it was hardly possible for her own parents to have treated her more tenderly, and. that it was from that time the business and pleasure of our lives to study how to oblige her, and how to alleviate the afflictions we were unable to remove; so we likewise found, that the seeds of our kindness could hardly be sown in a more promising and fruitful soil. I know not that either her aunt or I ever saw a cloud upon her countenance during the time she was with us. It is true we did not, we could not unnecessarily cross her; but if we thought it expedient to overrule any proposal she made, she acquiesced with a sweet smile: and we were certain that we should never hear of that proposal again. Her delicacy however was quicker than our observation; and she would sometimes say, when we could not perceive the least reason for it, " I am afraid I answered you peevishly; indeed I did; if I did, I ask your pardon. I should be very ungrateful, if I thought any pleasure equal to that of endeavouring to please you." It is no wonder that we dearly loved such a child.

Wonderful is the frame of the human heart. The Lord claims and deserves it all; yet there is still room for all the charities of relative life, and scope for their full play; and they are capable of yielding the sincerest

pleasures this world can afford, if held in subordination
to what is supremely due to him.

The hectic fever, cough, and sweats, which Eliza
brought with her from Scotland, were subdued in the
course of the summer, and there appeared no reason to
apprehend that she would be taken off very suddenly.
But still there was a worm preying upon the root of
this pretty gourd. She had seldom any severe pain, till
within the last fortnight of her life, and usually slept
well; but when awake she was always ill. I believe
she knew not an hour of perfect ease; and they who
intimately knew her state, could not but wonder to see
her so placid, cheerful, and attentive, when in company,
as she generally was. Many times, when the tears
have silently stolen down her cheeks, if she saw that her
aunt or I observed her, she would wipe them away,
come to us with a smile and a kiss; and say, " Do not
be uneasy, I am not very ill, I can bear it, I shall be
better presently ;" or to that effect.

Her case was thought beyond the reach of medicine,
and, for a time, no medicine was used. She had air
and exercise, as the weather and circumstances would
permit. For the rest, she amused herself as she could
with her guitar or harpsichord, with her needle, and
with reading. She had a part likewise, when able, in
such visits as we paid or received ; and our visits were
generally regulated by a regard to what she could bear.
Her aunt, especially, seldom went abroad but at such
times, and to such places, as we thought agreeable and

convenient to her. For we could perceive that she loved home best, and best of all when we were at home with her.

In April, 1784, we put her under the care of my dear friend Dr. Benamor. To the blessing of the Lord on his skill and endeavours, I ascribe the pleasure of having her continued with us so long. But what can the most efficacious medicines, or the best physicians, avail to prolong life, when the hour approaches, in which the prayer of the Great Intercessor must be accomplished, "Father, I will that they whom thou hast given me may be with me where I am to behold my glory?" This was the proper cause of my dear Eliza's death. The Lord sent this child to me to be brought up for him; he owned my poor endeavours: and when her education was completed, and she was ripened for heaven, he took her home to himself. He has richly paid me my wages, in the employment itself, and in the happy issue.

Dr. Benamor advising a trial of the salt water, we passed the month of August, 1784, with her, partly at Mr. Walter Taylor's, at Southampton, and partly at Charles Etty's, Esq., of Priestlands, near Symington. While she was with these kind and generous friends, she had every accommodation and assistance that could be thought of or wished for. And the bathing was evidently useful, so far as to give some additional strength to her very weak and relaxed frame, which assisted her in going more comfortably through the last winter. We

were, therefore, encouraged, and advised to repeat our
visit to Southampton this autumn. But the success was
not the same. Her feet and legs had already begun to
swell, and the evening before she took cold, which
brought on a return of the fever and cough; and though
Dr. Allen was successful in removing these symptoms
in about a fortnight, and she bathed a few times, she
could not persevere. However, the advantages of
situation, air, and exercise, being much greater than she
could have in London, and as we were with friends
whom she, as well as we, dearly loved, she continued
at Southampton six weeks; but she was unable to proceed to Mr. Etty's, who was very desirous of repeating
his former kindness. The Lord strengthened her to
perform her journey home without inconvenience. She
returned the sixteenth of September; then she entered
our door for the last time, for she went out no more,
till she was carried out to be put into the hearse.

I have thus put together, in one view, a brief account
of what relates to her illness, till within the last three
weeks of her pilgrimage. I now come to what is much
more important and interesting. Her excellent parents
had conscientiously endeavoured to bring her up in the
nurture and admonition of the Lord, and the principles
of religion had been instilled into her from her infancy.
Their labours were thus far attended with success,
that no child could be more obedient or obliging, or
more remote from evil habits or evil tempers; but I
could not perceive, when she came to us, that she had

any heart-affecting sense of divine things. But being under my roof, she of course, when her health would permit, attended on my ministry, and was usually present when I prayed and expounded the Scriptures, morning and evening, in the family. Friends and ministers were likewise frequently with us, whose character and conversation were well suited to engage her notice, and to help her to form a right idea of the Christian principles and temper. Knowing that she was of a thinking turn, I left her to make her own reflections upon what she saw and heard, committing her to the Lord from whom I had received her, and entreating him to be her effectual teacher. When I did attempt to talk with her upon the concerns of her soul, she could give me no answer but with tears. But I soon had great encouragement to hope that the Lord had both enlightened her understanding, and had drawn the desires of her heart to himself. Great was her delight in the ordinances; exemplary her attention under the preaching. To be debarred from going to hear prayer at our stated times, was a trial which, though she patiently bore, seemed to affect her more than any other, and she did not greatly care what she endured in the remainder of the week, provided she was well enough to attend the public worship. The judicious observations she sometimes made upon what had passed in conversation, upon incidents, books, and sermons, indicated a sound scriptural judgment, and a spiritual taste. And my hope was confirmed by her whole deportment, which was becoming the Gospel of Christ. So that had she died suddenly, on any day within about a year and a half past, I should have had no doubt that she had passed from death unto life. But I could seldom prevail with her to speak of herself: if she did, it was with the greatest diffidence and caution.

Soon after her return from Southampton, she became acquainted with acute pain, to which she had, till then, been much a stranger. Her gentle spirit, which had borne up under a long and languishing illness, was not so capable of supporting pain. It did not occasion any improper temper or language, but it wore her away apace. Friday the thirteenth of September, she was down stairs for the last time, and then she was brought down and carried up in arms.

It now became very desirable to hear from herself an explicit account of the hope that was in her; especially as, upon some symptoms of an approaching mortification, she appeared to be a little alarmed, and of course, not thoroughly reconciled to the thoughts of death. Her aunt waited for the first convenient opportunity of intimating to her the probability that the time of her departure was at hand. The next morning, Saturday the first of October, presented one. She found herself remarkably better; her pains were almost gone, her spirits revived; the favourable change was visible in her countenance. Her aunt began to break the subject to her by saying, "My dear, were you not extremely ill last night?" She replied, "Indeed I was." "Had you not been relieved, I think you could not have continued long." "I believe I could not." "My dear, I have been very anxiously concerned for your life." "But I hope, my dear aunt, you are not so now." She then opened her mind and spoke freely. I cannot repeat the whole; the substance was to this effect: "My views of things have been for some time very different from what they were when I came to you. I have seen and felt the vanity of childhood and youth." Her aunt said, "I believe you have long made a conscience of secret prayer." She answered, "Yes; I have long and earnestly sought the Lord, with reference to the change which is now approaching. I have not yet that full assurance which is so desirable; but I have a hope, I trust, a good hope, and I believe the Lord will give me whatever he sees necessary for me, before he takes me from hence. I have prayed to him to fit me for himself; and then, whether sooner or later, it signifies but little." Here was a comfortable point gained. We were satisfied that she had given up all expectation of living, and could speak of her departure without being distressed.

It will not be expected that a child at her age should speak systematically. Nor had she learnt her religion from a system or form of words, however sound. The Lord himself was her teacher. But, from what little she had at different times said to me, I was well satisfied that she had received a true conviction of the evil of sin, and of her own state by nature as a sinner.

42

When she spoke of the Lord, she meant the Lord JESUS CHRIST, the Great Shepherd, who gathers such lambs in his arms, and carries them in his bosom. She believed him to be God and man in one person; and that hope, of which she shall never be ashamed, was founded on his atonement, grace, and power. As I do not intend to put words into her mouth which she never spoke, I mention this lest any person should be disappointed at not finding a certain phraseology to which they may have been accustomed.

Her apparent revival was of short duration. In the evening of the same day, she began to complain of a sore throat, which became worse, and, before Sunday noon, threatened an absolute suffocation. When Dr. Benamor, who the day before had almost entertained hopes of her recovery, found her so suddenly and greatly altered, he could not at the moment prevent some signs of his concern from appearing in his countenance. She quickly perceived it, and desired he would plainly tell her his sentiments. When he had recovered himself he said, "You are not so well as when I saw you on Saturday." She answered, that she trusted all would be well soon. He replied, that whether she lived or died, it would be well and to the glory of God. He told me that he had much pleasing conversation with her that morning; some particulars of which he had committed to writing, but that he had lost the paper. From that time she may be said to have been dying, as we expected her departure from one hour to another.

When the doctor came on Wednesday, she entreated him to tell her how long he thought she might live. He said, "Are you in earnest, my dear?" She answered, "Indeed I am." At that time there were great appearances that a mortification had actually begun. He therefore told her, he thought it possible she might hold out till eight in the evening, but did not expect she could survive midnight at furthest. On hearing him say so, low as she was, her eyes seemed to sparkle with their former vivacity, and fixing them on him with an air of ineffable satisfaction, she said, "Oh, that is good news indeed." And she repeated it as such to a person who came soon after into the room, and said with lively emotions of joy, "The doctor tells me I shall stay here but a few hours more." In the afternoon she noticed and counted the clock, I believe, every time it struck; and when it struck seven, she said, "Another hour, and then!" But it pleased the Lord to spare her to us another day.

She suffered much in the course of Wednesday night, but was quite resigned and patient. Our kind servants, who, from their love to her and to us, watched her night and day with a solicitude and tenderness which wealth is too poor to purchase—were the only witnesses of the affectionate and grateful manner in which she repeatedly thanked them for their services and attention to her.

I was surprised on Thursday morning to find her not only alive, but in some respects better. The tokens of mortification again disappeared. This was her last day, and it was a memorable day to us. When Dr. Benamor asked her how she was, she answered, "Truly happy, and if this be dying, it is a pleasant thing to die." She said to me about ten o'clock, "My dear uncle, I would not change conditions with any person upon earth. Oh, how gracious is the Lord to me! Oh, what a change is before me!" She was several times asked, if she could wish to live, provided the Lord should restore her to perfect health? Her answer was, "Not for all the world," and sometimes "Not for a thousand worlds.* Do not weep for me, my dear aunt; but rather rejoice and praise on my account." We asked her if she would choose a text for her own funeral sermon? She readily mentioned, *Whom the Lord loveth he chasteneth.* "That," said she, "has been my experience; my afflictions have been many, but not too many; nor has the greatest of them been too great; I praise him for them all." But after a pause, she said, "Stay, I think there is another text which may do better; let it be *Blessed are the dead which die in the Lord.* That is my experience now." She likewise chose a hymn to be sung after the sermon.

But I must check myself, and set down but a small part of the gracious words which the Lord enabled her to speak in the course of the day. Though she was frequently interrupted by pains and agonies, she had

---

* The last time she was asked this question she said (as I have been since informed), "I desire to have no choice."

something to say, either in the way of admonition or consolation, as she thought most suitable, to every one she saw. To her most constant attendant she said, "Be sure you continue to call upon the Lord; and if you think he does not hear you now, he will at last, as he has heard me." She spoke a great deal to an intimate friend, who was with her every day, which I hope she will long remember as the testimony of her dying Eliza. Amongst other things she said, "See how comfortable the Lord can make a dying bed! Do you think that you shall have such an assurance when you come to die?" Being answered, "I hope so, my dear," she replied, "But do you earnestly and with all your heart pray to the Lord for it? If you seek him you shall surely find him." She then prayed affectionately and fervently for her friend, afterwards for her cousin, and then for another of our family, who was present. Her prayer was not long, but her every word was weighty, and her manner very affecting; the purport was, that they might all be taught and comforted by the Lord. About five in the afternoon, she desired me to pray with her once more. Surely I then prayed from my heart. When I had finished, she said, Amen. I said, "My dear child, have I expressed your meaning?" She answered, "Oh, yes!" and then added, "I am ready to say, *Why are his chariot wheels so long coming?* But I hope he will enable me to wait his hour with patience." These were the last words I heard her speak.

Towards seven o'clock, I was walking in the garden, and earnestly engaged in prayer for her, when a servant came to me, and said, "She is gone." O Lord, how great is thy power! how great is thy goodness! A few days before, had it been practicable and lawful, what would I not have given to procure her recovery! yet seldom in my life have I known a more heartfelt joy, than when these words, *She is gone*, sounded in my ears. I ran up stairs, and our whole little family were soon round her bed. Though her aunt and another person were sitting with their eyes fixed upon her, she was gone, perhaps, a few minutes before she was missed. She lay upon her left side, with her cheek gently reclining upon her hand as if in a sweet sleep. And I thought there was a smile on her countenance. Never, surely, did death appear in a more beautiful, inviting form! We fell upon our knees, and (I think I may say), I returned my most unfeigned thanks to God and my Saviour, for his abundant goodness to her, crowned in this last instance by giving her so gentle a dismission. Yes, I am satisfied, I am comforted. And if one of the tears involuntarily shed could have recalled her to life, to health, to an assemblage of all that this world could contribute to her happiness, I would have laboured hard to suppress it. Now my largest desires for her are accomplished. The days of her mourning are ended She is landed on that peaceful shore, where the storms of trouble never blow. She is for ever out of the reach of sorrow, sin, temptation, and snares. Now she is before the throne! she sees him, whom not having seen, she loved; she drinks of the rivers of pleasure, which are at his right hand, and shall thirst no more.

She was born at St. Margaret's, Rochester, February 6, 1771.

She breathed her spirit into her Redeemer's hands, a little before seven in the evening, on the 6th of October, 1785, aged fourteen years and eight months.

I shall be glad if this little narrative may prove an encouragement to my friends who have children. May we not conceive the Lord saying to us, as Pharaoh's daughter said to the mother of Moses, " Take this child and bring it up for me, and I will pay thee thy wages." How solemn the trust! how important and difficult the discharge of it! but how rich the reward if our endeavours are crowned with success! And we have everything to hope from his power and goodness, if, in dependence upon his blessing, we can fully and diligently aim at fulfilling his will. Happy they who will say at the last day, " Behold, here am I, and the children which thou hast given me."

The children of my friends will likewise see my narrative. May it convince them that it is practicable and good to seek the Lord betimes! My dear Eliza's state of languor prevented her from associating with young people of her own age, so frequently and freely as she might otherwise have done. But these papers will come into the hands of some such, whom she knew, and whom she loved. To them I particularly commend and dedicate this relation. Oh! my dear young friends, had you seen with what dignity of spirit she filled up the last scene of her life, you must have been affected by it! Let not the liveliness of your spirits, and the gayety of the prospects around you, prevent you from considering that to you likewise days will certainly come (unless you are suddenly snatched out of life), when you will say, and feel, that the world, and all in it, can afford you no pleasure. But there is a Saviour, and a mighty One, always near, always gracious to those who seek him. May you, like her, be enabled to choose him, as the Guide of your youth, and the Lord of your hearts. Then, like her, you will find support and comfort under affliction, wisdom to direct your conduct, a good hope in death, and by death a happy translation to everlasting life.

I have only to add my prayer, that a blessing from on high may descend upon the persons and families of all my friends, and upon all into whose hands this paper may providentially come.

JOHN NEWTON.

SCRIPTURAL SELECTIONS.

REMEMBER now thy Creator in the days of thy youth, while the evil days come not, nor the years draw nigh, when thou shalt say, I have no pleasure in them.—*Ecclesiastes*, xii. 1.

Father, I will that they also whom thou hast given me be with me where I am; that they may behold my glory, which thou hast given me: for thou lovedst me before the foundation of the world.—*John*, xvii. 24.

In my Father's house are many mansions: if it were not so, I would have told you.   I go to prepare a place for you.

And if I go and prepare a place for you, I will come again, and receive you unto myself: that where I am, there ye may be also.— *John*, xiv. 2, 3.

Precious in the sight of the Lord is the death of his saints.— *Ps*. cxvi. 15.

The righteous perisheth, and no man layeth it to heart; and merciful men are taken away, none considering that the righteous is taken away from the evil to come.

He shall enter into peace: they shall rest in their beds, each one walking in his uprightness.—*Isaiah*, lviii. 1, 2.

Weep not for Her!

Weep not for her! her span was like,the sky,
  Whose thousand stars shine beautiful and bright,
Like flowers that know not what it is to die,
  Like long-linked shadeless months of polar light,
Like music floating o'er a waveless lake,
While echo answers from the flowery brake,
          Weep not for her!

Weep not for her! she died in early youth,
  Ere hope had lost its rich romantic hues,
When human bosoms seemed the home of truth,
  And earth still gleamed with beauty's radiant dews.
Her summer prime waned not to days that freeze,
Her *wine* of life was not run to the lees,
          Weep not for her!

Weep not for her! By fleet or slow decay
  It never grieved her bosom's core to mark
The playmates of her childhood wane away,
  Her prospects wither, and her hopes grow dark.
Translated by her God with spirit shriven,
She passed, as 'twere on smiles, from earth to heaven;
          Weep not for her!

Weep not for her! It was not hers to feel
  The miseries that corrode amassing years,
'Gainst dreams of baffled bliss the heart to steel,
  To wander sad down age's vale of tears,

As whirl the withered leaves from friendship's tree,
And on earth's wintry world alone to be ;
   Weep not for her !

Weep not for her !   She is an angel now,
 And treads the sapphire floors of Paradise,
All darkness wiped from her refulgent brow,
 Sin, sorrow, suffering, banished from her eyes
Victorious over death, to her appears
The vista'd joys of heaven's eternal years ;
   Weep not for her !

Weep not for her !   Her memory is the shrine
 Of pleasant thoughts soft as the scent of flowers,
Calm as on windless eve the sun's decline,
 Sweet as the song of birds among the bowers,
Rich as a rainbow with its hues of light,
Pure as the moonlight of an autumn night :
   Weep not for her !

Weep not for her !   There is no cause of woe
 But rather nerve the spirit that it walk
Unshrinking o'er the thorny path below,
 And from earth's low defilements keep thee back.
So when a few fleet swerving years have flown,
She 'll meet thee at heaven's gate—and lead thee on :
   Weep not for her !

III.

The Noontide Eclipse.

"I will cause the sun to go down at noon, and I will darken the earth in the clear day."—
AMOS, VIII. 9.

THE sudden shutting out of sunlight by an eclipsing moon, is a solemn and impressive scene. The face of nature wears, at such times, a strange and peculiar aspect. The animal creation is overcome with instinctive dread, and man, even though science has taught him to unveil this mystery of the skies, is awe-struck and humbled by the sublime phenomenon.

As the earth enters the penumbra, and the rays of the sun are first shorn of their light and heat, there arises a general feeling of expectation mingled with fear. Millions of eyes are turned heavenward, and when at last the moon encroaches on the sun's eastern limb, and slowly but surely obscures his bright disc, nearly every face in the shadowy belt is gazing upon the apparently extinguished orb in wonder, and unwillingly admitted alarm.

And is not the going out of a great life like the noontide eclipse? Is there not in the covering up in the grave of a form, once noble, active, and influential, something like the obscuration of the midday sun? There certainly is, and it requires but a slight effort of imagination to seize upon many of the points of parallel.

In human estimation the horizon of life, that point where the confines of the two worlds, the present and the future, meet and intermingle, is the far-off period of old age. Every man looks forward to the setting of his sun of life behind that western horizon, and scarcely dreams that it may go out suddenly at midday. Hence, death, in the years of manhood or womanhood,—after the powers of mind and body have reached their meridian height, and before the shadows of the evening begin to be stretched out, may be termed a noontide eclipse— a going down of the sun at midday.

It seems, at times, strange to us that God should so often call away persons from the active and influential duties of middle life, when they are apparently in the very zenith of their usefulness, and most needed in the world. We can only stand by in mute wonder and submission, as we behold the great props of the state or the church stricken down, when their supporting shoulders were most needed to uphold the incumbent edifice; or witness the great lights of learning and science gradually fade away in the firmament when their beams were most vivifying and enlightening. We ponder with ourselves, how differently we should have arranged the event; we even, perhaps, question the wisdom of the deed, and we ask, with an ill-concealed repining at the Divine will, Why doeth God these things? But in this we are both ignorant and foolish. We are so accustomed to associate human machinery with divine purposes, that, when we behold a person occupying an important post in the councils of the church or nation, we at once associate the idea of such a necessary connexion between the two as to make his removal perfectly disastrous. Here is one surrounded by a large family—its supporting life and centre: to take him away is like removing the nave of a wheel—the radiating spokes have no support, and the felloe is crushed and splits asunder at the first revolution. Here is another, the head and leader of an important system of agencies for the extension of Christ's kingdom; nothing apparently can be done without his aid and counsel: and to remove him would derange a whole system of well-devised plans, and, perhaps, destroy them altogether. Here is another, a minister of Christ, the pastor of a large and influential congregation, the wielder of great moral strength, the doer of important service to the church, the motive power to a moral enginery, the value of which cannot be computed. His life seems essential to the church, vast schemes of benevolence are hinged on him, and to do without him is to have a noonday eclipse. He cannot be spared; he must live, or the cause he sustains, like a tower of strength, will fail. Such are, oftentimes, men's views of their fellow men, and taking it for granted that they are true, they act accordingly.

Several circumstances here conspire to make our views on this point exceedingly defective. One is, that

we look only at a small segment of the great circle of
life, while God regards, with omniscient eye, the whole
circumference of our being. How often has our own
experience taught us that things which we earnestly
desire, and even sinfully covet as necessary to our
usefulness or comfort, would have proved, had they
been granted to us, sources of real evil and permanent
sorrow! How often have we formed, as we supposed,
wise plans; secured, as we thought, their completion,
been suddenly disappointed in carrying them into full
execution, wept bitter tears perhaps over our failure,
and then found, a few months or years afterwards, that,
had those plans been successful, and our long-cherished
hopes been gratified, it would have been most disastrous
to our peace, and ruinous to our well-being! We make
these mistakes daily; we are continually correcting
and readjusting our hopes and aims, and all this arises
from the fact previously stated, that we look at our
life only in the small section which is presented to us
day by day, and cannot take those comprehensive views
which sweep around its entire circumference, and survey the whole at a glance. So when we see a standard-
bearer of truth, a mighty man of intellectual valour, a
great central light in the moral firmament, fall in the
midst of the battle, or faint in the heat of the conflict,
or go out like an eclipsed sun at midday, we feel too
much as if some great calamity had befallen our world
which could not be repaired, and are too often led into
murmuring as unseemly as it is unwise. Could we, for

a moment, occupy God's point of view, and see the plans of human existence as He sees them, we should immediately perceive the infinite wisdom of causing these dreaded eclipses in human life, and in thus cutting off our hopes at the moment of expected fruition.

Not only is our range of thought limited to a very small segment of life's circle, but we still further err in basing all our views on things as they appear on earth. We judge according to the worldly aspects of the case, according to its temporal influence; not considering that the relations of each individual, not only to this earth, but to time itself, are but a very small part of his outstanding relations to a world to come, and the eternity that stretches away beyond the grave. "No man," says the Apostle, "liveth to himself;" and we see, with our own eyes, how impossible it is for man to isolate himself from his fellows; and may it not be that other, though to us invisible connexions, may link us to other classes of beings, and to future cycles of existence, which render the breaks and interruptions of earth necessary; and hence, those things which seem to mar the harmonies of life, and make discords and woes in society, are requisite to the filling up of God's designs, which take in all worlds, all space, all duration. We are, certainly, not prepared to pronounce any event disastrous, evil, or unwise, until we have made ourselves acquainted with all the bearings and influences of that event in all worlds, through all space, and for all time; until, in fine, we occupy the stand point of Divinity itself. Could we but feel more seriously than we do, how small is the section of our knowledge, how short-sighted is our vision, what meagre minds we possess, what limits bound us on every side, we should not, methinks, be so arrogant, presumptuous, or dogmatic; we should not question God's wisdom, or impugn his justice, or asperse his mercy; we should not give way to such impatient repining, such fault-finding sorrow, such sinful despair. We should, on the contrary, comfort ourselves, under bereavements, with the thought that God doeth all things well; that though inscrutable to us, they were wisely ordered by him, and his course would yet be vindicated from all cavils before the assembled universe, when the multitudes that circle about the Great White Throne shall shout with one acclaim "God is right—God is true— God is just—God is love!" We shall then see how, while He made what we deemed our interest subservient to his glory, He yet made his glory our highest good, causing us to fulfil the great ends of being more and more as we aim to advance his glory, the reflected splendour of which constitutes the highest bliss of saint and seraph, in earth and heaven.

If then, the whole of life was summed up in what we see of it this side the grave—if we were made to be the dwellers for a little season on this earth alone— or if the great end of existence was to glorify and exalt ourselves, then, indeed, the removal of friends

44

in the meridian hour, or the sudden extinguishment
of hope when it flamed brightest in the zenith, might
be regarded as a dire calamity—a sad eclipse, and
we might even deem it cruel for God thus to cause
the sun to go down at noon, and to darken the earth
in the clear day. But as life here is but the dawn
of an eternal being; as the earth is but the proba-
tionary school of a higher existence; as God's glory,
and not self-interest, is man's chief end and aim, so
are we debarred, by this exalted Christian philosophy,
from unduly repining, or casting blame on God, when
he obscures to us the greater lights which rule in
the day of our moral, or social, or political firmament.
He never eclipses them until they have done all their
appointed work. If the sun goes down at noon, it is
because that was its ordained boundary. And not
only may we have this assurance, but we may add to
it another, namely, that God never removes his servants from earth until the hour has arrived when he
requires their service nearer to his person in heaven.

"Learn," says an old writer, "to pray moderately
for the lives of Christ's people. Who can tell but
what Christ and we are praying counter to one
another? He may be saying in heaven, 'Father, I
will have such an one to be with me where I am;' and
we saying on earth, 'Lord we would have him to be
with us where we are.' We saying 'we cannot spare
him as yet;' and Christ saying 'I will be no longer
without him.' It is the force of this prayer of Christ,

'I will have them to be with me where I am,' that is
the cause of the death of the godly. It is the force of
this prayer that carries away so many of the saints in
our day."

These are the enlarged views which it becomes us to
take of what, in their earthly aspect, may be called
noontide eclipses; especially when it respects our
Christian relatives and friends. Every other view is
narrow, unsatisfactory, and unscriptural. The coming
in of death between us and the dear objects of our love
and veneration, at a time when they appear to ride the
highest and shine the brightest in their career of usefulness and honour, does not for ever obscure their
light, or obliterate their beams, any more than the
intervening moon blots out the sun, which it yet for a
time hides from sight. For though these loved ones
are eclipsed to us, they are not obscured to the eye of
God. We cannot see them again in the flesh, for they
have passed within the veil; but they are still seen,
still loved by their Heavenly Father, their Ascended
Saviour, their Divine Comforter. They shine with
even a brighter light than before their obscuration; for
they are fuller of light in themselves, and their beams
are not dimmed by the clouds and vapours which so
obscured their earthly lustre. There is no eclipse in
heaven; the soul that once begins its lustrous glory
there, will ever emit the same holy rays, with a per-
petually increasing intensity of spiritual light.

STEVENS.

SCRIPTURAL SELECTIONS.

THEY meet with darkness in the day-time, and grope in the noon-day as in the night.—*Job*, v. 14.

One dieth in his full strength, being wholly at ease and quiet.—*Job*, xxi. 23.

For to me to live is Christ, and to die is gain.

For I am in a strait betwixt two, having a desire to depart, and to be with Christ; which is far better.—*Philippians*, i. 21, 23.

Therefore we are always confident, knowing that, whilst we are at home in the body, we are absent from the Lord:

(For we walk by faith, and not by sight):

We are confident, I say, and willing rather to be absent from the body, and to be present with the Lord.

Wherefore we labour, that, whether present or absent, we may be accepted of him —2 *Cor.* v. 6-9.

HE has gone to his God; he has gone to his home;
No more amid peril and error to roam:
 His eyes are no longer dim;
  His feet will no longer falter;
 No grief can follow him;
  No pang his cheek can alter.

There are paleness and weeping and sighs below;
For our faith is faint and our tears will flow;
 But the harps of heaven are ringing;
  Glad angels come to greet him,
 And hymns of joy are singing,
  While old friends press to meet him

O! honoured, beloved, to earth unconfined,
Thou hast soared on high, thou hast left us behind.
 But our parting is not for ever,
  We will follow thee by heaven's light,
 Where the grave cannot dissever
  The souls whom God will unite.

IV

The Setting Sun.

" *The shadows of the evening are stretched out.*"—Jeremiah, vi. 4.

THERE is something at once grand and solemn in a setting sun. It is the sinking to rest of the great king of day; the withdrawing from the busy world the light that has called out its activity, and the covering up with the veil of darkness the scenes that glistened with the radiance of noon.

As the sun rose in the morning, it awoke the world from slumber, and sent its teeming millions to their tasks and pleasures. As it poised itself for a moment in the meridian, it shone upon an active, bustling, life-filled hemisphere; and now that it touches the edge of the western sky, and gradually shuts its burning eye, it proclaims a day of work ended, a night of rest advancing, the cessation of toil and business, and the coming in of quiet, sleep, and silence. This change, though so little considered, is very marvellous and striking—from brightness to darkness—from noonday with its garish light, to midnight with its sombre blackness—from the din and bustle of intense activity, to the repose and silence of hushing slumber—from scenes gay and blithe in all the adornments of art, and

(350)

"And when Jacob had made an end of commanding his sons, he gathered up his feet into the bed, and yielded up the ghost." Gen. XLIX. 33.

decked with the painted splendours of meridian light, to scenes of stillness, darkness, and death-like sleep.

There is, however, in the setting of the sun of life that which is equally grand, still more solemn, and surpassingly sublime.　For

> The sun is but a spark of fire—
> A transient meteor in the sky,—
> The SOUL, immortal as its Sire,
> 　　　Shall never die.
>
> The SOUL, of origin divine,
> God's glorious image, freed from clay,
> In heaven's eternal sphere shall shine,
> 　　　A star of day.

Though the soul, by virtue of its immortality, and the eternal interests connected with it, is thus infinitely superior to the sun, which is but a mass of inanimate matter, and which, when it has served its purpose, shall be blotted out, yet there are several striking analogies between the setting of the sun of nature, and the setting of the sun of life, which suggest profitable considerations.　In speaking of a human sunset, we restrict our thoughts to those only who die in the Lord, and so sleep in Jesus.

The sun when it sets has run a whole day's circuit; his pathway has apparently traversed an entire arc of the heavens, and slowly, patiently, but surely, it has done its allotted work.　And so the aged Christian, when he dies, is described as having "run his race," as having "finished his course."　He has perhaps traversed the allotted distance of human life.　He has passed

each of its threescore-and-ten milestones, and now stands
at the verge of the horizon, waiting to sink to rest in
the everlasting arms. He has toiled a whole day of
life, and has come to his grave in a " good old age," having " finished the work which was given him to do;"
and though all his labours have been imperfectly done,
though he himself feels more deeply than he can express
his unprofitableness before God, yet he looks for acceptance, not to any merit or deservings of his own, but
only for Christ Jesus' sake, who of God and by faith
is made unto him " wisdom and righteousness, and sanctification, and redemption." We can contemplate with
satisfaction, then, the aged disciple, having " borne the
burden and heat of the day," patiently waiting for the
stretching out of the evening shadows, and the hour of
his own sunset. His life has been consecrated to Christ.
He has endeavoured to walk by faith, not by sight.
He has set the Lord always before him, and has run
with patience the Christian race, " looking unto Jesus."
He has relaxed his hold upon the world; he has re-
nounced all righteousness in and of himself. He looks
alone for salvation to the perfect and finished work of
his blessed Redeemer, and, resting his whole soul and
its eternal interests in the pierced hands of Him who
died that he might live, he quietly waits his appointed
time, and, strong in the abounding grace of God to all
who believe in Jesus Christ, he is enabled to say, with
a modest, though well assured triumph, " I have fought
a good fight, I have finished my course, I have kept
the faith; henceforth there is laid up for me a crown of

glory, which the Lord, the righteous Judge, will give me in that day."

Another point to be considered is, the fact that the setting of the sun is not always like the day which it closes. The morning may have been bright, and the evening hour dark with tempests; or the rising may have been obscured by clouds and mists, which gradually faded away and left a clear sky at sunset. How often, after nearly a whole day of rain and dullness, has the descending sun broken through the clouds on the horizon, and shone out between the rifted vapours with a gorgeousness all the more glorious, because of the preceding gloom! Nay, how have those very storm mists, which gathered around the west in dark and heavy folds, or which rolled upwards in murky convolutions, been so gilded with his light as to shine like burnished metal, as if the sky was plated with Solomon's "three hundred shields of beaten gold," making the whole west a scene of inexpressible glory.

So the sunset hour of Christian life does not always correspond to his previous day. We have seen the last hours of the believer shrouded in impenetrable gloom, and we have seen them gilded with hope and radiant with the forecast glories of the upper world. The way in which a Christian dies is not always an index of his spiritual condition. *He is to be judged by his life, not by his death.* The great virtues which make up Christian character are neither developed nor called into action on a dying bed; and it is not in the emotions and feelings manifested there, that we are

chiefly to look for evidences of a gracious state. Self
denial, the mortification of our passions, the crucifying
ourselves to the world, the resisting of earthly temptations, the putting into active exercise, and amidst
opposing difficulties, the whole class of Christian affections which flow out from the simple principle of loving
our neighbour as ourselves, and the manifestation of
that life of faith, of prayer, of holiness, of zeal, which
necessarily results from the constraining love of Christ
in the heart; all these qualities and tests of character
scarcely find a place on a dying bed, so that persons
thus situated have few opportunities to develop the
true evidences of the work of grace. We read, indeed,
of many marked and happy deathbeds, but we also
read of many closing hours of Christian life, where the
believer had no special manifestations of divine favour,
where no time even has been given for the utterance of
feelings, and where even a melancholy bordering on
despair has cast a sombre hue over the going down of
the disciple's sun. We have in our mind's eye cases of
each of these, where, however, not the slightest doubt
existed as to the real conversion of the individual, or
as to his final acceptance in the Beloved. There are
some Christians who may be called weepers and
mourners nearly all their days; their deep consciousness of sin, their extreme sensitiveness to evil, their
ever present fear to offend God, make their eyes to run
down with tears night and day; and so perhaps it continues until the evening sun bursts through the falling
mists, and paints a beautiful bow of promise on the

raindrops of penitential sorrow. There are others whose faith is blurred and indistinct ; they have no clear and well defined appreciation of the great truths of the Bible ; their sky of religious experience is overcast with a thin layer of cloud, which, while it does not shut out the light or heat of the sun, prevents the eye from viewing it distinctly, or from enjoying its unveiled splendour. They live, perhaps for years, in this almost twilight Christianity, but as they approach the grave the vapours become thinner and thinner, until a clear strip of blue lies above the horizon, and the descending sun shines out full-orbed and glorious ere he sinks to his evening rest. There are others, whose experience is April-like : a fleckered sky is over their heads, and alternate light and shade fall upon their path : and sometimes these come to the grave rejoicing, sometimes sorrowing, sometimes they go down amidst a blaze of golden glory, and sometimes massive doubts and fears are banked up like clouds over the west, so that they seem to set in darkness. These varieties of Christian experience are literally innumerable ; but whatever their nature, we must not judge of the validity of one's hope, or the genuineness of one's conversion, by his dying hour. Yet, when that dying hour accords with a long life of piety, or a true profession maintained in health and strength ; when it is but a concentrating within itself of the glories which have been more or less visible in the whole track of his experience, then is it eloquent in its revelations of the riches and peace and joy, which God generally gives to those who are faithful unto death :

and though we cannot order when or how our lives shall close upon earth, yet it should be our aim so to live as to secure, if God pleases, a serene, if not a triumphant exit, that our setting sun may, like the sun in the firmament, grow large and more resplendent as it declines, until passing away it shall leave behind it a trail of glory spread all over the place of our departure.

Another interesting thought connected with this subject is, that the sun is not lost or extinguished when it sets. This may seem a very trite remark concerning the natural sun, but it is not so trite when we speak of the soul-set in death. For are we not apt to grieve over the going down of our friends to the grave, as if they were to be for ever hidden in its dark chamber, or as if the bright spark of their immortality had been suddenly quenched? They have gone from us; the horizon of death shuts them out of view; their light of love, of hope, of piety, shines no more upon us, and we shall never again behold them in the flesh; but they are no more lost, than the sun is lost when his red disc rolls down behind the western hills; they are no more extinguished than the burning orb of day is quenched when he sinks beneath the waves of the ocean; for, as the sun leaving us in darkness still lights up other lands, so our departed ones shine in another sphere of existence still, not lost, not extinguished, but, if the friends of Christ, made to glow with a brighter light and a more enduring glory. When, therefore, we stand by their coffins, by their graves, or return sad and heavy-laden to their vacant dwellings, we should not mourn for them as those without hope, we should not give vent to grief as though they were lost to us altogether: they are hidden, but not lost, removed from our sight, but not extinct; they are still alive, only with a more exquisite vitality unfettered by sin, unencumbered by flesh, undefiled by the world, dwelling as redeemed spirits in the paradise of God.

And this remark leads us to make one final observation, viz. that when we see the sun set, we know that it will rise again; and so when we see the body of our friends borne to the voiceless dwelling of the tomb, we know that they also shall rise again.

Every night of death is followed by a resurrection morning. How precious is the thought as connected with God's people, that they shall rise from the dead! How rise? With glorified bodies, upon which the second death has no power. Rise by what power? By the mighty power of God. Rise when? When the Lord Jesus shall be revealed from heaven with all his mighty angels, then shall they be caught up to meet him in the air. Rise to what? To glory, honour, and immortality in the presence-chamber of God. How these thoughts light up with brightness every sepulchre of the righteous! How the doctrine of the resurrection throws a halo over every Christian's head-stone, and makes each open grave a little postern-gate leading into glory!

Reader, have you lost a father, mother, brother, sister, wife, husband, child, or lover, and were they Christ's before they died? Then lift up your heads, wipe away your tears, cheer up your hearts, for they shall come forth again before your face. Their sunset, though it left you in gloom and midnight sorrow, will soon be followed by the dawn of Resurrection day; and when the archangel's trump shall sound out over land and sea, awaking the myriads who slumber in earth's bosom, then shall your beloved ones who sunk to rest in Jesus, rise again, and go forth to meet and glorify their adorable Redeemer.

Thoughts like these cluster around the setting sun of the aged disciple of Jesus: Why should we wish to detain him? his work is done. Why desire to hold him back from the grave? it is through the gate and grave of death that he passes to his inheritance above. Why be inconsolable at his departure? he is not lost, neither is the light of his mind or heart extinguished. Why mourn as those who have no hope, beside his tombstone? He shall not lie there long. He is planted there in the likeness of Christ's death, that he may rise with Christ to the resurrection of eternal life; and not many more days shall roll over you, ere you and they shall all rise again; "they that have done good to the resurrection of life, and they that have done evil to the resurrection of damnation."

Rejoice rather when one you love, who is full of days and full of grace, sets like a sun behind the horizon of life. Rejoice, for he shall rise again; and when that morning of the resurrection dawns, it will usher in a day that has no clouds, a day that has no sunset, and a day that is followed by no night of sorrow or of death.

STEVENS.

SCRIPTURAL SELECTION.

[IN no pages, human or divine, has the decrepitude of age, and the gradual dying out of the physical powers of man, his sunset after a long day of life, been so graphically as well as poetically portrayed as in the twelfth chapter of the Book of Ecclesiastes.

The aim of Solomon in this chapter is to urge upon the young an early remembrance of God, and he enforces his exhortation by so setting forth the infirmities of age as to show that that period is entirely unfitted for the great work of turning unto God.]

"Remember now thy Creator in the days of thy youth, while the evil days come not, nor the years draw nigh, when thou shalt say, I have no pleasure in them.

"While the sun, or the light, or the moon, or the stars be not darkened, nor the clouds return after the rain:

"In the day when the keepers of the house shall tremble, and the strong men shall bow themselves, and the grinders cease because they are few, and those that look out of the windows be darkened.

"And the doors shall be shut in the streets, when the sound of the grinding is low, and he shall rise up at the voice of the bird, and all the daughters of music shall be brought low.

"Also when they shall be afraid of that which is high, and fears shall be in the way, and the almond-tree shall flourish, and the grass-hopper shall be a burden, and desire shall fail; because man goeth to his long home, and the mourners go about the streets:

"Or ever the silver cord be loosed, or the golden bowl be broken, or the pitcher be broken at the fountain, or the wheel broken at the cistern:

"Then shall the dust return to the earth as it was: and the spirit shall return unto God who gave it."—*Ecclesiastes*, xii. 1-7.

LIFE'S SUNSET.

As calmly sinks the setting sun
  To realms of gold in gorgeous skies,
When day and all its toils are done—
  In glorious peace the good man dies.

As glow the stars when darkness falls,
  To cheer the close of fading day,
So, brightening hopes, when death appals
  From Heaven gleam to light his way.

As peaceful clouds along the sky
  Retain the glories of the sun,
In memory bright are floating by
  His deeds of love in meekness done.

He dies!—as, passed the dreary night,
  The sun 'mid streams of light appears;
So, passed the vale, a holier light
  Bespeaks the glorious crown he wears.

O Thou, who art enthroned on high!
  To me Thy saving grace be given
To live, and like the GOOD MAN die;
  Like him, be crowned of thee in Heaven.

THE END.

ANOTHER RELATED TITLE FROM SGCB

MEMORIAL TRIBUTES
Classic Funeral Addresses

AN AID FOR PASTORS

A BOOK OF COMFORT FOR THE BEREAVED

First published in 1883, this volume is filled with wise and bold words spoken in the face of death by dozens of the leading evangelical ministers of the 19th century, including Charles H. Spurgeon, John Newton, William Jay, Gardiner Spring, W.B. Sprague, Wm. S. Plumer, William Taylor, D.L. Moody, J.R. Macduff, Horatius Bonar, Andrew Bonar, Charles Hodge, Thomas Binney, John Hall, John Todd, Francis Wayland, Theo. Cuyler, Thomas Guthrie, Canon H.P. Liddon, Alexander Dickson and many more.

Volume is divided into the following categories:

DEATH IN CHILDHOOD

DEATH OF A YOUTH

DEATH IN MIDDLE AGE

DEATH IN OLD AGE

MISCELLANEOUS CIRCUMSTANCES

Call us Toll Free at **1-866-789-7423**
Send us an e-mail at **sgcb@charter.net**
Visit us on line at **www.solid-ground-books.com**

LaVergne, TN USA
27 February 2011
217817LV00004B/1/A